LIFE AMONGST THE MODOCS:

UNWRITTEN HISTORY

LIFE AMONGST THE MODOCS:

UNWRITTEN HISTORY

by

JOAQUIN MILLER

Introduction by Malcolm Margolin

Afterword by Alan Rosenus

HEYDAY BOOKS / URION PRESS

Introduction and Afterword © 1996
Urion Press

Distributed to the trade by
Heyday Books
P.O. Box 9145
Berkeley, CA 94709

Publisher's Cataloging in Publication
(Prepared by Quality Books Inc.)

Miller, Joaquin, 1837-1913.
   Life amongst the Modocs : unwritten history / by Joaquin Miller ;
introduction by Malcolm Margolin ; afterword by Alan Rosenus.
   p. cm.
   Reprint. Originally published: 1873.
   Includes bibliographical references.
   ISBN 0-930588-79-7

   1. Modoc Indians--Fiction. I. Margolin, Malcolm. II. Rosenus,
Alan, 1940- III. Title.

PS2397.L49 1996   813'.4
                                        QBI96-1052

This book uses the complete
text of the first edition,
published in 1873.

                         Brief portions of the Afterword first
                    appeared in *Western American Literature*
                        (Volume II, No. 1), and in *Fifty Western
                            Writers* (Greenwood Press, 1982)
                      reprinted with permission of the editors.

TO

THE RED MEN OF AMERICA

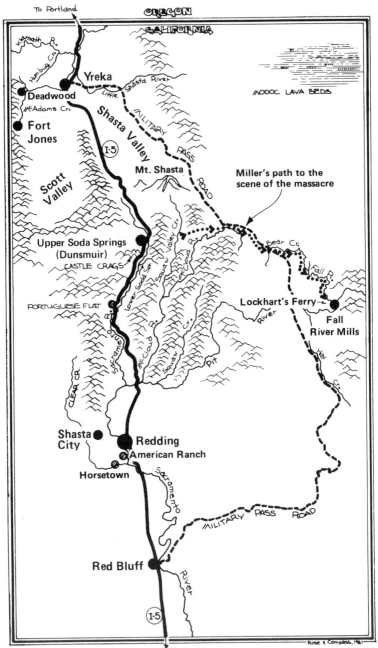

The locale of Joaquin Miller's activities in the Mount Shasta region, 1854–1860.

INTRODUCTION

On August 17, 1870, Joaquin Miller stepped off the ferry from New Jersey onto the wharves of New York City, thus ending his long-anticipated cross-country journey. The Transcontinental Railroad had been completed the previous year, and although he complained that the trip had been "incessant," in truth it had taken only two weeks—easy and even luxurious compared to the bone-rattling crossing of some eighteen years earlier, when at the age of fifteen he had traveled with his parents by covered wagon from Indiana to Oregon.

After a brief stay in New York, Miller boarded a ship for Europe, reaching the British Isles in fourteen days. The voyage among "cold seas and cold seamen" was undoubtedly disagreeable, as Miller depicted it in his journals; but by then steamship travel had long been established on the transatlantic routes, largely freeing tourists and merchants from the inconvenience of contrary winds, rendering the once fearsome voyage relatively safe and predictably on schedule.

In 1870 the world was shrinking fast. The voyages of Cook to the South Pacific, that had so startled Europe with depictions of scantily clad women and fiercely tattooed cannibal warriors, were now a century old. Two decades had elapsed since Sir Richard Burton's penetration into the strongholds of Mecca and Medina. Within months of Miller's arrival in London, Sir Henry Stanley would be setting forth to find Dr. David Livingstone and would virtually complete the exploration of the "dark" continent.

An era was drawing to a close so suddenly that few people realized it, and even fewer understood its significance. As colonial administrators, engineers, representatives of mercantile houses, and churchmen spread out from the capitals of Europe on missions of political, economic, and cultural domination, the great world—once of infinite mystery and terror—was shrinking with alarming rapidity to the dimensions of a Victorian parlor, its wondrous variety of humanity reduced to figurines on knickknack shelves.

This conquest of the globe by Europe created an appetite for the exotic—a romantic, yearning, sometimes almost pornographic curiosity about the lives of non-European people. It also produced in some a fear that the deep beauty and wealth of the earth were being plundered, and that the black coats, top hats, and constricted morality of the Fleet Street bankers would be the uniform of the future.

Perhaps there was something in the tone of the times that might help explain the conspicuous attire of the man who arrived from America in 1870. Joaquin Miller, then thirty-three years old, took to the London streets wearing a wide-brimmed sombrero, a flaming red flannel shirt, a blue polka-dot bandana, and—in case this wasn't enough—a gaudy sash tied around his waist. On some days he chose to wear cowboy pants with chaps; other days he donned more conventional trousers which he tucked into high-heeled boots upon which he affixed a set of spurs. He was much inclined to wear a pistol on his hip, but newfound friends advised him that this would be "going too far." He nevertheless did cultivate a swagger and cocksure attitude. Christened Cincinnatus Hiner Miller by his Quaker father and hymn-singing mother, he had even shed his given name for the swashbuckling "Joaquin."

Obviously, Miller wanted to be noticed, and he was. By 1871 he had published, at his own expense, a volume of poetry, *Songs of the Sierras*, which was received with great enthusiasm and gained him access to many of England's most illustrious poets, such as Robert Browning and Dante Gabriel Rossetti. His reputation was greatly enhanced when a couple of years later *Life Amongst the Modocs* was published to huge critical acclaim from his English audience. Subtitled *Unwritten History,* it purports to tell of his experiences among the Indians and miners of northernmost California.

From a character such as Miller, one would hardly expect a conventional book—safe, factual, and footnoted. Indeed, despite Miller's declaration that he had made the book "true in every particular," the work before us, while based on real incidents and actual experiences, is clearly as much a novel as it is a work of history. It is of utmost importance to recognize this fact when reading *Life Amongst the Modocs*. Those approaching it as a work of history—demanding that it be trustworthy in its details and sound in its conclusions—will find it wanting. Those, however, who understand it, at least in part, as a work of fiction, will find themselves hugely rewarded. The literary imagination has tremendous powers. It can leap with surety through a thousand details to the heart of a complex situation; it embraces contradiction and ambiguity without the encumbrance of interpretation; it can engage our emotions as can no mere assemblage of carefully footnoted facts. *Life Amongst the Modocs,* with its unique mixture of fact and fiction, is indeed such a work, presenting us with a daring view of this difficult era. It has such scope, and, in its odd way, such profound truthfulness, that its equal cannot be found anywhere else in the literature of the West.

Separating fact from fiction in *Life Amongst the Modocs* is no easy task. We know with certainty that Miller had indeed lived in the mining camps and among the Indians of northern California. He had married an Indian woman who taught him the Wintu language, and he had taken part in some of the skirmishes, battles, and even massacres of the 1850s. Characters and incidents in the book can be matched with people who actually lived and events that actually took place—a task which historian Alan Rosenus tackles in his valuable afterword to this volume.

Yet despite the factual core, Miller cannot seem to resist swaggering through the pages of the book, dressed in outlandish attitudes, any more than he could resist swaggering through the streets of London wearing colorful outfits. He struts, he lies, he boasts. On one page he presents himself as abjectly weak and passive, a few pages later he bursts forth as a decisive military leader. He wallows in his defects, parades his strengths, and in short pushes himself into the face of the reader every chance he can get.

Miller's vanity and self-obsession are great, sometimes ludicrous. As we read him, we sometimes see someone posing before a mirror, trying on different costumes, adopting different postures, admiring himself endlessly, exulting in his considerable powers as a poet and the freedom it allows—at liberty to blurt out the most outrageous and startling truths and fantasies. He is, at worst, an impossible egotist, self-absorbed and self-deluded. But it is not for his worst aspects that we still read Miller with fascination, even hunger. It is for his best aspects, and in these he is extraordinary.

The period covered by this book, the 1850s in northern California, was an era of upheaval, contradiction, and great complexity. Take, for example, the people whom Miller generally calls "Indians." Far from comprising a single culture or "tribe," the Indians of this part of California spoke four mutually incomprehensible languages: Wintu, Shasta, Modoc, and Pit River. Each of these languages had dialects, and within a dialect group were often many politically and culturally distinct peoples. Some of these people lived along salmon-rich rivers, some alongside lakes and marshes, some in pine forests, and some in high deserts. Their ways of living differed greatly, and they were variously at war or at peace with one or another of their neighbors.

Likewise, the white settlers were far from uniform. Only half the residents of the area, for example, listed their occupation as "miner" during the 1850s. Others were shopkeepers, farmers, blacksmiths, carpenters, soldiers, etc. While overwhelmingly white, the towns and mines of the Mount Shasta area also had blacks and Chinese, as well as a large foreign-born population from places such as Ireland, Scotland, France, Norway, Portugal, Mexico, and the various German principalities. Among the American-born were well-educated young men from the eastern seaboard, pious and sober young men from small New York and Pennsylvania farming communities, and the roughest of frontiersmen from the mountains of Tennessee and Kentucky.

The clash between the Indians and the white settlers was gruesome and soul-sickening. In later years the description of this confrontation would take on a brutal simplicity: the whites came, took over the land, and nearly annihilated the Indians. But to those who lived during this tumultuous era, the conflict, while brutal, was anything but simple. Whites, for example, did not only fight against the Indians, but they battled each other in endless duels, robberies, ambushes, and vigilante actions. Likewise, the Indians warred fiercely against each other as they had done for millennia. Neither side was innocent of mutilation, torture, or the murder of women and children. And when whites did fight against the Indians, they were often joined by "friendly" Indians who served as scouts or as soldiers.

In later years other writers would struggle to characterize the Indians of California and describe the horrors of their conflict with the white world. Borrowing concepts from anthropology, ethnohistory, linguistics, and other disciplines, drawing upon the accumulated writings of previous historians and literary people, they would over time develop a body of ideas, of frameworks, of language—in short, they would work out the highly evolved and largely acceptable way of describing Indians and the history of western settlement to which modern writers are heir and largely take for granted. But this would come later. Miller was a literary pioneer. There was for him no established school or scholarly tradition, no path to follow, no adequate language for describing what he had lived through. Embroiled in the chaotic events of the time; living partly within the white world of the mining camps, partly in Indian villages; a blond youth married to an Indian woman; an insider (at least by marriage) to regional Indian culture with ambition to make a name for himself in the world—Miller found himself without anything in the body of existing literature or conventional ways of thinking that could be used to describe his experiences.

He might, I suppose, have taken a different route—that of a journalist or historian, sticking to the facts with scrupulous attentiveness, weaving together strands of contradictory stories to get at some approximation of a complex truth. But this would have been for another personality. *Life Amongst the Modocs* is not a book of small, trustworthy, literal truths—of detailed ethnographic information about the Indian people of the area or strictly reliable accounts of conflicts and battles. These can be found elsewhere. What *Life Amongst the Modocs* offers is something more ambitious.

For the first readers of *Life Amongst the Modocs,* one of the big truths that jumped off the pages was one with which modern readers have become more familiar: namely, the horrifying accounts of the massacres of Indian people by whites. While such knowledge was not entirely absent in the 1870s—reports of massacres had been a staple of frontier newspapers for nearly two decades—previous accounts were brief and transitory, and in them Indians were presented largely as nameless and pitiful victims. Bodies of men, women, and children might be counted, but virtually nothing was said or known about who these people were. Not only did *Life Amongst the Modocs* provide a book-length treatment of this hideous period of American history, but for the first time in Western literature the Indians who were being massacred were portrayed not just as Indians but as people—people with whom Miller had lived, people whom he knew and admired.

Also new to his early readers were the huge, sweeping, poetic depictions of nature. In this period before John Muir, exultant descriptions of western wilderness were rare, and even rarer was a sense of what we now call ecology—a recognition that the environmental degradation caused by mining had affected the herds of elk and the spawning of salmon, and in doing so had reduced to starvation the Indians who depended upon them. As modern people we are all too familiar with this line of thought. But for most of the original readers, "progress" and economic development were still unmitigated virtues, wilderness was something to be tamed, and Indians clearly needed to be conquered. For them Miller's way of thinking was something of an eye-opener.

Also startling for readers of the 1870s, and perhaps even more so for readers of today, is Miller's literary rather than scientific approach to history. Ordinarily we read history to give a sense of order to the past. That is what historians tend to do: they bring order, define themes, show that the chaos of the past is only apparent and that beneath it are larger purposes, causes, inevitabilities. Miller, however, does not set out to tame the chaos, to fit it into theories, to explain it and deaden it with the language of the dispassionate historian.

Rather, Miller embraces the chaos. We feel in *Life Amongst the Modocs* the raw crosscurrents of violence and love, of divided people and split loyalties, of delicacy and brutality, all presented to us full face. In quick and astoundingly energetic strokes, piling incident upon incident, image upon image, he captures the movement and the emotion of the times. Reading other accounts from more conventional historians we get the feeling that we are standing at a safe distance looking back upon stormy times. *Life Amongst the Modocs,* however, gives us the feeling of having entered the storm itself.

In a review of *Life Amongst the Modocs,* critic Hamlin Garland once commented: "Such pictures as these were unknown to our literature when they were written, and they stand unsurpassed today in their largeness of movement and their mass of light and shade." Like others, Garland borrows the language of art criticism to describe *Life Amongst the Modocs*. And for good reason. In the early 1870s, Impressionism was taking hold of the European imagination, and in 1870 Monet and Pissarro, fleeing the Franco-Prussian War, took up residence in England. Their paintings were shown in London in 1871. Whether or not Miller was directly influenced by this school of painting is not clear, but he certainly shared its goals. Just as the Impressionistic painter might avoid a "realistic" portrayal of solid objects in order to capture the fleeting qualities of light and motion, Miller in his writing seems to avoid fidelity to historic detail in order to explore other aspects of experience. *Life Amongst the Modocs,* rather than providing us with reliable reportage, gives us instead a rendering of elusive states of mind. Miller was the first of the western writers to attempt to portray the emotional landscape of early California, to deal with themes such as loneliness and defeat, melancholy and rage, weakness and strength, joy and loyalty—the insubstantial but all-important parts of life that modern writers who cover this era have all but forgotten to ask about, let alone describe.

Central to *Life Amongst the Modocs* is Miller's fascination with what he calls "the real Indian." What he means by this is something quite specific—not the Indian "willing to mix with us on the border," but rather the "Indian who retreats from the white man when he can." Miller had indeed caught a glimpse of this real Indian. He had lived among a people whose personalities had been formed before the coming of whites and who were still leading a largely traditional life. The quest to describe the real Indian haunted him, just as it was to haunt other writers for the better part of a century—not only white writers, but Indian writers as well.

Perhaps it was the shrinking world in which Miller was writing that gave this need a certain urgency. It seemed inevitable to Miller and his contemporaries that Indians would soon disappear, and even the memory of them would become yet another trophy of European culture, to survive only within the constructs of the conqueror. Miller, however, knew that he had seen another kind of being, and in the pages before us one senses him as almost desperate to find a language with which he can describe the people he knew, throwing himself at the task again and again in his attempts to convey something of what he had witnessed.

The real Indian, Miller tells us, was "a druid and a dreamer—the mildest and tamest of beings. I saw him as no man can see him now... the worst and the best of men, the tamest and the fiercest of beings. The world cannot understand the combination of these two qualities."

We read such descriptions with a sense of great surprise. This is not the language to which our ears have become accustomed. Instead of delineating kinship systems and analyzing material culture, he talks of things like mildness and fierceness, melancholy and joy. We sense that there is something new coming off the page here, and we almost hold our breath to see if Miller, with all his outlandishness, can bring it off.

He does bring it off to an amazing degree, and indeed one cannot help but feel that he succeeds in the larger task to which he applied himself—to present the unwritten history of his era. He succeeds because of his powers as a poet, his courage as a writer, and yet something else. The reason *Life Amongst the Modocs* still holds our attention and, despite its flaws, holds our great respect is that it is pervaded by something that might be called (if we are not too embarrassed to give it its proper name) love. A strange and wonderful love seems to fill the book, and it is, I feel, this quality that makes the vanities, the foolish posturings, even the outright lies bearable. He was, as Ambrose Bierce would later say, "the greatest-hearted man I ever knew," and it is this greateartedness that helps carry the reader, transfixed, through the book.

There is for the modern reader brought up on more cautious and conventional scholarly works something wonderfully liberating about reading *Life Amongst the Modocs*—as if for too long our thoughts and feelings were moving in narrow channels, and we can now see the possibilities of plunging into deeper, perhaps more dangerous, but infinitely more exciting waters. Among the grand sweeps of the book, the dashing forays into truths, the startling asides and odd, uncensored thoughts, the mind feels enlarged, refreshed, and enlivened.

Miller clearly recognized a certain roughness within himself. In the work before us he writes:

> I think what I most needed in order to understand, get on and not be misunderstood, was a long time at school, where my rough points could be ground down. The schoolmaster should have taken me between his thumb and forefinger and rubbed me about till I was as smooth and as round as the others. Then I should have been put out in the society of other smooth pebbles, and rubbed and ground against them till I got as smooth and pointless as they. You must not have points or anything about you singular or noticeable if you would get on. You must be a pebble, a smooth, quiet pebble. Be a big pebble if you can, a small pebble if you must. But be a pebble, just like the rest, cold, and hard, and sleek, and smooth, and you are all right. But I was as rough as the lava rocks I roamed over, as broken as the mountains I inhabited.

Life Amongst the Modocs, like its remarkable author, is not a smooth pebble, ground and polished, sleek, hard, and cold. The book before us has not been smoothed out, edited for good taste, correct thoughts, or even factual accuracy. It is rough and jagged, and even after so many years it still has the power to catch us and move us as no other work of this era can.

Malcolm Margolin
Berkeley, 1996

LIFE AMONGST THE MODOCS: UNWRITTEN HISTORY

CHAPTER I

ONELY as God, and white as a winter moon, Mount Shasta starts up sudden and solitary from the heart of the great black forests of Northern California.

You would hardly call Mount Shasta a part of the Sierras ; you would say rather that it is the great white tower of some ancient and eternal wall, with here and there the white walls overthrown.

It has no rival! There is not even a snow-crowned subject in sight of its dominion. A shining pyramid in mail of everlasting frosts and ice, the sailor sometimes, in a day of singular clearness, catches glimpses of it from the sea a hundred miles away to the west ; and it may be seen from the dome of the capital 300 miles distant. The immigrant coming from

the east beholds the snowy, solitary pillar from afar
out on the arid sage-brush plains, and lifts his
hands in silence as in answer to a sign.

Column upon column of storm-stained tamarack,
strong-tossing pines, and warlike-looking firs have
rallied here. They stand with their backs against
this mountain, frowning down dark-browed, and con-
fronting the face of the Saxon. They defy the advance of civilization into their ranks. What if these
dark and splendid columns, a hundred miles in depth,
should be the last to go down in America! What
if this should be the old guard gathered here, marshalled around their emperor in plumes and armour,
that may die but not surrender!

Ascend this mountain, stand against the snow
above the upper belt of pines, and take a glance below. Toward the sea nothing but the black and
unbroken forest. Mountains, it is true, dip and
divide and break the monotony as the waves break
up the sea; yet it is still the sea, still the unbroken
forest, black and magnificent. To the south the
landscape sinks and declines gradually, but still main-
tains its column of dark-plumed grenadiers, till the
Sacramento Valley is reached, nearly a hundred
miles away. Silver rivers run here, the sweetest in
the world. They wind and wind among the rocks
and mossy roots, with California lilies, and the yew
with scarlet berries dipping in the water, and trout
idling in the eddies and cool places by the basket-
ful. On the east, the forest still keeps up unbroken

rank till the Pit River valley is reached ; and even there it surrounds the valley, and locks it up tight in its black embrace. To the north, it is true, Shasta valley makes quite a dimple in the sable sea, and men plough there, and Mexicans drive mules or herd their mustang ponies on the open plain. But the valley is limited, surrounded by the forest, confined and imprisoned.

Look intently down among the black and rolling hills, forty miles away to the west, and here and there you will see a haze of cloud or smoke hung up above the trees; or, driven by the wind that is coming from the sea, it may drag and creep along as if tangled in the tops.

These are mining camps. Men are there, down in these dreadful cañons, out of sight of the sun, swallowed up, buried in the impenetrable gloom of the forest, toiling for gold. Each one of these camps is a world in itself. History, romance, tragedy, poetry in every one of them. They are connected together, and reach the outer world only by a narrow little pack trail, stretching through the timber, stringing round the mountains, barely wide enough to admit of footmen and little Mexican mules with their apparajos, to pass in single file. We will descend into one of these camps by-and-by. I dwelt there a year, many and many a year ago. I shall picture that camp as it was, and describe events as they happened. Giants were there, great men were there.

They were very strong, energetic and resolute,

and hence were neither gentle or sympathetic.
They were honourable, noble, brave and generous,
and yet they would have dragged a Trojan around
the wall by the heels and thought nothing of it.
Coming suddenly into the country with prejudices
against and apprehensions of the Indians, of whom
they knew nothing save through novels, they of
course were in no mood to study their nature.
Besides, they knew that they were in a way,
trespassers if not invaders, that the Government
had never treated for the land or offered any
terms whatever to the Indians, and like most men
who feel that they are somehow in the wrong, did not
care to get on terms with their antagonists. They
would have named the Indian a Trojan, and dragged
him around, not only by the heels but by the scalp,
rather than have taken time or trouble, as a rule, to
get in the right of the matter.

I say that the greatest, the grandest body of men
that have ever been gathered together since the
siege of Troy, was once here on the Pacific. I
grant that they were rough enough sometimes. I
admit that they took a peculiar delight in periodical
six-shooter war dances, these wild-bearded, hairy-
breasted men, and that they did a great deal of
promiscuous killing among each other, but then they
did it in such a manly sort of way !

There is another race in these forests. I lived
with them nearly five years. A great sin it was
thought then, indeed. You do not see the smoke of

their wigwams through the trees. They do not smite the mountain rocks for gold, nor fell the pines, nor roil up the waters and ruin them for the fishermen. All this magnificent forest is their estate. The Great Spirit made this mountain first of all, and gave it to them, they say, and they have possessed it ever since. They preserve the forest, keep out the fires, for it is the park for their deer.

I shall endeavour to make this sketch of my life with the Indians—a subject about which so much has been written and so little is known—true in every particular. In so far as I succeed in doing that I think the work will be novel and original. No man with a strict regard for truth should attempt to write his autobiography with a view to publication during his life; the temptations are too great.

A man standing on the gallows, without hope of descending and mixing again with his fellow men, might trust himself to utter "the truth, the whole truth, and nothing but the truth," as the law hath it; and a Crusoe on his island, without sail in sight or hope of sail, might be equally sincere, but I know of few other conditions in which I could follow a man through his account of himself with perfect confidence.

This narrative, however, while the thread of it is necessarily spun around a few years of my early life, is not particularly of myself, but of a race of people that has lived centuries of history and never yet had a historian; that has suffered nearly four hundred years of wrong, and never yet had an advocate.

I must write of myself, because I was among these people of whom I write, though often in the background, giving place to the inner and actual lives of a silent and mysterious people, a race of prophets ; poets without the gift of expression—a race that has been often, almost always, mistreated, and never understood—a race that is moving noiselessly from the face of the earth ; dreamers that sometimes waken from their mysteriousness and simplicity, and then, blood, brutality, and all the ferocity that marks a man of maddened passions, women without mercy and without reason, brand them with the appropriate name of savages.

But beyond this, I have a word to say for the Indian. I saw him as he was, not as he is. In one little spot of our land, I saw him as he was centuries ago in every part of it perhaps, a Druid and a dreamer—the mildest and the tamest of beings. I saw him as no man can see him now. I saw him as no man ever saw him who had not the desire and patience to observe, the sympathy to understand, and the intelligence to communicate his observations to those who would really like to understand him. He is truly " the gentle savage ;" the worst and the best of men, the tamest and the fiercest of beings. The world cannot understand the combination of these two qualities. For want of a truer comparison let us liken him to a jealous woman—a whole-souled uncultured woman, strong in her passions and her love. A sort of Parisian woman, now made desperate by a long siege and an endless war.

A singular combination of circumstances laid his life bare to me. I was a child and he was a child. He permitted me to enter his heart.

As I write these opening lines here to-day in the Old World, a war of extermination is declared against the Modoc Indians in the New. I know these people. I know every foot of their once vast possessions, stretching away to the north and east of Mount Shasta. I know their rights and their wrongs. I have known them for nearly twenty years.

Peace commissioners have been killed by the Modocs, and the civilized world condemns them. I am not prepared to defend their conduct. This narrative is not for their defence, or for the defence of the Indian, or any one ; but I could, by a ten-line paragraph, throw a bombshell into the camp of the civilized world at this moment, and change the whole drift of public opinion. But it would be too late to be of any particular use to this one doomed tribe.

Years and years ago, when Captain Jack was but a boy, the Modocs were at war with the whites, who were then scouring the country in search of gold. A company took the field under the command of a brave and reckless ruffian named Ben Wright.

The Indians were not so well armed and equipped as their enemies. The necessities of the case, to say nothing of their nature, compelled them to fight from behind the cover of the rocks and trees. They were hard to reach, and generally came out best in the few little battles that were fought.

In this emergency Captain Wright proposed to meet the chiefs in council, for the purpose of making a lasting and permanent treaty. The Indians consented, and the leaders came in. "Go back," said Wright, "and bring in all your people ; we will have council, and celebrate our peace with a feast."

The Indians came in in great numbers, laid down their arms, and then at a sign Wright and his men fell upon them, and murdered them without mercy. Captain Wright boasted on his return that he had made a *permanent* treaty with at least a thousand Indians.

Captain Jack was but a boy then, but he was a true Indian. He was not a chief then. I believe he was not even of the blood which entitles him to that place by inheritance, but he was a bold, shrewd Indian, and won the confidence of the tribe. He united himself to a band of the Modocs, worked his way to their head, and bided his time for revenge. For nearly half a lifetime he and his warriors waited their chance, and when it came they were not unequal to the occasion.

They have murdered, perhaps, one white man to one hundred Indians that were butchered in the same way, and not so very far from the same spot. I deplore the conduct of the Modocs. It will contribute to the misfortune of nearly every Indian in America, however well some of the rulers of the land may feel towards the race.

With these facts before you, considering our

superiority in understanding right and wrong, and all that, you may not be so much surprised at the faithful following in this case of the example we set the Modoc Indians, which resulted in the massacre, and the universal condemnation of Captain Jack and his clan.

To return to my reason for publishing this sketch at this time. You will see that treating chiefly of the Indians, as it does, it may render them a service, that by-and-by would be of but little use, by instructing good men who have to deal with this peculiar people.

I know full well how many men there are on the border who are ready to rise up and contradict everything that looks like clemency or an apology for the Indian, and have therefore given only a brief account of the Ben Wright treachery and tragedy, and only such an account as I believe the fiercest enemy of the Indians living in that region admits to be true, or, at least, such an account as Ben Wright gave and was accustomed to boast of.

The Indian account of the affair, however, which I have heard a hundred times around their camp fires, and over which they seemed to never tire of brooding and mourning, is quite another story. It is dark and dreadful. The day is even yet with them, a sort of St. Bartholomew's Eve, and their mournful narration of all the bloody and brutal events would fill a volume.

They waited for revenge, a very bad thing for

Indians to do, I find; though a Christian king can wait a lifetime, and a Christian nation wait a century. They saw their tribe wasting away every year; every year the hordes of white settlers were eating into the heart of their hunting grounds, still they lay in their lava beds or moved like shadows through the stormy forests and silently waited, and then when the whites came into their camp to talk for peace, as they had gone into the camp of the whites, they showed themselves but too apt scholars in the bloody lesson of long ago.

The scene of this narrative lies immediately about the base of Mount Shasta. The Klamat river with its tributaries flows from its snows on the north, and the quiet Sacramento from the south. The Shasta Indians, now but the remnant of a tribe at one time the most powerful on the Pacific, live at the south base of the mountain, while the Modocs and Pit River Indians live at the east and north-east, with the Klamats still to the north. The other sides and base of the mountain is disputed territory, since the driving out of its original owners, between settlers and hunters, and the roving bands of Indians.

It was late in the fall. I do not know the day or even remember the month; but I do know that I was alone, a frail, sensitive, girl-looking boy, almost destitute, trying to make my way to the mines of California, and that before I had ridden my little spotted Cayuse pony half way up the ten-mile trail that then crossed the Siskiyou mountains, I met little patches of snow; and that a keen, cold wind came pitching down between the trees into my face from the Californian side of the summit.

At one place I saw where a moccasin track was in the snow, and leading across the trail; a very large track I thought it was then, but now I know that it was made by many feet stepping in the same impression.

My dress was scant enough for winter, and it was chill and dismal. A fantastic dress, too, for one looking to the rugged life of the miner ; a sort of cross between an Indian chief and a Mexican vaquero, with a preference for colour carried to extremes.

As I approached the summit the snow grew deeper, and the dark firs, weighted with snow, reached their sable and supple limbs across my path as if to catch me by the yellow hair, that fell, like a school-girl's, on my shoulders. Some of the little firs were covered with snow, and were converted into pyramids and snowy pillars.

I crossed the summit in safety, with a dreamy sort of delight, a half-articulated " Thank God! " and began to descend. Here the snow disappeared on the south side of the mountain, and a generous flood of sunshine took its place.

After a while I turned a sharp-cut point in the trail, with dense woods hanging on either shoulder, and an open world before me. I lifted my eyes and looked away to the south.

Mount Shasta was before me. For the first time I

now looked upon the mountain in whose shadows so
many tragedies were to be enacted; the most comely
and perfect snow peak in America. Nearly a hundred
miles away, it seemed in the pure, clear atmosphere
of the mountains to be almost at hand. Above the
woods, above the clouds, almost above the snow, it
looked like the first approach of land to another
world. Away across a grey sea of clouds that arose
from the Klamat and Shasta rivers, the mountain
stood, a solitary island; white and flashing like a
pyramid of silver! solemn, majestic and sublime!
Lonely and cold and white. A cloud or two about
his brow, sometimes resting there, then wreathed and
coiled about, then blown like banners streaming in
the wind.

I had lifted my hands to Mount Hood, uncovered
my head, bowed down and felt unutterable things,
loved, admired, adored, with all the strength of an
impulsive and passionate young heart. But he who
loves and worships naturally and freely, as all strong,
true souls must and will do, loves that which is most
magnificent and most lovable in his scope of vision.
Hood is a magnificent idol; is sufficient, if you do
not see Shasta.

A grander or a lovelier object makes shipwreck
of a former love. This is sadly so.

Jealousy is born of an instinctive knowledge of
this truth. . . .

Hood is rugged, kingly, majestic, immortal! But
he is only the head and front of a well-raised family.

He is not alone in his splendour. Your admiration is divided and weakened. Beyond the Columbia St. Helen's flashes in the sun in summer or is folded in clouds from the sea in winter. On either hand Jefferson and Washington divide the attention; then farther away, fair as a stud of fallen stars, the white Three Sisters are grouped together about the fountain springs of the Willamette river;—all in a line—all in one range of mountains; as it were, mighty milestones along the way of clouds!—marble pillars pointing the road to God!

Mount Shasta has all the sublimity, all the strength, majesty, and magnificence of Hood; yet is so alone, unsupported, and solitary, that you go down before him utterly, with an undivided adoration—a sympathy for his loneliness and a devotion for his valour—an admiration that shall pass unchallenged.

I dismounted and stood in the declining sun, hat in hand, and looked long and earnestly across the sea of clouds. Now and then long strings of swans went by to Klamat lakes. I could hear them calling to each other. Far and faint and unearthly their echoes seemed, and were as sounds that had lost their way, and come to me for protection.

I looked and listened long but uttered not a sound; strangely mute for a boy; besides, exclamation at such a time is a sacrilege.

At last I threw a kiss across the sea of clouds, as the red banners and belts of gold streamed from the summit in the setting-sun, and turned, took up my lariat, mounted, and proceeded down the mountain.

Should ever your fortune lead you to cross the Chinese wall that divides the people of Oregon from the people of California, stop at the Mountain House and ask for the old mountain trail. Take the direction and stop at the top of what is called the first summit of the Siskiyou mountains, for there you will see to the left hand by the trail a pile of rocks high as your head, put there to mark where a party fell a few days after.

Dismount and contribute a stone to the monument from the loose rocks that lie up and down the trail. It is a pretty Indian custom that the whites sometimes adopt and cherish. I never fail to observe it here, for this spot means a great deal to me.

I uncover my head, take up a stone and lay it on the pile, then turn my face to Mount Shasta and kiss my hand, for the want of some better expression.

CHAPTER II

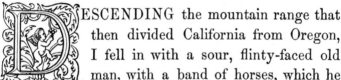ESCENDING the mountain range that then divided California from Oregon, I fell in with a sour, flinty-faced old man, with a band of horses, which he was driving to the lower settlements of California. He was short of help, and proposed to take me into his employ for the round trip, promising to pay me whatever my services were worth. Glad of an opportunity to do something at least in a new land, I scarcely thought of the consideration, but eagerly accepted his offer, and was enrolled as a vaquero along with a motley set of half Indians from the north, and Mexicans from the south.

Our duties were light, and the employment pleasant and congenial to my nature. It was, in fact, about the only thing I was then fit for in that strange new country, boiling and surging with hosts of strong men, rushing hither and thither in search of gold. Our work consisted in keeping the saddle eight or ten hours a day, leading or following after the horses, camping under the trees, and now and then keeping alternate watch over the stock by night.

We were miserably fed, and half frozen while in the mountains, but we soon descended into the quiet Sacramento valley, where the nights are warm with perpetual summer.

The old drover, whose great vice was avarice, quarrelled with his men at Los Angelos, whither he had gone to get a herd of Mexican horses after disposing of the American stock, to take with him on the back trip, and only escaped by adroitly suing out warrants, and leaving them all there in gaol for threatening his life. The cause of the trouble was the old man's avarice. He had made a loose contract with the roving vaqueros, and on settlement refused to pay them scarcely a tithe of their earnings. I remained with him. We returned to the north with a great herd of half-wild horses, driven by a band of almost perfectly wild men : men of all nationalities and conditions, though chiefly Mexicans, all anxious to reach the rich mines of the north.

Drovers in this country always leave the line of travel and all frequented roads that they may obtain fresh grass for their stock. In the long, long journey north we passed through many tribes of Indians, and except in the mountains, I noticed that all the Indians from Southern to Northern California were low, shiftless, indolent, and cowardly. The moment you touched the mountains you seemed to touch a new current of blood.

The old man left his motley army of vaqueros mostly to me, and I was practically captain of the caravan. Not unfrequently, of a morning, we would find ourselves short of a Mexican, who had disappeared in the night with one of the best horses. Sometimes in the daytime these men would get sulky and cross with the cold and cruel old master, and ride off before his face. These men would have to be replaced by others, picked up here and there, of a still more questionable character.

We reached Northern California after a long and lonely journey, through wild and fertile valleys, with only the smoke of wigwams curling from the fringe of trees that hemmed them in, or from the river bank that cleft the little Edens to disprove the fancy that here might have been the Paradise and here the scene of the expulsion.

We crossed flashing rivers, still white and clear, that since have become turbid yellow pools with barren banks of boulders, shorn of their overhanging foliage, and drained of flood by ditches that the resolute miner has led even around the mountain top.

On entering Pit River Valley we met with thousands of Indians, gathered there for the purpose of fishing, perhaps, but they kindly assisted us across the two branches of the river, and gave no signs of ill-will.

We pushed far up the valley in the direction of Yreka, and there pitched camp, for the old man wished to recruit his horses on the rich meadows of wild grass before driving them to town for market.

We camped against a high spur of a long timbered hill, that terminated abruptly at the edge of the valley. A clear stream of water full of trout, with willow-lined banks, wound through the length of the narrow valley, entirely hidden in the long grass and leaning willows.

The Pit River Indians did not visit us here, neither did the Modocs, and we began to hope we were entirely hidden, in the deep narrow little valley, from all Indians, both friendly and unfriendly, until one evening some young men, calling themselves Shastas, came into the camp. They were very friendly, however, were splendid horsemen, and assisted to bring in and corral the horses like old vaqueros.

Our force was very small, in fact we had then less than half-a-dozen men; and the old man, for a day or two, employed two of these young fellows to attend and keep watch about the horses. One morning three of our vaqueros mounted and rode off, cursing my sour old master for some real or fancied wrong, and then he had but one white person with him beside myself, so that the two young Indians had to be retained.

Some weeks wore on pleasantly enough, when we began to prepare to strike camp for Yreka. Thus far we had not seen the sign of a Modoc Indian.

It was early in the morning. The rising sun was streaming up the valley, through the fringe of fir and cedar trees. The Indian boys and I had just returned from driving the herd of horses a little way down the stream. The old man and his companion were sitting at breakfast, with their backs to the high bare wall with its crown of trees. The Indians were taking our saddle-horses across the little stream to tether them there on fresh grass, and I was walking idly towards the camp, only waiting for my tawny young companions. Crack ! crash ! thud !!

The two men fell on their faces and never uttered a word. Indians were running down the little lava mountain side, with bows and rifles in their hands, and the hanging, rugged brow of the hill was curling in smoke. The Ben Wright tragedy was bearing its fruits.

I started to run, and ran with all my might towards where I had left the Indian boys. I remember distinctly thinking how cowardly it was to run and desert the wounded men with the Indians upon them, and I also remember thinking that when I got to the first bank of willows I would turn and fire, for I had laid hold of the pistol in my belt, and could have fired, and should have done so, but I was thoroughly frightened, and no doubt if I had succeeded in reaching the willows I would have thought it best to go still further before turning about.

How rapidly one thinks at such a time, and how distinctly one remembers every thought.

All this, however, was but a flash, the least part of an instant. Some mounted Indians that had been stationed up the valley darted out at the first shot, and one of them was upon me before I saw him, for I was only concerned with the Indians pouring down the little hill out of the smoke into the camp.

I was struck down by a club, or some hard heavy object, maybe the pole of a hatchet, possibly only a horse's hoof, as he plunged in the air.

When I recovered, which must have been some minutes after, an Indian was rolling me over and pulling at the red Mexican sash around my waist. He was a powerful savage, painted red, half-naked, and held a tomahawk in his hand. I clutched tight around one of his naked legs with both my arms. He tried to shake me off, but I only clutched the tighter. I looked up, and his terrible face almost froze my blood. I relaxed my hold from want of strength. I shut my eyes, expecting the tomahawk to crash through my brain and end the matter at once, but he only laughed, as much as an Indian ever allows himself to laugh, and winding the red sash around him strode down the valley.

My pistol was gone. I crept through the grass into the stream, then down the stream to where it nearly touched the forest, and climbed over and slipped into the wood.

From the timber rim I looked back, but could see nothing whatever. The band of horses was gone, the Indians had disappeared. All was still. It was truly the stillness of death.

The Indian boys, my companions, had escaped with the ponies into the wood, and I stole up the edge of the forest till I struck their trail, and following on a little way, weak and bewildered, I met them stealing back on foot to my assistance.

My mind and energy both now seemed to give way. We reached the Indian camp somehow, but I have but a vague and shadowy recollection of what passed during the next few weeks. For the most part, as far as I remember, I sat by the lodges or under the trees, or rode a little, but never summoned spirit or energy to return to the fatal camp.

I asked the Indians to go down and see what had become of the two bodies, but they would not think of it. This was quite natural, since they will not revisit their own camp after being driven from it by an enemy, until it is first visited by their priest or medicine man, who chaunts the death-song and appeases the angered spirit that has brought the calamity upon them. The Indian camp was a small one, and made up mostly of women and children. It was in a vine-maple thicket, on the bend of a small stream called by the Indians Ki-yi-mem, or white water. By the whites I think it is now called Milk Creek. A singular stream it is; sometimes it flows very full, and then is nearly dry; sometimes it is almost white with ashes and fine sand, and then it is perfectly clear with a beautiful white sand border and bottom. The Indians say, that it is also sometimes so hot as to burn the hand, and then again is as cold as the McCloud; but this last phenomenon I never witnessed. The changes however, whatever they are, are caused by some internal volcanic action of Mount Shasta, from which the stream flows in great springs.

The camp was but a temporary one, and pitched here for the purpose of gathering and drying a sort of mountain camas root from the low marshy springs of this region. This camas is a bulbus root shaped much like an onion, and is prepared for food by roasting in the ground, and is very nutritious. Sometimes it is kneaded into cakes and dried. In this state if kept dry it will retain its sweetness and fine properties for months.

I could not have been treated more kindly even at home. But Indian life and Indian diet are hardly suited to restore a shattered nervous system and organization so delicate as my own, and I got on slowly. Perhaps after all I only needed rest, and it is quite likely the Indians saw this, for rest I certainly had, such as I never had before or since. It was as near a life of nothingness down there in the deep forest as one well could imagine. There were no birds in the thicket about the camp, and you even had to go out and climb a little hill to get the sun.

This hill sloped off to the south with the woods open like a park, and here the children and some young women sported noiselessly or basked in the sun.

If there is any place outside of the tomb that can

be stiller than an Indian camp when stillness is required, I do not know where it is. Here was a camp made up mostly of children, and what is usually called the most garrulous half of mankind, and yet all was so still that the deer often walked stately and unconscious into our midst.

No mention was made of my going away or remaining. I was permitted as far as the Indians were concerned to forget my existence, and so I dreamed along for a month or two and began to get strong and active in mind and body.

I had dreamed a long dream, and now began to waken and think of active life. I began to hunt and take part with the Indians, and enter into their delights and their sorrows.

Did the world ever stop to consider how an Indian who has no theatre, no saloon, no whisky shop, no parties, no newspaper, not one of all our hundreds of ways and means of amusement, spends his evening? Think of this! He is a human being, full of passion and of poetry. His soul must find some expression; his heart some utterance. The long, long nights of darkness, without any lighted city to walk about in, or books to read. Think of that! Well, all this mind, or thought, or soul, or whatever it may be, which we scatter in so many directions, and on so many things, they centre on one or two.

What if I told you that they talk more of the future and know more of the unknown than the Christian? That would shock you. Truth is a great galvanic battery.

No wonder they die so bravely, and care so little for this life, when they are so certain of the next.

After a time we moved camp to a less dangerous quarter, and out into the open wood. I now took rides daily or hunted bear or deer with the Indians. Yet all this time I had a sort of regretful idea that I must return to the white people and give some account of what had happened. Then I reflected how inglorious a part I had borne, how long I had remained with the Indians, though for no fault of my own, and instinctively knew the virtue of silence on the subject.

In this new camp I seemed to come fully to my strength. I took in the situation and the scenery and began to observe, to think, and reflect.

Here, for the first time, I found myself alone in an Indian camp without any obligation or anything whatever binding me or calling me back to the Saxon. I began to look on the romantic side of my life, and was not displeased. I put aside the little trouble of the old camp and became as careless as a child.

The wood seemed very very beautiful. The air was so rich, so soft and pure in the Indian summer, that it almost seemed that you could feed upon it. The antlered deer, fat, and tame almost as if fed in parks, stalked by, and game of all kinds filled the woods in herds. We hunted, rode, fished and rested beside the rivers.

What a fragrance from the long and bent fir boughs;

what a healthy breath of pine! All the long sweet
moonlight nights the magnificent forest, warm and
mellow-like from sunshine gone away, gave out
odours like burnt offerings from censers swinging in
some mighty cathedral.

If I were to look back over the chart of my life for
happiness, I should locate it here if anywhere. It is
true that there was a little cast of concern in all this
about the future, and some remorse for wasted time;
and my life, I think, partook of the Indian's melancholy, which comes of solitude and too much thought,
but the memory of these few weeks always appeals
to my heart, and strikes me with a peculiar gentleness and uncommon delight.

The Indians were not at war with the whites, nor
were they particularly at peace. In fact, they assert
that there has never been any peace since they or
their fathers can remember. The various tribes,
sometimes at war, were also then at peace, so that
nothing whatever occurred to break the calm repose
of the golden autumn.

The mountain streams went foaming down among
the boulders between the leaning walls of yew and
cedar trees toward the Sacramento. The partridge
whistled and called his flock together when the sun
went down; the brown pheasants rustled as they ran
in strings through the long brown grass, but nothing
else was heard. The Indians, always silent, are unusually so in autumn. The majestic march of the
season seems to make them still. They moved

like shadows. The conflicts of civilization were
beneath us. No sound of strife; the struggle for
the possession of usurped lands was far away, and I
was glad, glad as I shall never be again. I know I
should weary you, to linger here and detail the life
we led; but as for myself I shall never cease to
relive this life. Here I go for rest when I cannot
rest elsewhere.

With nothing whatever to do but learn their
language and their manners, I made fast progress,
and without any particular purpose at first, I soon
found myself in possession of that which, in the
hands of a man of culture would be of great
value. I saw then how little we know of the
Indian. I had read some flaming picture books of
Indian life, and I had mixed all my life more or less
with the Indians, that is, such as are willing to mix
with us on the border, but the real Indian, the
brave, simple, silent and thoughtful Indian who
retreats from the white man when he can, and fights
when he must, I had never before seen or read a
line about. I had never even heard of him. Few
have. Perhaps ten years from now the red man, as
I found him there in the forests of his fathers, shall
not be found anywhere on earth. I am now certain
that if I had been a man, or even a clever wide-awake
boy, with any particular business with the Indians, I
might have spent years in the mountains, and known
no more of these people than others know. But lost
as I was, and a dreamer, too ignorant of danger to fear,

they sympathized with me, took me into their inner life, told me their traditions, and sometimes showed me the " Indian question " from an Indian point of view.

After mingling with these people for some months, I began to say to myself, Why cannot they be permitted to remain here? Let this region be un-traversed and untouched by the Saxon. Let this be a great national park peopled by the Indian only. I saw the justice of this, but did not at that time conceive the possibility of it.

No man leaps full-grown into the world. No great plan bursts in full and complete magnificence and at once upon the mind. Nor does any one sud-denly become this thing or that. A combination of circumstances, a long chain of reverses that refuses to be broken, carries men far down in the scale of life, without any fault whatever of theirs. A similar but less frequent chain of good fortune lifts others up into the full light of the sun. Circumstances which few see, and fewer still understand, fashion the destinies of nearly all the active men of the plastic west. The world watching the gladiators from its high seat in the circus will never reverse its thumbs against the successful man. Therefore, succeed, and have the approval of the world. Nay! what is far better, deserve to succeed, and have the approval of your own con-science.

CHAPTER III

NOW stood face to face with the outposts of the great events of my life. Here were the tawny people with whom I was to mingle. There loomed Mount Shasta, with which my name, if remembered at all, will be remembered. I had not sought this. I did not dream even then that I should mix with these people, or linger longer here in the shadows of Shasta than I had lingered in camps before.

I visited many of the Indian villages, where I received nothing but kindness and hospitality. They had never before seen so young a white man. The Indian mothers were particularly kind. My tattered clothes were replaced by soft brown buckskins, which they almost forced me to accept. I was not only told that I was welcome, and that they were glad to see me, but I was made to feel that this was the case. Their men were manly, tall, graceful.

Their women were beautiful in their wild and natural, simple and savage beauty beyond anything I have since seen, and I have gone well-nigh the circuit of the earth since I first pitched camp at the base of Shasta.

I came to sympathize thoroughly with the Indians. Perhaps, if I had been in a pleasant home, had friends, or even had the strength of will and capacity to lay hold of the world, and enter the conflict successfully, I might have thought much as others thought, and done as others have done ; but I was a gipsy, and had no home. I did not fear or shun toil, but I despised the treachery, falsehood, and villany, practised in the struggle for wealth, and kept as well out of it as I could.

All these old ideas of mine seem very singular now for one so young. Yet it appears to me I always had them ; may be, I was born with a nature that did not fit into the mould of other minds. At all events, I began to think very early for myself, and nearly always as incorrectly as possible. Even at the time mentioned I had some of the thoughts of a man ; and at the present time, perhaps, I have many of the thoughts of a child. My life on horseback and among herds from the time I was old enough to ride a horse, had made me even still more thoughtful and solitary than was my nature, so that on some things I thought a great deal, or rather observed, while on others—practical things—I never bestowed a moment's time. I had never been a boy, that is, an orthodox, old-

fashioned boy, for I never played in my life. Games
of ball, marbles, and the like, are to me still mysterious as the rites in a Pagan temple. I then knew
nothing at all of men. Cattle and horses I understand thoroughly. But somehow I could not understand or get on with my fellow man. He seemed to
always want to cheat me—to get my labour for
nothing. I could appreciate and enter into the heart of
an Indian. Perhaps it was because he was natural;
a child of nature; nearer to God than the white man.
I think what I most needed in order to understand,
get on and not be misunderstood, was a long time at
school, where my rough points could be ground down.
The schoolmaster should have taken me between his
thumb and finger and rubbed me about till I was as
smooth and as round as the others. Then I should
have been put out in the society of other smooth
pebbles, and rubbed and ground against them till I
got as smooth and pointless as they. You must not
have points or anything about you singular or noticeable if you would get on. You must be a pebble, a
smooth, quiet pebble. Be a big pebble if you can, a
small pebble if you must. But be a pebble just like
the rest, cold, and hard, and sleek, and smooth, and
you are all right. But I was as rough as the lava
rocks I roamed over, as broken as the mountains I
inhabited; neither a man nor a boy.

How I am running on about myself, and yet how
pleasant is this forbidden fruit ! The world says you
must not talk of yourself. The world is a tyrant.

The world no sooner discovered that the most delightful of all things was the pleasure of talking about one's self, even more delightful than talking about one's neighbour, than straightway the world, with the wits to back it, pronounced against the use of this luxury.

Who knows but it is a sort of desire for revenge against mankind for forbidding us to talk as much as we like about ourselves, that makes us so turn upon and talk about our neighbours.

Be that as it may, I know very well that if all men were permitted to talk about themselves as much as they liked, they would not talk so much about their neighbours. They would not have time.

Even ages ago, whenever any man dared come out and talk freely, naturally and fully as he desired about himself, the wits nailed him to the wall with their shafts of irony, until the last man was driven from the green and leafy Eden of egotism, and no one has yet had courage to attempt to retake it.

Now I like this great big letter " I," standing out boldly alone like a soldier at his post. It is a sort of granite pillar, it seems to me, set up at each mile, even every quarter if you like, to face you, to be familiar, to talk to you as you proceed, without an interpreter or the intervention of a third party.

Modest Cæsar! The man who writes of a third person when he means the first is a falsehood. The man who says "we" when he means "I," is a coward, and afraid to go alone. He winces before the wits, and takes shelter behind the back of another person. I would rather see a man stand up like Homer's heroes, or a North American Indian, and tell all his deeds of valour and the deeds of all his ancestors even back to the tenth generation, than this.

J despise this contemptible little wishy-washy editorial "we." The truth is, it is ten times more pompous than the bold naked soldier-like "I." Besides, it has the disadvantage of being a falsehood; a slight, slight disadvantage in this age, it is true, but still a disadvantage.

I edited a little paper once for a brief period. I was owner, editor, and proprietor. This was distinctly stated at the head of the first column of the paper. It would have been clear to all, even had I desired to take shelter under the editorial "we," that its use was a naked and notorious falsehood. I was young then. I knew nothing of civilization. My education had been greatly neglected, and I could not lie. I stood up the great big pronoun on the paper as thick as pickets around a garden fence. The publication died soon after, it is true, but this proves nothing against the use of the great and popular pronoun.

Winter now was approaching; and while I should have been welcome with the Indians to the end, I preferred to consider my stay with them in the light of a visit, and decided to go on to Yreka (a mining camp then grown to the dignity of a city), and try my fortune in the mines.

It was unsafe to venture out alone, if not impossible to find the way ; but the two young men who had assisted as vaqueros in the valley set out with me and led the way till we touched the trail leading from Red Bluffs to Yreka on the eastern spurs of Mount Shasta. Here they took a tender farewell, turned back, and I never saw them again. They were murdered before I returned to their village.

The facts of the cruel assassinations are briefly these. The following summer the young men went down into Pit River Valley, then filling up rapidly with white settlers, and there took to themselves wives from the Pit River tribe, with whom the Shastas were on the best of terms.

These young fellows had a fondness for the whites, and were very frequently about the settlements. They finally made a camp near some men who were making hay, and put in their time and supported themselves by hunting and fishing, at the same time keeping up friendly relations with the whites by liberal donations of game.

One day one of these Indians, with his young wife, went out among the hay makers, and while he was standing there, watching the men at work, two men came up from a neighbouring part of the prairie and shot him down in cold blood, saying only that they knew him and that he was "a damned bad Injin."

This is, or was at that time, considered quite sufficient excuse for taking an Indian's life on the Pacific.

They hid the body under a haycock, and carried his young and terrified wife to their camp.

That evening the other Indian, returning from the hills, came to look after his companion. The two men told him they would show him where he was; and the young man, still unsuspicious, walked out with them; but when near the hayfield one of the two, who had fallen behind, shot him in the back.

The Indian was good mettle, however, and for the first time discerning the treachery, sprang forward upon the other now a little in advance and brought him to the ground. But the poor boy had been mortally shot, and died almost instantly after.

The plain cold truth of the matter is these men had seen the two young Indian women, wanted them, and got them after this manner, as did others in similar ways, and no one said nay.

This account I had from the lips of one of the very two men alluded to. His name is Fowler. He told it by way of a boast, repeatedly, and to numbers of men, while we were engaged in the Pit river war. This Fowler is now married to a white woman, and lives in Shasta county, California.

Of such deeds grew the Pit river valley massacre hereinafter narrated.

I rode down and around the northern end of the deep wood, and down into Shasta valley.

If I was unfit to take my part in the battle of life when I left home, I was now certainly less so. My wandering had only made me the more a dreamer.

My stay with the Indians had only intensified my dislike for shopkeepers, and the commercial world in general, and I was as helpless as an Indian.

I was so shy, that I only spoke to men when compelled to, and then with the greatest difficulty and embarrassment. I remember, lonely as I was in my ride to Yreka, that I always took some by-trail, if possible, if about to meet people, in order to avoid them, and at night would camp alone by the wayside, and sleep in my blanket on the ground, rather than call at an inn, and come face to face with strangers.

I left the Indians without any intention of returning, whatever. I had determined to enter the gold mines, dig gold for myself, make a fortune, and return to civilization, or to such civilization as I had known.

Stronger men than I have had that same plan. Perhaps one out of twenty has succeeded.

I must here make a long digression from the Indian trail. In spite of my resolution to boldly enter the camp or city and bear my part there, as I neared the town my heart failed me, and I made on to Cottonwood, a mining camp twenty miles distant, on the Klamat, and a much smaller town.

After two or three days of unsuccessful attempts to find some opening, I determined to again marshal courage and move upon Yreka. I accordingly, on a clear frosty morning, mounted my pony, and set out alone for that place.

I rode down to the banks of the beautiful, arrowy Klamat — misspelled Klamath — with a thousand peaceful Indians in sight.

A deep, swift stream it was then, beautiful and blue as the skies; but not so now. The miners have filled its bed with tailings from the sluice and tom; they have dumped, and dyked, and mined in this beautiful river-bed till it flows sullen and turbid enough. Its Indian name signifies the "giver" or "generous," from the wealth of salmon it gave the red men till the white man came to its banks.

The salmon will not ascend the muddy water from the sea. They come no more, and the red men are gone.

As I rode down to the narrow river, I saw a tall, strong, and elegant-looking gentleman in top boots and red sash, standing on the banks calling to the ferryman on the opposite side.

Up to this moment, it seemed to me I had never yet seen a perfect man. This one now before me seemed to leave nothing to be desired in all that goes to make the comely and complete gentleman. Young—I should say he was hardly twenty-five— and yet thoroughly thoughtful and in earnest. There was command in his quiet face and a dignity in his presence, yet a gentleness, too, that won me there, and made it seem possible to approach as near his heart as it is well for one man to approach that of another.

This, thought I, as I stood waiting for the boat, is

no common person. He is surely a prince in disguise; may be he is the son of a president or a banker, wild and free, up here in the mountains for pleasure. Then I saw from the dark and classic face that he was neither an American, German, nor Irishman, and vaguely I associated him with Italian princes dethroned, or even a king of France in exile. He was surely splendid, superb, standing there in the morning sun, in his gay attire, by the swift and shining river, smiling, tapping the sand in an absent-minded sort of way with his boot. A prince! truly nothing less than a prince! The man turned and smiled good-naturedly, as I dismounted, tapped the sand with his top-boot, gently whistled the old air of " '49," but did not speak.

This man was attired something after the Mexican style of dress, with a wealth of black hair on his shoulders, a cloak on his arm, and a pistol in his belt.

The boatman came and took us in his narrow little flat, and set his oars for the other side. A sort of Yankee sailor was this boatman, of a very low sort too; blown up from the sea as sea-gulls are sometimes found blown out even in the heart of the plains: a suspicious-looking, sallow, solemn-faced, bald-headed man in gum-boots, duck-breeches, blue shirt with the front all open, showing his hairy bosom, and with a lariat tied about his waist in the form of a sash.

The tall, fine-looking man stepped ashore with a

quiet laugh as the boat touched the sand, and said, "Chalk that." These were the first words I had ever heard him utter.

The solemn-faced ferryman tied his boat in a second, and, stepping boldly up under the nose of the tall man, said fiercely:—

"Look here, what do you play me for? Do you think I'm a Chinaman? You high-toned, fine-haired gamblers don't play me—not much, you don't!"

" Don't want to play you, my friend."

" Then pay me. Why don't you pay me, and be off ?"

" Haven't got the tin. Can't come to the centre! Haven't got the dust. Can't liquidate. That's the reason why."

And here the good-natured tall gentleman again tapped the sand with his boot, and looked down at the river and at the bullying ferryman under his nose.

" Then leave your coat; leave your—your pistol, till you come again."

The tall man shifted his cloak from his right arm to his left. The ferryman fell back toward his boat. Sailors know the signs of a storm.

"Look here," began the tall man, mildly, " I crossed here yesterday, did I not ? I gave you a whole cart-wheel, did I not ? a clean twenty dollar, and told you to keep the change and use it in crossing poor devils that were out of tin. You don't know me now with no mule and no catenas filled with tin. Forgot what I told you, I should think. Now, you count out my change, or by the holy spoons, I'll pitch you in there, neck and crop, among the salmon."

And here the tall man reached for the man in blue who in turn turned red and white and black, and when he had retreated to the water's edge and saw the tall man still advancing and reaching for him, thrust his hand into his capacious pocket and counted down the coin in a very methodical and business-like way, into the hand of the other.

Then the tall man laughed good-naturedly, bade the boatman good-bye, came up and coolly tied his coat on behind my saddle, and we set forward up the trail.

The tall man hummed an air as he followed in the trail behind my pony, the boatman swore a little as he untied his boat, and the arrowy, silver river shot away towards the sea between its rocky walls, with its thousands of listless, dreamy Indians on its banks.

I take it to be a good sign if a strong, good-natured man who has a fair opportunity, does not talk to you much, at first. In fact, as a rule, you should be cautious of over-talkative strangers. Such persons have either not sense enough to keep quiet; not brains enough to ballast their tongues, as it were, or are low and vicious people who feel their littleness and feel that they must talk themselves into some consequence.

After we had gone on in silence for some time, on turning a point in the trail we saw a man approaching from the other direction. A strong, fine-looking man was this also, mounted on a sleek, well-fed mule with his long ears set sharply forward; a sure sign that he was on good terms with his rider. The mule brayed lustily, and then pointed his two ears keenly at us as if they were opera-glasses, and we a sort of travelling theatre.

The man was richly dressed, for the mountains; sported a moustache, top-boots, fur vest, cloth coat, a broad palm hat, and had diamonds in the bosom of his shirt. A costly cloak on his shoulders, yellow buckskin gauntlets, a rich, red sash around his waist, where swung a pair of Colt's new patent, and a great gold chain made up by linking specimens of native gold together, made up this man's attire. His great hat sheltered him like a palm.

CHAPTER IV

THE man did not notice me, but made straight up to my companion until his mule's opera-glasses nearly touched the tall man's nose, who was now in a little trail at my side.

Then the man under the palm-leaf let go the reins, leaned back as the mule stopped, put his two hands on the saddle pommel, and slowly, emphatically, and with the most evident surprise, as he raised one hand and pushed back the palm-leaf clear off his eyes to get a good square look at my companion, said :—

"Well—blast—my sister's cat's-tail to the bone! Is this you, Prince Hal, or is it Hamlet's daddy's ghost? You back from the war-path, afoot and alone! Angels and ministers of grace defend us! Spirits of the"——

And here as if the mention of the first-named in the sentence had suddenly inspired him with a new thought, he leaned forward, unfastened his catenas, and drew forth a long-necked bottle. He drew the cork with his teeth, then held the bottle up to the sun, shut one eye, looked at the contents as if to see that they had the desired bead, handed it to the man he had called Prince Hal, said "Boston's best," and bowed down his head.

The Prince took the bottle solemnly, held it up to the light, placed three fingers on a level with the top of the contents, and then slowly raised the bottom towards the sun.

A gurgling sound, then the telescope descended, and the Prince took a long breath as he handed the bottle on to me.

I had not yet learned the etiquette of the mountain traveller, and shook my head.

A hand reached out from under the broad hat, as the Prince returned the bottle in that direction, took it by the neck, shook it gently, tilted it over as the broad hat fell back, and consulted the oracle; then stuck it back in the catenas.

When he had replaced the bottle, he stood in his great wooden stirrups, rattled the bells of steel on his great Spanish spurs, and again eyed my companion.

"Well damn old roper!" he again broke forth, "money, mule, and watch all gone, and you afoot and alone! Well, how on earth did it happen? And is it really so? Just to think that Prince Hal, the man of all others who always made it particular hell for the rest of us, should travel all the way from Yreka to Cottonwood to get a game, and then get cleaned out cleaner than a shot-gun! Too jolly for anything! And are you really dead-broke?"

"Skinned clean down to the bed-rock. Haven't got the colour," said the Prince, laconically, as he again tapped the dust with his boot.

"Well now, do tell a fellow how it happened. I shall hang up at Cottonwood to-night, and if I don't make the sports *ante*, my name ain't Boston. What did you go through on?"

"Four aces!"

"Four devils! and what did the other fellow have?"

"A pair!"

"A pair of what? You let him take your money on a pair when you had four aces? Now come! On the square—how on earth did you get sinched, any-how? and did you really have four aces?"

"Yes."

"And the other fellow?"

"A pair."

"Of what ?"

"Six-shooters!" calmly answered the laconic Prince, still tapping at the dust and looking sidewise like, to the right.

"Now look here," said Boston earnestly, as he dismounted, stood on one foot and leaned against his mule, with the broad hat pressed back and his right arm over the animal's neck, "do for the love of Moses tell me all about how this happened!"

Here the Prince stopped looking around, held up his head, laughed a little, and proceeded to state that the night before he had a game with two new gamblers, who claimed to have just come up from Oregon, long-haired and green, as he supposed, as Willamette grass, at twenty dollars a corner. That about midnight he fell heir to four aces, and staked all his fortune, money, mule and watch on the hand. " I really felt sorry for the boys," added the Prince. " It seemed like robbing, to take their money on four aces, and I told them to not set it too deep, but they said they would mourn as much as they liked at their own funeral, and so came to the centre and called me to the board."

" What have you got?"

" Four aces!"

" Four aces! and what else? Skin 'em out, skin 'em out!"

" I put down my four aces before their eyes, when one of them coolly put his finger down on my fifth card, pushed it aside, and there lay the sixth card!"

Boston gave a long whistle, and as he could not push his panama any further back, he pulled it forward, and looked up with his nose at Mount Shasta.

This was my first lesson in gambling. Here for the first time I learned that any one caught cheating at cards forfeits his stakes.

Cheat all you like, but don't get caught. A game at cards, you see, is much like many other things in this respect.

The Prince of course remonstrated, but it was no use. He had not been cheating; they had waxed his cards together and he did not detect it till too late.

Appearances were against him; besides a pair of pistols cocked and at hand, decided the matter. He acknowledged himself beat. Took a drink good-naturedly with the crafty gamblers and retired.

For the benefit of ladies whose husbands may profess ignorance on this subject, I may state that four aces in a game of poker make a " corner" that cannot be broken.

The man in the broad hat slowly mounted his mule, set his feet in the stirrups, stretched his long legs in the tapideros, unbuckled the catenas, and again reached the contents of the right-hand pocket to the Prince, and leaning back as my companion took a refreshing drink again, said " Well—blast my sister's cat's tail to the bone !"

" Well, Prince," said Boston, as he drove the cork home with his palm and replaced the bottle, " you and I have set against each other, night after night, and I have found you a hard nut to crack, you bet your life, but to see you skinned to the bed-rock, and by Oregonians at that, is too rough; and here's my hand on that. You was always best, and I second best, of the two you know, but no matter; take this." And he put his hand down in the other pocket of his catenas, and drew forth a handful of twenties. " Take them, I tell you," as the Prince declined. "You must and shall take them as a friend's loan if nothing else. That is, I intend to force you to take these few twenties, and won't take no for an answer."

The Prince took the coins, carelessly dropped them into his pocket, and again tapped the dust with his boot, and looked up at the sun as if he wished to be on his way.

Neither of the men had counted the money, or seemed to take any note of the amount.

The bottle was again uncorked and exchanged. Boston gathered up the reins from the neck of his mule, settled himself in the saddle, stuck his great spurs in the sinch, and the mule struck out, ambling and braying as he went, with his opera-glasses held directly on the river below.

I had not been mentioned, or noticed further. I might have been invisible as air, so far as my presence was concerned, after I declined to take a drink.

California gamblers these, of the old and early type! And they were men! There is no doubt of that. They were brave, honest, generous men. But let it be distinctly understood, that the old race is extinct.

These men described were the cream of their calling, even at that time when gold was plenty and manhood was not rare. Such men were the first to give away their gains, the first to take part in any good enterprise, not too much freighted with the presence of a certain type of itinerants, so-called "Methodist ministers." In these few first years, they went about from camp to camp, and won or lost their money as the men above described.

The man who keeps a gambling den to-day is another manner of man. The professional gambler through most of the Pacific cities of to-day is a low character. The would-be "sport" who would imitate these men of the early time is usually a broken-down barber, bar-tender, or waiter in disgrace.

A sudden and short-lived race were these. Gay old sports, who sprung up mushroom-like from the abundance and very heaps of gold. Men who had vast sums of money from some run of fortune, and no great aim in life, and having no other form of excitement, sat down and gambled for amusement, until they came to like it and followed it as a calling, for a time, at least.

All men have a certain amount of surplus energy that must be thrown off against some keen excitement. You see how very naturally very good men became gamblers in that time. Their successors, however, gamble for gold and gain; too idle to toil and too cowardly to rob, they follow a calling, about the mining camps particularly, that is now as disreputable as it was once respectable, or rather aristocratic.

The good old days are gone. The gay gamblers with their open pockets and ideas of honour; the fast women who kept the camps in turmoil and commotion, are no more. Their imitators are there, but in camps where men would be glad to pay a woman well to wash his shirt, and where every man strong enough to swing a pick can get employment, there is no excuse for the one nor apology for the other.

Water will seek its level. As a rule, the low are low—avoid them, particularly in America, more particularly on the Pacific side of America. Give a man five years, and, with unfortunate exceptions of course, he will find his level on the Pacific, and his place, whether high or low, as naturally as a stream of water. Many of our old gamblers took up the law. A great many took to politics; some advanced far into distinction, even to Congress, and were heard when they got there. Many fell in Nicaragua. One or two became ministers, and made some mark in the world. One is even now particularly famous for his laconic sword-cuts of speech, born of the gambling table, when he is excited and earnestly addressing his congregation of miners in the mountains.

As a rule, these men remained true to the Pacific, and refused to leave it. The miners gathered up their gold, and returned to their old homes; the merchants did the same as the camps went down, but these men remained. They have, to use their own expression, mostly " passed in their checks," but what few of them are still found, no matter what they follow, are honest, brave old men.

Nature had knighted them at their births as of noble blood, and they could not but remain men even in the calling of knaves.

It was late in the day when we passed, on one side of the dusty road we had been travelling but a short distance, a newly-erected gallows, and a populous grave-yard on the other. Certain evidences, under the present order of things, of the nearness of civilization and a city.

Mount Shasta is not visible from the city. A long butte, black and covered with chapparal, lifts up before Yreka, shutting out the presence of the mountain.

It was a strange sort of inspiration that made the sheriff come out here to construct his gallows—out in the light, as it were, from behind the little butte and full in the face of Shasta.

A strange sort of inspiration it was, and more beautiful, that made the miners bring the first dead out here from the camp, from the dark, and dig his grave here on the hill-side, full in the light of the lifted and eternal front of snow.

Dead men are even more gregarious than the living. No one lies down to rest long at a time alone, even in the wildest parts of the Pacific. The dead will come, if his place of rest be not hidden utterly, sooner or later, and even in the wildest places will find him out, and one by one lie down around him.

The shadows of the mountains in mantles of pine were reaching out from the west over the thronged busy little new-born city, as we entered its populous streets.

The kingly sun, as if it was the last sweet office on earth that day, reached out a shining hand to Shasta, laid it on his head till it became a halo of gold and glory, withdrew it then and let the shadowy curtains of night come down, and it was dark almost in a moment.

The Prince unfastened his cloak from the macheers behind my saddle, and as he did so, courteously asked if I was "all right in town," and I boldly answered, "Oh yes, all right now." Then he bade me good bye, and walked rapidly up the street.

If I had only had a little nerve, the least bit of practical common-sense and knowledge of men, I should have answered, " No, sir; I am not all right, at all. I am quite alone here. I do not know a soul in this city or any means of making a living. I have nothing in the world but a half-dollar and this pony. I am tired, cold, hungry, half-clad, as you see. No, sir, since you ask me, that is the plain truth of the matter. I am not all right at all."

Had I had the sense or courage to say that, or any part of that, he would have given me half, if not all, the coins given him on the trail, and been proud and happy to do it.

I was alone in the mines and mountains of California. But what was worse than mines and mountains, I was alone in a city. I was alone in the first city I had ever seen. I could see nothing here that I had ever seen before, but the cold far stars above me. There was nothing, no one there that had ever heard of, known, or cared for me before, but . . . . God.

I pretended to be arranging my saddle till the Prince was out of sight, and then seeing the sign of a horse with hind legs like the knees of a ship, and other points displaying equal artistic skill, swinging before a stable close at hand, I led my tired pony there, and asked that he should be cared for.

A negro kept this stable, a Nicaragua negro, with one eye, and an uncommon long beard for one of his race. He had gold enough hung to his watch-chain in charms and specimens to stock a ranch, and finger-rings like a pawn-dealer. He was very black, short and fat, and insolent to the white boy who tended his horses. I was afraid of this man from the first, instinctively, and without any reason at all.

When you fear a man or woman instinctively, follow your instincts. I shrank from this short, black, one-eyed scoundrel, with his display of gold, in a strange way. When he came up and spoke to me, as I was about to go out, I held my head down under his one eye, as if I had stolen something and dared not look into it.

Permit me to say here that the popular idea that the honest man will look you in the face and the knave will not, is one of the most glaring of popular humbugs that I know. Ten chances to one the knave will look you in the eye till you feel abashed yourself, while the honest, sensitive man or woman will merely lift the face to yours, and the eyes are again to the ground.

" Look me in the eye and tell me that, and I will believe you," is a favourite saying. Nonsense! there is not a villain in the land but can look you in the eye and lie you blind.

CHAPTER V

THINK I was ill. I remember some things but vaguely which took place this night, and the day and night that followed.

I am certain that something was wrong all this time; for, as a rule, when we first land from a voyage, or reach a journey's end, the mind is fresh and strong—a blank ready to receive impressions and to retain them.

If you will observe or recall the fact, you will find that the first city you visited in China, or the first sea-port you touched at in Europe, is fixed in your mind more perfectly than any other. But my recollection of this time, usually clear and faultless, is shadowy and indistinct. I was surely ill.

This black man to me was a nightmare. I stood before him like a convict before his keeper. I felt that he was my master. Had he told me to do this or that I would have gone and done it, glad to get from under his one and dreadful eye, that seemed to be burning a hole in my head.

The one-eyed black villain knew very well he was torturing me. He took a delight in it. Understand he had not said a word. I had not lifted my eyes.

At last he hoisted his black fat hand to his black thick head and turned away. I walked with an effort out into the street. This man had taken my strength; he had absorbed me into his strong animal body.

Here is a subject that I do not understand at all. I will only state a fact. There are men that exhaust me. There are men that if they come into a room and talk to me, or even approach closely, take my strength from me more speedily, and as certainly, as if I spent my force climbing a hill. There are men that I cannot endure; their presence is to me an actual physical pain. I have tried to overcome this—in vain. I have found myself dodging men in the street, hiding around the corner, or flying like a pick-pocket into a crowd to escape them. Good honest men are they—some of them, no doubt, yet they use me up; they absorb, exhaust me; they would kill me dead in less than a week.

I stole away from the stable and reached the main street. A tide of people poured up and down, and across from other streets, as strong as in a town of the East. The white people on the side walks, the Chinese and mules in the main street. Not a woman in sight, not a child, not a boy. People turned to look at me as at something new and out of place.

I was very hungry, faint, miserable. The wind pitched down from the white-covered mountains, cold and keen, and whistled above the crowds along the streets. I got a biscuit for my half-dollar, walked on, ate it unobserved, and was stronger.

Brick houses on either hand, two and three stories high. A city of altogether, perhaps, five thousand souls. I was utterly overcome by the magnitude of the place and the multitude of people. There being but one main street, I kept along this till the further end was reached, then turned back, and thus was not lost or bewildered. I returned to the stable, stronger now, yet almost trembling with fear of meeting the black man with one eye.

As a rule, beware of one-eyed people, who have not a strong moral anchor; also beware of cripples, unless they too have a good and patient nature. Fate has put them at a disadvantage with the world, and they can only battle and keep pace with their fellows by cunning. Nine times out of ten they instinctively take to treachery and tricks to overcome this disadvantage. That is only natural.

On the same principle, woman, who is not so strong as man, resorts to strategy to match him. What she lacks in strength, she makes up in being more than his equal in craftiness. The strong grizzly goes boldly upon his prey, crushing through the chapparal like the march of an army; the panther lies on a limb, waiting to take it to a disadvantage. A deaf and dumb person is usually a lovable person;

so is one who is totally blind, for these live somewhat more within themselves and do not go out to battle with the world, or at least, do not attempt to match it in the daily struggle; but you put a one-eyed man or a cripple in the fight, and unless he is very good, he is very bad indeed.

I went up to my pony, standing on three legs with his nose in the hay, put my arms around his neck, talked baby-talk to him, and felt as with an old friend. There was a little opening overhead, a place where they put hay down from the loft. I looked up. An idea struck me. I looked over my shoulder for the negro. No one was there. I climbed up like a cat; found a hump of hay, crept into it, and was soon fast asleep.

It was not a pleasant bed. The wind whistled through the loft, and though I crept and cowered into the very heart of the hay-pile, the frost followed me up unmercifully. I descended with the dawn, lest the negro should be there, and was on the street even before the Chinamen, and long before the sun. A frost was on the ground, and a taste of winter in the air and wind.

To the west the pine hills were brown with the dead grass, then farther up, green with pine and fir, then white with frost and snow.

I walked up the single long street in that direction, the hills began to flash back the sun that glowed from Shasta's helmet, and my heart rose up with the sun. I said, " The world is before me.

Here is a new world being fashioned under my very feet. I will take part in the work, and a portion of it shall be mine."

All this city had been built, all this country opened up, in less than two years. Twenty months before, only the Indian inhabited here; he was lord absolute of the land. But gold had been found on this spot by a party of roving mountaineers; the news had gone abroad, and people poured in and had taken possession in a day, without question and without ceremony.

And the Indians? They were pushed aside. At first they were glad to make the strangers welcome; but when they saw where it would all lead, they grew sullen and concerned. Then trouble arose; they retreated, and Ben Wright took the field and followed them, as we have seen.

I hurried on a mile or so to the foot-hills, and stood in the heart of the placer mines. Now the smoke from the low chimneys of the log cabins began to rise and curl through the cool, clear air on every hand, and the miners to come out at the low doors; great hairy, bearded, six foot giants, hatless, and half-dressed.

They stretched themselves in the sweet, frosty air, shouted to each other in a sort of savage banter, washed their hands and faces in the gold-pan that stood by the door, and then entered their cabins again, to partake of the eternal beans and bacon and coffee, and coffee and bacon and beans.

The whole face of the earth was perforated with holes; shafts sunk and being sunk by these men in search of gold, down to the bed-rock. Windlasses stretched across these shafts where great buckets swung, in which men hoisted the earth to the light of the sun by sheer force of muscle.

The sun came softly down, and shone brightly on the hillside where I stood. I lifted my hands to Shasta, above the butte and town, for he looked like an old acquaintance, and I again was glad.

It is one of the chiefest delights of extreme youth, and I may add of extreme ignorance, to bridge over rivers with a rainbow. And one of the chief good things of youth and verdancy is buoyancy of spirits. You may be twice vanquished in a day, and if you are neither old nor wise you may still be twice glad.

A sea of human life began to sound and surge around me. Strong men shouldered their picks and shovels, took their gold pans under their arms, and went forth to their labour. They sang little snatches of songs familiar in other lands, and now and then they shouted back and forth, and their voices arose like trumpets in the mountain air.

I went down among these men full of hope. I asked for work. They looked at me and smiled, and went on with their labour. Sometimes, as I went from one claim to another, they would ask me what I could do. One greasy, red-faced old fellow, with a green patch over his left eye, a check shirt, yellow with dirt, and one suspender, asked—

" What in hell are you doing here anyhow?" . . . .

My spirit mercury fell to freezing point before night.

At dusk I again sought the rude half-open stable, put my arms around my pony's neck, caressed him and talked to him as to a brother. I wanted, needed something to love and talk to, and this horse was all I had.

I trembled lest the negro should be near, and hastened to climb again into the loft and hide in my nest of hay.

It was late when I awoke. I had a headache and hardly knew where I was. When I had collected my mind and understood the situation, I listened for the negro's voice. I heard him in the far part of the stable, and, frightened half to death, hastened to descend.

When a young bear up a tree hears a human voice at the root it hastens down, though it be perfectly safe where it is, and will reach the ground only to fall into the very arms of the hunter.

My conduct was something like that of the young bear. I can account for the one about as clearly as for the other.

My hat was smashed in many shapes, my clothes were wrinkled, and there were fragments of hay and straw in my hair. My heart beat audibly, and my head ached till I was nearly blinded with pain as I hastened down.

There was no earthly reason why I should fear

this negro. Reason would have told me it was not in his power to harm me; but I had not then grown to use my reason.

There are people who follow instinct and impulse, much as a horse or dog, all through rather eventful lives, and, in some things, make fewer mistakes than men who act only from reason.

A woman follows instinct more than man does, and hence is keener to detect the good or bad in a face than man, and makes fewer real mistakes.

When I had descended and turned hastily and half blinded to the door, there stood the one-eyed negro, glaring at me with his one eye ferociously.

"What the holy poker have you been a doin' up there? Stealin' my eggs, eh? Now look here, you better git. Do you hear?" And he came toward me, keeping between me and the door as I tried to pass. "I know you; do you hear? I know'd you stole dat hoss, I did. Now you git."

Here he stepped aside, levelled his one eye at me like a single-barrelled shot-gun as I fled past him, half expecting he would take me on the wing.

What should I do? What did I do? I ran! A boy's legs, like a mule's heels, answer many arguments. They are his last resort, and often his first. Deprive him of everything else, but leave him his legs, and he will get on.

I was not strong. I was not used to making my way through a crowd, and got on slowly. I ran against men coming down the street with picks

and pans, and they swore lustily. I ran against
Chinamen, with great baskets on their bamboo poles,
who took it in good part and said nothing. I expected every moment this black man would seize me
in his black hands and lug me off to a prison. I was
surely delirious.

At last, when near the hotel, I took time to look
over my shoulder. I could see nothing of him; he
perhaps had not left the stable.

As I passed the hotel the Prince came out. He
had slept and rested the day before, after his night
and day of sport and travel, and looked fresh as the
morning.

" How-dy-do?" said the Prince, in his quiet, good-
humoured way. " How-dy-do? Take a drink?"
And he led me into the bar-room. I followed
instinctively.

In most parts of America the morning salutation
is, " How d'ye do? How's the folks?" But on
the Pacific it is, " How-dy-do? Take a drink?"

There was a red sign over the door of the hotel—
a miner with a pick, red shirt, and top boots. I
lifted my face and looked at that sign to hide my expression of concern from the Prince.

" Hullo, my little chicken, what 's up ? You look as
pale as a ghost. Come, take a smash! It will strengthen
you up. Been on a bender last night; ı   cried
an old sailor, glass in hand.

There was an enormous box-stove there in the
middle of the room, with a drum like a steam boiler

above, and a great wood fire that cracked and roared like a furnace.

The walls were low, of painted plank, and were hung around with cheap prints in gay colours—of race-horses, prize-fighters, and bull-dogs. One end of the room was devoted to a local picturing, on a plank half the size of a barn door, which was called a Mexican Bull. This name was prudently written at the bottom, perhaps to prevent mistakes. The great picture of the place, however, was that of a grizzly bear and hunter, which hung at the back of the man who dealt out the tumblers behind the bar. This picture was done by the hunter himself. He was represented clasped in the bear's embrace, and heroically driving an enormous knife to his heart. The knife was big and broad as a hand-saw, red and running with blood. The bear's fore legs were enormous, and nearly twice as long and large as his hind ones. It may be a good stroke of genius to throw all the strength and power in the points to which the attention will most likely be directed. At least that seemed to be the policy adopted by this artist of the West.

An Indian scalp or two hung from a corner of this painting. The long matted hair hung streaming down over the ears of the bear and his red open mouth. A few sheaves of arrows in quivers were hung against the wall, with here and there a tomahawk, a scalping-knife, boomerang and war-club, at the back of the " bar-keep."

Little shelves of bottles, glasses, and other requisites of a well-regulated bar, sprang up on either side of the erect grizzly bear; and on the little shelf where the picture rested lay a brace of pistols, capped and cocked, within hand's reach of the cinnamon-haired bar-keeper. This man was short, thickset, and of enormous strength, strength that had not remained untrained. He had short red hair, which stuck straight out from the scalp; one tooth out in front, and a long white scar across his narrow red forehead. He wore a red shirt, open at the throat, with the sleeves rolled up his brawny arms to the elbows.

All this seems to be before me now. I believe I could count and tell with a tolerable accuracy the number of glasses and bottles there were behind the bar.

Here is something strange. Everything that passed, everything that touched my mind through any source whatever, every form that my eyes rested upon, in those last two or three minutes before I broke down, remained as fixed and substantial in the memory, as shafts of stone.

Is it not because they were the last? because the mind, in the long blank that followed, had nothing else to do but fix those last things firmly in their place; something as the last scene on the land or the last words of friends are remembered when we go down on a long journey across the sea.

I have a dim and uncertain recollection of trying

hard to hold on to the bar, of looking up to the
Prince for help in a helpless way; the house seemed
to rock and reel, and then one side of the room is
lifted up so high I cannot keep my feet—cannot see
distinctly, cannot hear at all, and then all seemed to
recede; and all the senses refused to struggle longer
against the black and the blank sea that came over
me, and all things around me.

The Prince, I think, put out his strong arms and
took me up, but I do not know. All this is painful to
recall. I never asked anything about it when I got
up again, because I tried to forget it. That is
impossible. I see that bar, bar-keeper, and grizzly-
bear so distinctly this moment, that if I were a
painter I could put every face, every tumbler, everything there, on canvas as truthfully as they could
be taken by a photograph.

I remember the room they took me to up-stairs.
They spoke kindly, but I do not think I could
answer. Every now and then, through it all and in
all things, I could see the one-eyed negro. I lay
looking at the double-barrelled shot-gun against the
wall by the bed, and the bowie-knife that lay beside
a brace of pistols on the table; some decanters on a
stand, and a long white pole, perhaps a sort of pick-
handle, in the corner, are all that I remember. And
yet all this fixed on the mind in an instant; for
soon my remaining senses went away, and returned
no more for many, many weeks.   .   .   .

There was a little Chinaman, tawny, moon-eyed,

and silent, sitting by the bed ; but when he saw me lift my hands and look consciously around, his homely features beamed with delight. He sprung up from my side, spun around the room a time or two in his paper slippers, hitched up his blue, loose trousers, and seemed as glad as a country child when a parent comes home from town. Then he took up my hand, moved my head, fixed the pillow, and again spun around the room, grinning and showing his white teeth.

This little, moon-eyed heathen belonged to that race we send so many tracts and missionaries to across the seas; and was one of those little wretches that the dear children in the cities of the Pacific pelt and pound on Sabbath days with cobble stones, rotten apples, hymn-books, bibles, and whatever comes convenient, as they return home from church and Sunday school.

At last, this diminutive Chinaman seemed to come to his senses, and shot out of the door and down the stairs as if flying for a wager, and I slept then and dreamed sweet and beautiful dreams.

When I awoke the little heathen had returned. The Prince, more earnest and thoughtful, it seemed to me, than before, was at my side, and with him a sallow, sickly-looking physician in green glasses, and a ruffled shirt. Miners were coming in and going out on tip-toe, holding their slouch hats stiffly in both hands, and making long measured steps as they moved around the bed.

I looked for the shot-gun on the wall but it was gone; a fancy-picture too had disappeared, or possibly, I had only dreamed that such a picture hung on the wall across by the window. The pistols had been taken away, too, from the stand, and the bowie-knife was gone. There was only a book on the stand—a brown, old, leather-bound book. The decanters had been taken away, and a short junk-bottle stood there, doing service for a vase, with a bunch of wild autumn blossoms, and a green fir-twig or two to relieve the yellow of the blooms.

CHAPTER VI

 CHANGE had certainly come over the actions and, I may say, the mind of the Prince, in the long weeks of my illness. I had fallen into his hands so helplessly and so wholly that I was in a way absolutely his. He did not shift the responsibility, nor attempt to escape it.

I could not, of course, then understand why my presence, or the responsibility of a young person thrown on him in this way, could have influenced him for good or evil, or have altered his plans or course of life in any way at all. I think I can now. I did not stop to inquire then. It so happens that when very young we are not particular about reasons for anything.

It is often a fortunate thing for a man that the fates have laid some responsibility to his charge. From what I could learn the Prince was utterly alone;—had no one depending on him; had formed no very ardent attachments; expected, of course, to leave the mountains sometime, and settle down as all others were doing, but did not just then care to fix the time, or assume any concern about it.

Naturally noble and generous in all his instincts, he fell to planning first for me, and then for himself and me together. He saw no prospect better than that of an honest miner. He shrunk from initiating any one into the art of his own temporary calling, and resolved to possess a mining claim, build a cabin, and enter upon a real life. This made him a new man—a more thoughtful, earnest man, perhaps—no better. Besides, a recollection of his reverses at the Klamat possibly had a little to do in this making up the decision to turn over a new leaf in his life. Not the losses, either—he could not care for that; but, rather, that he felt ashamed to have to do with a calling where men would stoop so low and go to such lengths to procure money.

After casting about for many days in the various neighbouring localities, the Prince finally decided to pitch his tent on the Humbug, a tributary of the Klamat, and the most flourishing, newly-discovered camp of the north. It lay west of the city, a day's ride down in a deep, densely-timbered cañon, out of sight of Mount Shasta, out of sight of everything—even the sun; save here and there where a land-slide had ploughed up the forest, or the miners had mown down the great evergreens about their cabins, or town sites in the camp.

Do not doubt or be surprised at this name of Humbug. Get your map and you will see it there— fifty miles or more west of Mount Shasta, twenty miles from Greenhorn, thirty miles from Deadwood, and about the same distance from Rogue's Gulch. Hogem, Hardscrabble, and Hell-bent were adjoining, and intervening mining camps of lesser note.

I asked the Prince to go down and see about my pony when we were about to set out, but the negro had confiscated him long since—claimed to have disposed of him for his keeping. " He's eat his cussed head off," said he, and I saw my swift patient little companion no more.

On a crisp clear morning, we set out from the city, and when we had reached the foot-hills to the west, we struck a fall of snow, with enormous hare, ears as large almost as those of Mexican mules, crossing here and there, and coyotes sitting on the ground, tame as dogs, looking down on the cabins and camp below.

We had, strapped on our saddles behind us, blankets, picks, shovels, frying-pans, beans, bacon, and coffee,—all, of course, in limited quantities.

The two mules snuffed at the snow, lifted their little feet gingerly, spun around many times like tops, and brayed a solemn prayer or two to be allowed to turn back.

Snow is a mule's aversion. Give him sand, the heat of a furnace, and only sage-brush to subsist upon, and he will go on patient and uncomplaining ;

but snow goes against his nature. We began to leave the world below—the camps, the clouds of smoke, and the rich smell of the burning juniper and manzanita.

The pines were open on this side of the mountain, so that sometimes we could see through the trees to the world without and below. Over against us stood Shasta. Grander, nearer, now he seemed than ever, covered with snow from base to crown.

If you would see any mountain in its glory, you must go up a neighbouring mountain, and see it above the forests and lesser heights. You must see a mountain with the clouds below you, and between you and the object of contemplation.

Until you have seen a mountain over the tops and crests of a sea of clouds, you have not seen, and cannot understand, the sublime and majestic scenery of the Pacific.

Never, until on some day of storms in the lower world you have ascended one mountain, looked out above the clouds, and seen the white snowy pyramids piercing here and there the rolling nebulous sea, can you hope to learn the freemasonry of mountain scenery in its grandest, highest, and most supreme degree. Lightning and storms and thunder underneath you ; calm and peace and perfect beauty about you ! Typical and suggestive.

Sugar-pines, tall as pyramids, on either hand as we rode up the trail, through the dry bright snow, with great burrs or cones, long as your arm, swaying from the tips of their lofty branches; and little pine squirrels, black and brown, ran up and down, busy with their winter hoard.

Once on the summit we dismounted, drew the sinches till the mules grunted and put in a protest with their teeth and heels, and then began the descent.

The Prince had been silent all day, but as we were mounting the mules again, he said—

"We may have a rocky time down there, my boy. The grass is mighty short with me, I tell you. But I have thought it all out, clean down to the bed-rock, and this is the best that can be done. If we can manage to scratch through this winter, we will be all right for a big clean up by the time the snows fly over again ; and then, if you like, you shall see another land. There ! look down there," he said, as we came to the rim of a bench in the mountain, and had a look-out below, "that is the place where we shall winter. Three thousand people there ! not a woman, not a child ! Two miles below, and ten miles a-head !"

Not a woman ? Not much of a chance for a love affair. He who consents to descend with me into that deep dark gorge in the mountains, and live the weary winter through, will see neither the light of the sun, nor the smiles of woman. A sort of Hades. A savage Eden, with many Adams walking up and down, and plucking of every tree, nothing forbidden here; for here, so far as it would seem, are neither laws of God or man

When shall we lie down and sleep, and awake and find an Eve and the Eden in the forest? An Eve untouched and unstained, fresh from the hand of God, gazing at her reflection in the mossy mountain stream, amazed at her beauty, and in love with herself; even in this first act setting an example for man that he has followed too well for his own peace!

This cañon was as black as Erebus down there—a sea of sombre firs; and down, down as if the earth was cracked and cleft almost in two. Here and there lay little nests of clouds below us, tangled in the tree-tops, no wind to drive them, nothing to fret and disturb. They lay above the dusks of the forest as if asleep. Over across the cañon stood another mountain, not so fierce as this, but black with forest, and cut and broken into many gorges—scars of earthquake shocks, and sabre-cuts of time. Gorge on gorge, cañon intersecting cañon, pitching down towards the rapid Klamat—a black and boundless forest till it touches the very tide of the sea a hundred miles to the west.

Our cabin was on the mountain side. Where else could it have been but on the mountain top? Nothing but mountains. A little stream went creeping down below,—a little wanderer among the boulders —for it was now sorely fretted and roiled by the thousands of miners up and down.

There was a town, a sort of common centre, called The Forks ; for here three little streams joined hands, and went down from there to the Klamat together. Our cabin stood down on the main stream, not far from the river.

The Forks had two butcher's shops; and each of the rival houses sent up and down the streams two mules each day, laden with their meats; left so much at each claim as directed, weighed it out themselves, kept the accounts themselves ; and yet, never to my knowledge, in any of the mining camps, did the butcher betray his trust. A small matter this, you say. No doubt it is. Yet it is true and new. Any new truth is always worthy of attention. I mention this particularly as an item of evidence confirmative of my belief, that we have only to trust man to make him honest, and, on the other hand, to watch and suspect him to make him a knave.

The principal saloon of The Forks was the "Howlin' Wilderness;" an immense pine-log cabin, with higher walls than most cabins, earth floor, and an immense fire-place, where crackled and roared, day and night, a pine-log fire, that refreshes me even to this day to remember.

It is true the Howlin' Wilderness was not high-toned, was not even first-class in this fierce little mining camp of The Forks; but it was a spacious place—always had more people in it and a bigger fire than other places, and so was a power and a centre in the town. Besides, all the important fights took place at the Howlin' Wilderness, and if you wanted to be well up in the news, or to see the

Saturday evening entertainment, you had to have some regard for the Howlin' Wilderness.

The proprietors, who stood behind the bar, had bags of sand laid up in a bullet-proof wall inside the counter, between them and the crowd, so that when the shooting set in, and men threw themselves on the floor, fled through the door, or barricaded their breasts with monte-tables and wooden benches, they had only to drop down behind the bags of sand, and lie there, pistols in hand, till the ball was over.

These men were wisely silent and impartial in all misunderstandings that arose. They always seemed to try to quell a trouble, and prevent a fight; perhaps they did. At all events, when the battles were over, they were always the first to take up the wounded, and do what they could for the dying and the dead. There was a great puncheon, hewn from sugar-pine, that had once been a monte-table, back on the outside by the chimney. This was stained with the blood of many. Many bodies had been laid out, in the course of a year, to stiffen on this board.

"We will have a man for breakfast to-morrow," some one would say, when shots were heard in the direction of the Howlin' Wilderness; and the prophecy was nearly always fulfilled.

There was a tall man, a sort of half sport and half miner, who had a cabin close to town, who seemed to take a special interest in these battles. He was known as "Long Dan," always carried a pistol, and took a pride in getting into trouble.

"Look here," said Prince to him one evening,

after he had been telling his six-shooter adventures, with great delight, by the cabin fire, "Look here, Dan, some of these days you will die with your boots on. Now see if you don't, if you keep on slinging your six-shooter around loose in this sort of a way, you will go up the flume as slick as a salmon —die with your boots on before you know it."

Dan smiled blandly as he tapped his ivory pistol-butt, and said, "Bet you the cigars, I don't! Whenever my man comes to the centre, I will call him, see if I don't, and get away with it, too."

Now to understand the pith of the grim joke which Dan played in the last act, you must know that "dying with the boots on" meant a great deal in the mines. It is the poetical way of expressing the result of a bar-room or street-battle.

Let me here state that while the wild, semi-savage life of the mines and mountains has brought forth no dialect to speak of, it has produced many forms of expression that are to be found nowhere else.

These sharp sword-cuts are sometimes coarse, sometimes wicked, but always forcible and driven to the hilt. They are even sometimes strangely poetical, and when you know their origin, they carry with them a touch of tenderness beyond the reach of song.

Take, for example, the last words of the old Sierra Nevada stage-driver, who, for a dozen years, had sat up on his box in storm or sun, and dashed down the rocky roads, with his hat on his nose, his foot on the break, and the four lines threaded through his fingers.

The old hero of many encounters with robbers and floods and avalanches in the Sierras, was dying now. His friends gathered around him to say farewell. He half raised his head, lifted his hands as if still at his post, and said:—

" Boys, I am on the down grade, and can't reach the break!" and sank down and died.

And so it is that " the down grade," an expression born of the death of the old stage-driver, has a meaning with us now.

A Saturday or so after the conversation alluded to between Long Dan and the Prince, there were heard pistol-shots in the direction of the Howlin' Wilderness saloon, and most of the men rushed forth to see what Jonah fate had pitched upon to be thrown into the sea of eternity, and be the "man for breakfast" this time.

Nothing "draws" like a bar-room fight of California. It is a sudden thing. Sharp and quick come the keen reports, and the affair has the advantage of being quite over by the time you reach the spot, and all danger of serving the place of barricades for a stray bullet is past.

I have known miners standing on their good behaviour, who resisted the temptations of hurdy-gurdy houses, bull-fights, and bull and bear encounters, who always wrote home on Sundays, read old letters, and said the Lord's Prayer; but I never yet knew one who could help going to see the dead man or the scene of the six-shooter war-dance, whenever the shots were heard.

The Prince rushed up. The house was full; surging and excited men with their hats knocked off, their faces red with passion, and their open red shirts showing their strong, hairy bosoms.

"It is Long Dan," some one called out; and this made the Prince, who was his neighbour, push his way more eagerly through the men. He reached the wounded man at last, and the crowd, who knew the Prince as an acquaintance of the sufferer, fell back and gave him a place at his side.

The proprietors of the Howlin' Wilderness had set up the monte-table, which had been overthrown in the struggle, and laid the dying Dan gently there with an old soldier overcoat under his head.

When the Prince took up the helpless hand of the poor fellow, so overthrown in his pride and strength, and spoke to him, he slowly opened his eyes, looked straight at the Prince with a smile, only perceptible, hardly as distinct as the tear in his eye, and said in a whisper, as he drew the Prince down to his face:

"Old fellow, Prince, old boy, take off my boots."

The Prince hastened to obey, and again took his place at his side.

Again Long Dan drew him down, and said, huskily,

"Prince, Prince, old boy, I've won the cigars! I've won 'em, by the holy poker!"

And so he died.

CHAPTER VII

UCH fearful scenes were the chief diversions of the camp. True, the miners did not, as a rule, take part in these bloody carnivals, but were rather the spectators in the circus. The men at The Forks, gamblers and the like, were the gladiators.

Of course, we had some few papers, very old ones, and there were some few novels on the creek; but there was no place of amusement, no neighbours with entertaining families, nothing but the monotony of camp and cabin-life of the most ungracious kind.

As for ourselves, I know the Prince had often hard work to keep his commissary department in tack. The butchers no longer competed for his patronage, and but for fear of his influence to their disadvantage, backed by something of real heart, as these mountain butchers mostly possess to an uncommon degree for men in their calling, they would have left him long ago.

We had a claim down among the boulders big as a barn, at the base of the cabin, in the creek; but if it contained any gold worth mentioning we had not yet had any real evidence of it.

We toiled—let that be understood—we two together. I, of course, was not strong, and not worth much; but he, from dawn till dark, never took rest at all. He was in earnest—a thoughtful man now. He was working on a new problem, and was concerned. Often at night, by the light of the pine-log fire, I would see the severe lines of thought across his splendid face, and wished that I, too, was a strong man, and such a man as this.

Sometimes he would talk to me of myself, lay plans for us both, and be quite delighted to find that I left all to him. I think he was half glad to find I was so helpless and dependent.

It was a severe and cruel winter. I remember one Sunday I went down to the claim and found a lot of Californian quails frozen to death in the snow. They had huddled up close as possible; tried to keep warm, but perished there, every one. Maybe this was because we had cut away all the under-brush up and down the creek and let in the cold and snow, and left the birds without a shelter.

The Prince was entirely without money now, and anything in the shape of food was fifty cents and a dollar a pound. The gay gambler was being put to the test. It was a great fall from his grand life of the year before. It remained to be seen if he would be consumed in the fire, or would come out only brightened and beautified.

The cold weather grew sharply colder. One morning when I arose and went down to the stream to wash my hands and face, and snuff the keen, crisp air, the rushing mountain stream was still; not even the plunge and gurgle underneath the ice. It was frozen stiff and laid out in a long white shroud of frost and ice, and fairy-work by delicate hands was done all along the border; but the stream was still—dead, utterly dead.

The strip of sky that was visible above us grew dark and leaden. Some birds flew frightened past, crossing the cañon above our heads and seeking shelter; and squirrels ran up and down the pines and frozen hillsides in silence and in haste. We instinctively, like the birds, began to prepare for the storm, and stored in wood all day till a whole corner of the cabin was filled with logs of pine and fir, sweet-smelling juniper and manzanita to kindle with, and some splinters of pitch, riven from a sugar pine seamed and torn by lightning, up the hill.

The Prince kept hard at work, patient and cheerful all day, but still he was silent and thoughtful. I did not ask him any questions; I trusted this man, loved him, leaned on him, believed in him solely. It was strange, and yet not strange, considering my fervid, passionate nature, my inexperience and utter ignorance of men and things. But he was worthy. I had never seen a full, splendid, sincere, strong man like this. I had to have some one—some thing—to love; it was a necessity of my nature. This man answered all, and I was satisfied. Had he called to me some morning and said, " Come, we will start north now, through this snow ;" or, " Come, let us go to the top of Mount Shasta, and warm us by the furnace of the volcano there," I had not hesitated a moment, never questioned the wisdom and propriety of the journey, but followed him with the most perfect faith and undoubting zeal and energy.

The next morning there was a bank of snow against the door when I opened it. The trail was level and obliterated. Snow! Snow! Snow! The stream that had lain all day in state, in its shroud of frost and fairy-work, was buried now, and beside the grave, the alder and yew along the bank bent their heads and drooped their limbs in sad and beautiful regret; a patient, silent sorrow!

Over across from the cabin the mountain side shot up at an angle almost frightful to look upon, till it lost its pine-covered summit in the clouds, and lay now a slanting sheet of snow.

The trees had surrendered to the snow. They no longer shook their sable plumes, or tossed their heads at all. Their limbs reached out no more triumphant in the storm, but drooped and hung in silence at their sides—quiet, patient, orderly as soldiers in a line, with grounded arms. Back of us the same scene was lifted to the clouds. Snow! Snow! Snow!

nothing but snow! To right and to left, up and
down the buried stream, were cabins covered with
snow, white and cold as tombs and stones of marble
in a churchyard.

And still the snow came down steadily and white,
in flakes like feathers. It did not blow or bluster
about as if it wanted to assert itself. It seemed as
if it already had absolute control; rather like a king,
who knows that all must and will bow down before
him. Steady and still, strong and stealthy, it
came upon us and possessed the earth. Not even a
bird was heard to chirp, or a squirrel to chatter or
protest. High over head, in the clouds as it seemed,
or rather back of us, a little on the steep and stupendous mountain, it is true a coyote lifted his nose
to the snow, and called out dolefully ; but that, may
be, was a call to his mate across the cañon, in the
clouds on the hill-top opposite. That was all that
could be heard.

The trail was blocked, and the butcher came no
more. This was a sad thing to us. I know that
more than once that morning the Prince went to the
door, and looked up sharply toward the point where
the mule made his appearance when the trail was
open, and that his face expressed uncommon concern
when he had settled in his mind that the beef supply
was at an end.

It is pretty certain that the two butchers had been
waiting for some good excuse to shut up shop without offending the miners, until their claims should

be opened in the spring. This they now had, and at once took advantage of the opportunity.

In these days no man thought of refusing credit. A man who had said "No credit!" would have had "no business" in the mines. Any merchant, saloon-keeper, or butcher, who had had the littleness and audacity to have put up the sign "No tick," now so frequent in mining camps and border towns, at that time would have stood a first-rate chance of having his house pulled down about his ears. These men had a strangely just way of doing things in the early days. They did not ask for credit often, but when they did they wanted it, needed it, and woe then to the man who refused. Every man in the camp was told of it, in no modified form, you may be sure; and that shop and that man were, at the least, shunned thereafter, as if one had been a pest-house and the other the keeper of it.

We could mine no more, could pick-and-shovel no more, with frosty fingers, in the frozen ground, by the pine-log fire, down by the complaining, troubled little stream. The mine was buried with the brook.

I used to think some strange and sympathetic things of this stream, even in our hardest battles for a respectable existence on its banks, that gloomy, weary winter. That stream was never satisfied. It ran, and foamed, and fretted, hurried and hid under the boughs and bushes, held on to the roots and grasses, and lifted little white hands as it ran toward the Klamat, a stronger and braver brother, as if there were grizzlies up the gorge where it came from. At best, it had but a sorry time, even before the miners came. It had to wedge itself in between the foot-hills, and elbow its way for every inch of room. It was kicked and cudgelled from this foot-hill to that ; it ran from side to side, and worked, and wound, and curved, and cork-screwed on in a way that had made an angler sorry. Maybe, after all, it was glad to fold its little icy hands across its fretted breast, and rest, and rest, and rest, stiff and still, beneath the snow, below the pines and yew and cedar trees that bent their heads in silence by the sleeper.

The Kanaka sugar-mat was empty ; the strip of bacon that had hung in the corner against the wall was gone, and the flour-sack grew low and suggestive.

Miners are great eaters in the winter. Snuff the fierce frost weather of the Sierras, run in the snow, or delve in the mine through the day, and roast by a great pine fire through the evening, and you will eat like an Englishman.

The snow had fallen very fast ; then the weather settled cold and clear as a bell. The largest and the brightest stars, it seemed to me, hang about and above Mount Shasta in those cold, bright winter nights of the north. They seem as large as California lilies ; they flash and flare, and sparkle and dart their little spangles ; they lessen and enlarge, and seem to make signs, and talk and understand each other, in their beautiful blue home, that seems in the winter time so near the summit of the mountain.

The Indians say that it is quite possible to step from this mountain to the stars. They say that their fathers have done so often. They lay so many great achievements to their fathers. In this they are very like the white man. But maybe, after all, some of their fathers have gone from this mountain-top to the stars. Who knows ?

We could do nothing now but get wood, cook, and eat. It did not take us long to cook and eat.

The bill of fare was short enough. Miners nearly always lay in a great store of provisions—enough to last them through all the winter, as no stores or supply posts are kept open when the mines are closed, as they were then. With us that was impossible. All the others up and down the stream, with few exceptions, had complete supplies on hand, and had a good and jovial time generally.

They got wood, made snow shoes, cleared off race tracks, and ran races by hundreds on great shoes, twelve and fifteen feet in length, or made coasting places on the hillsides, and slid down hill.

At night, many would get out the old greasy pack of cards, sit before the fire, and play innocent games of old sledge, draw poker, euchre or whist, while some would read by the pine-log light; others, possessed with a little more devilment, or restlessness, maybe, or idle curiosity, would take the single deep-cut trail that led to The Forks, and bring up down at the crackling, cheerful fire-place of the Howlin' Wilderness.

The Prince and I sometimes went to town too. It was dull work sitting there, us two, in the warm little log-cabin, covered all up in snow, with nothing to read, nothing in common to talk of, and him, full of care and anxiety about the next day's rations, and the next; and it was a blessed relief to sometimes go out, mix in a crowd and see the broad-breasted, ruddy-faced men, and hear their strong and hearty voices, even though the utterances of some were often thick with oaths and frequent violations of the laws of grammar.

One morning we had only bread for breakfast. The Prince was gloomy and silent as we sat down. He did not remain long at the table. He stood by the fire and watched my relish of the little breakfast with evident satisfaction.

" Little one," said he, at last, " it is getting mighty rocky. I tell you the grass is shorter than it ever was with us before, and what to do next I do not know."

There was something affecting in the voice and manner. My breakfast was nearly choking me, and I tried to hide my face from his. I got up from the table, went to the door and looked across into the white sheet of snow hung upon the mountain opposite, got the air, came back, kicked the fire vigorously, and turned and stood by his side with my back to the fire also.

The weather was still clear and cold. There was, of course, no absolute need of going hungry there, as far as we two were concerned, if we had had the courage, or rather the cowardice, to ask for bread.

But this man was a proud man and a complete man, I take it; and when a man of that nature gets cornered, he is going to endure a great deal before he makes any sign. A true man can fight, he can kill, but he cannot ask for quarter. Want only makes such a man more sensitive. Distress only intensifies his proud and passionate nature, and he prepares himself for everything possible but an appeal to man. Besides, this man was not altogether a miner. He had never felt that he had won his place among the brawny, broad-shouldered men, who from the first, and all through life, had borne and accepted the common curse that fell on man through the first transgression, and he had always held himself somewhat aloof.

Perhaps he was fighting a battle with himself. Who knows? It seems to me now, although I had no thought of such a thing then, that he had made a resolve within himself to make his bread by the sweat of his brow, to set a good example to one whom fate had given into his charge, and never turn back or deviate from the one direction. To have asked for help from men of the old calling would have meant a great deal that he was not willing to admit, even if help had been forthcoming, which, as I have said, was extremely problematical.

What that man must have felt would be painful to consider. As for myself, I did not take in all the situation, or really half of it. This man, somehow, stood to me like a tower. I had no fear.

The weather was still intensely cold. That afternoon the Prince said:

"Come, we will go to town."

CHAPTER VIII

HERE was a tribe of Indians camped down on the rapid, rocky Klamat river—a sullen, ugly set were they, too: at least so said The Forks. Never social, hardly seeming to notice the whites, who were now thick about them, below them, above them, on the river and all around them. Sometimes we would meet one on the narrow trail; he would gather his skins about him, hide his bow and arrows under their folds, and, without seeming to see any one, would move past us still as a shadow. I do not remember that I ever saw one of these Indians laugh, not even to smile. A hard-featured, half-starved set of savages, of whom the wise men of the camp prophesied no good.

The snow, unusually deep this winter, had driven them all down from the mountains, and they were compelled to camp on the river.

The game, too, had been driven down along with

the Indians, but it was of but little use to them.
Their bows and arrows did poor competition with the
rifles of the whites in the killing of the game. The
whites fairly filled the cabins with deer and elk, got all
the lion's share, and left the Indians almost destitute.

Another thing that made it rather more hard on
the Indians than anything else, was the utter failure
of the annual run of salmon the summer before, on
account of the muddy water. The Klamat, which
had poured from the mountain lakes to the sea as
clear as glass, was now made muddy and turbid from
the miners washing for gold on its banks and its
tributaries. The trout turned on their sides and
died; the salmon from the sea came in but rarely on
account of this; and what few did come were pretty
safe from the spears of the Indians, because of the
coloured water; so that supply, which was more than
all others their bread and their meat, was entirely
cut off.

Mine? It was all a mystery to these Indians as
long as they were permitted to live. Besides, there
were some whites mining who made poor headway
against hunger. I have seen them gather in groups
on the bank above the mines and watch in silence for
hours as if endeavouring to make it out; at last they
would shrug their shoulders, draw their skins closer
about them, and stalk away no wiser than before.

Why we should tear up the earth, toil like gnomes
from sun-up to sun-down, rain or sun, destroy the
forests and pollute the rivers, was to them more than

a mystery—it was a terror. I believe they accepted it as a curse, the work of evil spirits, and so bowed to it in sublime silence.

This loss of salmon was a greater loss than you would suppose. These fish in the spring-time pour up these streams from the sea in incalculable swarms. They fairly darken the water. On the head of the Sacramento, before that once beautiful river was changed from a silver sheet to a dirty yellow stream, I have seen between the Devil's Castle and Mount Shasta the stream so filled with salmon that it was impossible to force a horse across the current. Of course, this is not usual, and now can only be met with hard up at the heads of mountain streams where mining is not carried on, and where the advance of the fish is checked by falls on the head of the stream. The amount of salmon which the Indians would spear and dry in the sun, and hoard away for winter, under such circumstances, can be imagined; and I can now better understand their utter discomfiture at the loss of their fisheries than I did then.

A sharp, fierce winter was upon them; for reasons above stated they had no store of provisions on hand, save, perhaps, a few dried roots and berries; and the whites had swept away and swallowed up the game before them as fast as it had been driven by the winter from the mountains. Yet I do not know that any one thought of all this then. I am sure I did not; and I do not remember hearing any allusion made to these things by the bearded men of the camp, old enough, and wise enough too, to look at the heart of things. Perhaps it was because they were all so busy and intent on getting gold. I do remember distinctly, however, that there was a pretty general feeling against the Indians down on the river—a general feeling of dislike and distrust.

What made matters worse, there was a set of men, low men, loafers, and of the lowest type, who would hang around those lodges at night, give the Indians whiskey of the vilest sort, debauch their women, and cheat the men out of their skins and bows and arrows. There was not a saloon, not a gambling den in camp that did not have a sheaf of feathered, flint-headed arrows in an otter quiver, and a yew bow hanging behind the bar.

Perhaps there was a grim sort of philosophy in the red man so disposing of his bow and arrows now that the game was gone and they were of no further use. Sold them for bread for his starving babes, maybe. How many tragedies are hidden here? How many tales of devotion, self-denial, and sacrifice, as true as the white man lived, as pure, and brave, and beautiful as ever gave tongue to eloquence or pen to song, sleep here with the dust of these sad and silent people on the bank of the stormy river!

In this condition of things, about mid-winter, when the snow was deep and crusted stiff, and all nature seemed dead and buried in a ruffled shroud, there was a murder. The Indians had broken out! The prophesied massacre had begun! Killed by the Indians!

It swept like a telegram through the camp. Confused and incoherent, it is true, but it gathered force
and form as the tale flew on from tongue to tongue,
until it assumed a frightful shape.

A man had been killed by the Indians down at the
rancheria. Not much of a man, it is true. A "capper;"
sort of tool and hanger-on about the lowest gambling
dens. Killed, too, down in the Indian camp when he
should have been in bed, or at home, or at least in
company with his kind.

All this made the miners hesitate a bit as they
hurriedly gathered in at The Forks, with their long
Kentucky rifles, their pistols capped and primed, and
bowie knives in their belts.

But as the gathering storm that was to sweep the
Indians from the earth took shape and form, these
honest men stood out in little knots, leaning on their
rifles in the streets, and gravely questioned whether,
all things considered, the death of the " Chicken," for
that was the dead man's name, was sufficient cause
for interference.

To their eternal credit these men mainly decided
that it was not, and two by two they turned away,
went back to their cabins, hung their rifles up on the
rack, and turned their thoughts to their own affairs.

But the hangers-on about the town were terribly
enraged. "A man has been killed!" they proclaimed aloud. " A man has been murdered by the
savages!! We shall all be massacred! butchered!
burnt!!"

In one of the saloons where men were wont to meet at night, have stag-dances, and drink lightning, a short, important man, with the print of a glass-tumbler cut above his eye, arose and made a speech.

"Fellow-miners (he had never touched a pick in his life), I am ready to die for me country! (He was an Irishman sent out to Sydney at the Crown's expense.) What have I to live for? (Nothing whatever, as far as anyone could tell.) Fellow-miners, a man has been kilt by the treacherous savages—kilt in cold blood! Fellow-miners, let us advance upon the inemy. Let us—let us—fellow-miners, let us take a drink and advance upon the inemy."

This man had borrowed a pistol, and held or flourished it in his hand as he talked to the crowd of idlers, rum-dealers, and desperadoes—to all of whom any diversion from the monotony of camp-life, or excitement, seemed a blessing.

"Range around me. Rally to the bar and take a drink, every man of you, at me own ixpense." The bar-keeper, who was also proprietor of the place, a man not much above the type of the speaker, ventured a mild remonstrance at this wholesale generosity; but the pistol, flourished in a very suggestive way, settled the matter, and, with something of a groan, he set his decanters to the crowd, and became a bankrupt.

This was the beginning; they passed from saloon to saloon, or, rather, from door to door; the short, stout Irishman making speeches and the mob gathering force and arms as it went, and then, wild with drink and excitement, moving down upon the Indians, some miles away on the bank of the river.

" Come," said the Prince to me, as they passed out of town, " let us see this through. Here will be blood. We will see from the hill overlooking the camp. I hope the Indians are ' on it '—hope to God they are 'heeled,' and that they will receive the wretches warmly as they deserve." The Prince was black with passion.

Maybe his own wretchedness had something to do with his wrath; but I think not. I should rather say that had he been in strength and spirits, and had his pistols, which had long since been disposed of for bread, he had met this mob face to face, and sent them back to town or to the place where they belonged.

We followed not far behind the crowd of fifty or sixty men armed with pistols, rifles, knives, and hatchets.

The trail led to a little point overlooking the bar on which the Indian huts were huddled.

The river made a bend about there. It ground and boiled in a crescent blocked with running ice and snow. They were out in the extreme curve of a horse-shoe made by the river, and we advanced from without. They were in a net. They had only a choice of deaths; death by drowning, or death at the hands of their hereditary foe.

It was nearly night; cold and sharp the wind blew up the river and the snow flew around like feathers. Not an Indian to be seen. The thin blue smoke came slowly up, as if afraid to leave the wigwams, and the traditional, ever watchful and wakeful Indian dog was not to be seen or heard. The men hurried down upon the camp, spreading out upon the horse-shoe as they advanced in a run.

" Stop here," said the Prince; and we stood from the wind behind a boulder that stood, tall as a cabin, upon the bar. The crowd advanced to within half a pistol shot, and gave a shout as they drew and levelled their arms. Old squaws came out—bang! bang! bang! shot after shot, and they were pierced and fell, or turned to run.

Some men sprung up, wounded, but fell the instant; for the whites, yelling, howling, screaming, were among the lodges, shooting down at arm's length man, woman, or child. Some attempted the river, I should say, for I afterwards saw streams of blood upon the ice, but not one escaped; nor was a hand raised in defence. It was all done in a little time. Instantly as the shots and shouts began we two advanced, we rushed into the camp, and when we reached the spot only now and then a shot was heard within a lodge, dispatching a wounded man or woman. The few surviving children—for nearly all had been starved to death—had taken refuge under skins and under lodges overthrown, hidden away as little kittens will hide just old enough to spit and hiss, and hide when they first see the face of man. These were now dragged forth and shot. Not all these men who made this mob, bad as they were, did this—only a few; but enough to leave, as far as they could, no living thing. Christ! it was pitiful! The babies did not scream. Not a wail, not a sound. The murdered men and women, in the few minutes that the breath took leave, did not even groan.

As we came up a man named " Shon"—at least, that was all the name I knew for him—held up a baby by the leg, a naked, bony little thing, which he had dragged from under a lodge—held it up with one hand, and with the other blew its head to pieces with his pistol.

I must stop here to say that this man Shon soon left camp, and was afterwards hung by the Vigilance Committee at Lewiston, Idaho Territory; that he whined for his life like a puppy, and died like a coward as he was. I chronicle this fact with a feeling of perfect delight.

He was a tall, spare man, with small, grey eyes, a weak, wicked mouth, colourless and treacherous, that was for ever smiling and smirking in your face.

Shun a man like that. A man who always smiles is a treacherous-natured, contemptible coward.

He knows, himself, how villainous and contemptible he is, and he feels that you know it too, and so tries to smile his way into your favour. Turn away from the man who smiles and smiles, and rubs his hands as if he felt, and all men knew, that they were really dirty.

You can put more souls of such men as that inside of a single grain of sand than there are dimes in the national debt.

This man threw down the body of the child among the dead, and rushed across to where a pair of ruffians had dragged up another, a little girl, naked, bony, thin as a shadow, starved into a ghost. He caught her by the hair with a howl of delight, placed the pistol to her head and turned around as if to point the muzzle out of range of his companions who stood around on the other side.

The child did not cry—she did not even flinch. Perhaps she did not know what it meant; but I should rather believe she had seen so much of death there, so much misery, the steady, silent work of the monster famine through the village day after day, that she did not care. I saw her face: it did not even wince. Her lips were thin and fixed, and firm as iron.

The villain, having turned her around, now lifted his arm, cocked the pistol, and—

"Stop that, you infernal scoundrel! Stop that, or die! You damned assassin, let go that child, or I will pitch you neck and crop into the Klamat."

The Prince had him by the throat with one hand, and with the other he wrested the pistol from his grasp and threw it into the river. The Prince had not even so much as a knife. The man did not know

this, nor did the Prince care, or he had not thrown
away the weapon he wrung from his hand. The
Prince pushed the child behind him, and advanced
towards the short, fat Sydney convict, who had now
turned, pistol in hand, in his direction.

"Keep your distance, you Sydney duck, keep your
distance, or I will send you to hell across lots in a
second."

There are some hard names given on the Pacific;
but when you call a man a "Sydney duck" it is
well understood that you mean blood. If you call a
man a liar to his face you must prepare to knock him
down on the spot, or he will perform that office for
you. If he does not, or does not attempt it, he is
counted a coward and is in disgrace.

When you call a man a "Sydney duck," however,
something more than blows are meant; that means
blood. There is but one expression, a vile one, that
cannot well be named, that means so much, or carries
so much disgrace as this.

The man turned away cowed and baffled. He had
looked in the Prince's face, and saw that he was born
his master.

As for myself, I was not only helpless, but, as was
always the case on similar occasions, stupid, awkward,
speechless. I went up to the little girl, however,
got a robe out of one of the lodges—for they had not
yet set fire to the village—and put it around her
naked little body. After that, as I moved about
among the dead, or stepped aside to the river to see

the streams of blood on the snow and ice, she followed close as a shadow behind me, but said nothing.

Suddenly there was a sharp yell, a volley of oaths, exclamations, a scuffle and blows.

" Scalp him! Scalp him! the little savage! Scalp him and throw him in the river!"

From out the piles of dead somewhere, no one could tell exactly where or when, an apparition had sprung up—a naked little Indian boy, that might have been all the way from twelve to twenty, armed with a knotted war-club, and fallen upon his foes like a fury.

The poor little hero, starved into a shadow, stood little show there, though he had been a very Hercules in courage. He was felled almost instantly by kicks and blows; and the very number of his enemies saved his life, for they could neither shoot nor stab him with safety, as they crowded and crushed around him.

How or why he was finally spared, was always a marvel. Quite likely the example of the Prince had moved some of the men to more humanity. As for Shon and Sydney, they had sauntered off with some others towards town at this time, which also, maybe, contributed to the Indian boy's chance for life.

When the crowd that had formed a knot about him had broken up, and I first got sight of him, he was sitting on a stone with his hands between his naked legs, and blood dripping from his long hair, which fell down in strings over his drooping forehead. He

had been stunned by a grazing shot, no doubt, and
had fallen among the first. He came up to his work,
though, like a man, when his senses returned, and
without counting the chances, lifted his two hands to
do with all his might the thing he had been taught.

Valour, such valour as that, is not a cheap or common thing. It is rare enough to be respected even by
the worst of men. It is only the coward that affects
to despise such courage. He is moved to this altogether by the lowest kind of jealousy. A coward
knows how entirely contemptible he is, and can
hardly bear to see another dignified with that
noble attribute which he for ever feels is no part
of his nature.

So this boy sat there on the stone as the village
burned, the smoke from burning skins, the wild-rye
straw, willow-baskets and Indian robes, ascended,
and a smell of burning bodies went up to the Indians'
God and the God of us all, and no one said nay, and
no one approached him; the men looked at him from
under their slouched hats as they moved around,
but said nothing.

I pitied him. God knows I pitied him. I clasped
my hands together in grief. I was a boy myself,
alone, helpless, in an army of strong and unsympa-
thetic men. I would have gone up and put my arms
about the wild and splendid little savage, bloody and
desperate as he was, so lonely now, so intimate with
death, so pitiful! if I had dared, dared the reproach
of men-brutes.

But besides that there was a sort of nobility about him; his recklessness, his desire to die, lifting his little arms against an army of strong and reckless men, his proud and defiant courage, that made me feel at once that he was above me, stronger, somehow better, than I. Still, he was a boy and I was a boy— the only boys in the camp; and my heart went out, strong and true, towards him. The work of destruction was now too complete. There was not found another living thing—nothing but two or three Indians that had been shot and shot, and yet seemed determined never to die, that lay in the bloody snow down towards the rim of the river. Naked nearly, they were, and only skeletons, with the longest and blackest hair tangled and tossed, and blown in strips and strings, or in clouds out on the white and the blood-red snow, or down their tawny backs, or over their hairy breasts, about their dusky forms, fierce and unconquered, with the bloodless lips set close, and blue, and cold, and firm, like steel.

The dead lay around us, piled up in places, limbs twisted with limbs in the wrestle with death; a mother embracing her boy here; an arm thrown around a neck there; as if these wild people could love as well as die.

CHAPTER IX

NOT a dog in camp. All had been eaten, I suppose, long before. Children die first in their famines ; then the old men, then the young men. The endurance of an Indian woman is a marvel.

In the village, some of the white men claimed to have found something that had been stolen. I have not the least idea there was any truth in it. I wish there was; then there might be some shadow of excuse for all the murders that made up this cruel tragedy, all of which is, I believe, literally true; truer than nine-tenths of the history and official reports written, wherein these people are mentioned; and I stand ready to give names, dates, and detail to all whom it may concern.

Let me not here be misunderstood. An Indian is no better than a white man. If he sins let him suffer. But I do protest against this custom of making up a case—this custom of deciding the case against him in favour of the white man, for ever, on the evidence of the white man only; even though that custom be, in the language of the law, so old "that the memory of man runneth not to the contrary."

The white man and the red man are much alike, with one great difference, which you must and will set down to the advantage of the latter.

The Indian has no desire for fortune; he has no wish in his wild state to accumulate wealth; and it is in his wild state that he must be judged, for it is in that condition that he is said to sin. If "money is the root of all evil," as Solomon hath it, then the Indian has not that evil, or that root of evil, or any desire for it.

It is the white man's monopoly. If an Indian loves you, trusts you, or believes in you at all, he will serve you, guide you through the country, follow you to battle, fight for you, he and all his sons and kindred, and never think of the pay or profit. He would despise it if offered, beyond some presents, some tokens of remembrance, decorations, or simplest articles of use.

Again, I do vehemently protest against taking the testimony of border Indians or any Indians with whom the white man comes in constant contact, and to whom he has taught the use of money and the art of lying.

And most particularly I do protest against taking these Indians—turn-skins and renegades—who affiliate, mix, and strike hands with the whites, as representative Indians. Better take our own

" camp followers " as respectable and representative soldiers.

When you reflect that for centuries the Indians in almost every lodge on the continent, at almost every council, have talked of the whites and their aggressions, and of these things chiefly, and always with that bitterness which characterizes people who look at and see only one side of a case, then you may come to understand, a little, their eternal hatred of their hereditary enemy—how deeply seated this is, how it has become a part of their nature, and, above all, how low, fallen, and how unlike a true Indian one must be who leaves his retreating tribe and lingers in a drunken and debauched fellowship with the whites, losing all his virtues and taking on all the vices of his enemy.

A pot-house politician should represent us at the court of St. James's, if such an Indian is to be taken as a representative of his race.

The true Indian retires before the white man's face to the forest and to the mountain tops. It is very true he leaves a surf, a sort of kelp and drift-wood, and trash, the scum, the idlers, and the cowards and prostitutes of his tribe, as the sea leaves weeds and drift and kelp.

Judge not the sea by this, I protest. This is not the sea, but the refuse and dregs of the sea. The misfortune of it is, however, that this is about all that those who have written and pronounced upon the character of the Indian have ever seen.

And, again, why hold the whole race, from Cariboo

to Cape Saint Lucas, responsible for a single sin? Of course, we may deplore the death of the white man on the border. But for every white man that falls the ghosts of a hundred Indians follow. A white man is killed (half the time by a brother white man) and the account of it fills the land. Telegraph and printing-press reiterate, day after day, the whole details, and who shall say that they grow less as they spread to every household? The artist is called in. His ingenuity is taxed and tortured to put the horrible affair before the world in flaming illustrations, and a general cry goes up against the Indians, no matter where.

All right enough, no doubt; but who tells the tale when the Indian falls, or who tells his side of the story? A hundred Indians are killed in cold blood by the settlers, and the affair is never heard of outside the county where it occurs.

If we wish for justice let us, at least, try to be just. If we do wrong it seems to me to take half the sin away to be brave enough to admit it. At all events, it shows that if we have a great sin we have also one virtue—Valour!

Killed by the Indians! Yes, many good men have been killed by the Indians with cause and without cause. Many good men have also died of fevers. I think a man is about as likely to die a natural death in New York, New Orleans, or any other city, if he remains there, as he is to be killed by the Indians, should he travel or remain amongst them.

Take one case in point. I happen to know an old man who has lived more than forty years on the frontier and among the Indians. More than twenty years ago he took his little family of children and made the six months' journey across the great plains, almost alone and entirely unarmed. I happen to know that this old man, owing to his singularly quiet nature and Quaker-like love of peace, never fired a gun or pistol in his life for any purpose whatever. I happen to know that he made many journeys through the Indian countries; lived and still lives on the border, always unarmed and utterly helpless in the use of arms, and yet never received so much as an uncivil word from an Indian. I am not mistaken in this, for the old man referred to is my father.

Twenty years' observation ought to enable one to speak with intelligence on this subject; and I am free to say that grandmothers never hold up before naughty children a bigger or more delusive bug-a-boo than this universal fear of Indians.

The village was soon consumed; and as the smoke went up, black and sullen, from its embers, we turned away towards our cabin. Most of the men had already gone. A sort of chill had fallen over all, and they scarcely spoke to each other now. They were more than sober.

The blood, the burning camp, the cold and cruel butchery, the perfect submission, the savage silence in which the wretches died, the naked, bony forms in the snow, had gone to the hearts of the men, and they were glad to get away when all was over.

There was not an adventure, not an achievement, not a hazard or escape of any one to allude to. The only heroic act was that of the little skeleton savage with his club. I think they almost wished they had butchered and scalped this boy as they had threatened. To think that the only achievement of the whole affair worth mentioning was that of an Indian, and an Indian boy at that! They did not mention it.

The men were nearly all gone now, stringing up along the snowy trail by twos and threes, toward The Forks. A few still lingered about the smouldering wigwams, or stood looking down into the river, grinding its blocks of ice in its mighty, rocky jaws.

The boy had not moved. I believe he had not lifted his eyes. The sharp wind, pitching up and down and across, cut him no doubt, on the one hand, while the burning wigwams scorched him on the other; but he did not move.

The Prince had stood there all this time like a king, turning sometimes to watch this man or that, but never going aside, never giving way an inch for any one. They went around him, they avoided him, or deferred to him in every way possible. From the very moment he came down from the bluff to the bank of the river, and they saw him in their midst, they felt the presence of a master and a man.

I had always said to myself, this man is of royal blood. This man was born to lead and control. To me he had always stood, like Saul, a head and shoulders above his fellows. I had always believed him a king of men, and now I knew it.

He took the little girl by the hand, folded her robe about her gently as if she had been a Christian born, looked to her moccasins, and then cast about to see who should take and provide for the boy. The last man was going—gone!

There was a look of pain and trouble in the face of the Prince. There was not a crust of bread in the cabin: a poor place to which to take the two starved children, to be sure.

The cast of care blew on with the wind; and with the same old look of confidence and self-possession he went up to the Indian boy, took him by the thin little arm, and bade him arise and follow.

The boy started. He did not understand, and yet he understood perfectly. He stood up taller than before. His face looked fierce and bitter, and his hands lifted as if he would strike. The Prince smiled, stooped and picked up his club, and put it in his hand. This conquered him. He stood it against the stone on which he had sat, took up a robe that lay under his feet, fastened his moccasin strings, and we moved away together and in silence.

The little girl would look up now and then, and endeavour to be pleasant and do cunning things; but this boy with his club tucked under his robe did not look up, nor down, nor around him.

There were some dead that lay in the way; he did

not notice them. He walked across them as if they had been clay. What could he have been thinking of?

I know very well what I do; how unpopular and unprofitable it is to speak a word for this weak and unfriended people. A popular verdict seems of late to have been given against them. Fate, too, seems to have the matter in hand, for in the last decade they have lost more ground than in the fifty preceding years. Cannon are mounted on their strongholds, even on the summits of the Rocky Mountains. Bayonets bristle in their forests of the north, and sabres flash along the plains of the Apache. There is no one to speak for them now, not one. If there was I should be silent.

Game and fish have their seasons to come and go, as regular as the flowers. Now the game go to the hills, now to the valleys, to winter, to have their loves, to bring forth their young. You break in upon their habits by pushing settlements here and there. With the fish you do the same by building dams and driving steam-boats, and you break the whole machinery of their lives and stop their increase. Then the Indians must starve, or push over on to the hunting and fishing grounds of another tribe. This makes war. The result is they fight—fight like dogs! almost like Christians! Here is the whole trouble with this doomed race, in a nut-shell.

Let us, sometimes, look down into this thing honestly, try and find the truth, and understand.

Even the ocean has a bottom.

These rude red men love their lands and their homes. The homes for which their fathers fought for a thousand generations, where their fathers lie buried with their deeds of daring written all over the land, every mountain pass a page of history; every mountain peak a monument to some departed hero; every mountain stream a story and a tradition. They love and cherish these as no other people can, for their lands, their leafy homes, are all they have to love.

I know very well they have never received so much as a red blanket for all the matchless and magnificent Willamette valley; and, I may add, that the whites never took that in war, and so cannot claim it as a conquest. No white man's blood ever stained that great and fertile valley at the hands of an Indian.

True, there are Reservations over on the sea, forty and fifty miles away from the valley; but the interior Indian had as soon descend silently to his grave as go there to live. Hundreds have so chosen and acted on the choice. The sea-coast Indians are "fish-eaters." "They stink!" say the valley Indians, "while we of the interior eat venison and acorns."

Their feuds and wars were fierce, and reached farther back than their traditions. Fancy these valley Indians being induced to go over there on their enemies' lands to make a home. Their own sense of justice revolted at it. Besides, they knew they would be murdered, one by one, in spite of the promises and half-extended protection of the Government.

Let Germans, to-day, enter, helpless and unarmed, even into civilized Paris, and sit down there without ample protection, and see how it would be! Compel certain celebrated leaders of the North to go down unarmed and pitch their tents under the palm-trees of the Ku-Klux, and mark what would follow!

The Indian agent of this Reservation by the sea, who had Indians gathered in from a thousand miles of territory, could not understand why Indians would fight among themselves. " Ah! but they are a vile set," he said: " they fight among themselves like dogs. They are a low set. They will soon kill each other off." And so they did.

The miserable heathens were as bad as the Christians of the North and South. They fought amongst each other. The ungrateful wretches! To fight amongst themselves after all the Government had done for them! Why did they not keep quiet, and die of small-pox and cholera in the little pens built for them, all at the expense of the Government?

If the Government invites settlers to a place, and sells or gives away land that does not yet belong to the Government, and a difficulty arises between the immigrant and the Indian, and the whites get the worst of it, why, send in a thousand young lieutenants, thirsting for glory, and they will soon bring them to terms, at a cost to the Government only a few hundred times more than it would take to set the

Indians up comfortably for life. But if the Indians
get the worst of any little misunderstanding that
may arise, why—why, they get the worst of it, and
what is the use to interfere!

I was present once when the superintendent sent
a delegation of half-civilized Indians into the mountains to the chief of the Shastas, old Worrotetot, called
Black-beard by the whites, for he was bearded like
a prophet, to ask him to surrender and go on to the
Reservation.

" Where is the Superintendent, the man of
blankets?"

" Down in the valley, at the base of the Shasta
mountain."

" Well, that is all right, I suppose. Let him stay
there, if he likes, and I will stay here."

" But we must take him an answer. Will you go
or not?"

" What can I do if I go?"

" You shall have a house, a farm, and horses."

" Where?"

" Down at the Reservation, by the sea."

" Bah! give me a piece of land down by the sea?
Where did he get it to give? Tell me that. The
white men took it from the Indians, and now want to
give it to me. I won't have it. It is not theirs to
give. They drove the Indians off, and stole their
land and camping places. I could have done that
myself. No. You go and tell your great father,
the blanket-maker, I do not want that land. I have

got land of my own high up here, and nearer to the Great Spirit than his. I do not want his blankets: I have a deer-skin; and my squaws and my children all have skins, and we build great wood fires when it snows. No, I will not go away from this mountain. But you may tell him if he will take this mountain along, I will go down by the sea and live on the Reservation."

We reached the cabin, and built a roaring fire.

"Stand your war-club there in the corner, Klamat," said the Prince to the boy, "and come to the fire. This is your home now." The boy did as he was bid, not as a slave, but proud and unbending as a chief in council.

The little girl had washed her hands and face, thrown back her long luxuriant hair, and stood drying herself by the fire, quite at home.

Two more mouths to feed, and where was the bread to come from!

Soon the Prince went out and left us there. He returned in a little while with a loaf of bread.

Where on earth did he get it? I never knew. Maybe he stole it.

He divided it with a knife carefully into three pieces, gave first to the Indian boy, then to the Indian girl, and then to me. Then he stood there a moment, looked a little abashed, but finally said something about wood and went out.

We ate our bread as the axe smote and echoed against the pine-log outside.

A certain strong magnet attracts from out the grains of gold all the ironstone and black sand to itself. It seemed there was something in the nature of this man that attracted all the helpless, and weak, and friendless to his side. He had not sought these little savages. That would have been folly, if not an absolute wrong to them. There was, perhaps, not another man in camp as little capable of caring for them as he. He had rather tried to avoid them, particularly the boy; but when they fell into his hands, when fate seemed to put them there, he took them proudly, boldly, and trusted to fortune, as all brave men will trust it, and without question.

To see those Indians eat—daintily, only a little bit at a time, then put it under the robe, stealthily, and look about; then a memory, and the head would bend and the eyes go down; then the little piece of bread would be withdrawn, eyed wistfully, a morsel broken off, and then the piece again returned beneath the robe, to be again withdrawn as they found it impossible to resist the hunger that consumed them.

But Indians are strangely preservative, and these had just endured a bitter school. They had learned the importance of hoarding a bit for to-morrow, and even the next morning had quite a piece of bread still. How could they suppose that any one would provide, or attempt to provide, for them the next day?

The Prince came in at last from the dusk, and we all went out and helped to bring the wood from the snow.

I am bound to say that I suddenly grew vastly in my own estimation that evening. Up to this time I had been the youngest person in all the camp, the most helpless, the least of all. Here was a change. Here were persons more helpless than myself; some one now that I could advise, direct, dictate to and patronize.

There must be a point in each man's life when he becomes a man—turns from the ways of a boy.

I dare say any man can date his manhood from some event, from some little circumstance that seemed to invest him with a sort of majesty, and dignify him, in his own estimation, at least, with manhood. A man must first be his own disciple. If he does not first believe himself a man, he may be very sure the world, not one man or woman of the world, will believe it.

We sat late by the fire that night. The little girl leaned against the wall by the fire-side and slept, but the boy seemed only to brighten and awake as the night went on. He looked into the fire. What did he see? What were his thoughts? What faces were there? Fire, and smoke, and blood—the dead!

Down before the fire in their fur-robes we laid the little Indians to sleep, and sought our blankets in the bunks against the wall.

Through the night one arose and then the other, and stirred the fire silently and lay down. Indians never let their fires go out in their lodges in time of peace. It is thought a bad omen, and then it is inconvenient, and certainly not the thing to do in the winter.

The Prince was up early the next morning. He could not sleep. Why? Starve yourself a week and you will understand. I did not think or ask myself then why he could not sleep. I know now.

He went to town at day-break. Then when we had rolled a back log into the spacious fire-place, and built a fire under my direction, a new style of architecture to the Indians, with a fore-stick on the stone and irons, and a heap of kindling wood in the centre, I induced Klamat to wash his face, and helped him to wash the blood from his hair in a pan of tepid water.

The little girl without any direction made her toilet, poor child, in a simple, natural way, with a careful regard for the effect of falls of dark hair on her brown shoulders and about her face ; and then we all sat down and looked at the fire and at each other in silence.

Soon the Prince returned, and wonderful to tell, he had on his shoulder a sack of flour. All flour in the mines is put in fifty-pound sacks, so as to be easily packed and unpacked, in the transportation over the mountains on the backs of mules, and is branded " Fifty Pounds, Self-rising, Warranted Superfine."

The Prince's face was beaming with delight. He took the sack from his shoulder gently, set it on the empty flour-bench in the corner, as carefully and tenderly as if it had been a babe—as if it had been his own firstborn.

The "Doctor" came with him. Not on a professional visit, however, but as a friend, and to see the Indians.

Now this Doctor was a character, a special part of The Forks. Not a lovely part or an excellent part in the estimation of either saloon-men or miners, but he filled a place there that had been left blank had he gone away, and that was not altogether because he was the only doctor in the place, but because he was a man of marked individuality.

A man who did not care three straws for the good or ill-will of man, and, as a consequence, as is always the fortune of such men when they first appear in a place, was not popular. He was a foreigner of some kind; maybe a German. I know he was neither an American nor an Irishman. He was too silent and reserved to have been either of these.

He was a small, light-haired man, a sort of an invalid, and a man who had no associates whatever. He was always alone, and never spoke to you if he could help it.

How the Prince made this man's acquaintance I do not know. Most likely he had gone to him that morning deliberately, told him the situation of things, asked for help, and had it for the asking. For my part, I had rather have seen almost anyone else enter the cabin. I did not like him from the first time that I ever saw him.

"Come here, Paquita," said the Doctor, as he sat down on the three-legged stool by the fire, and held out his hand to the Indian girl. She drew her robe modestly about her bosom and went up to the man, timid but pleasantly.

I knew no more of this Doctor, or his name, than of the other men around me.

He came into the camp as a doctor, and had pill bags and a book or two, and was called The Doctor.

Had another doctor come, he would have been called Doctor Brown, or Smith, or Jones, provided that neither of these names, or the name given him by the camp, was the name given him by his parents. I know a doctor who wore the first beaver hat into a camp, and was called Doctor Tile. He could not get rid of that name. If he had died in that camp, Doctor Tile would have been the name written on the pine board at his head.

I can hardly account for this habit of nick-naming men in the mines. Maybe it was done in the interest of those who really desired and felt the need of a change of name. No doubt it was a convenient thing for many; but for this wholesale re-naming of men, I see no sufficient reason. Possibly it was because these men, in civilization, had become tired of Col. William Higginson, The Hon. George H. Ferguson, Major Alfred Percival Brown, and so on to the end and exhaustion of handles and titles of men, and determined out here to have it their own way, to set up a sort of democracy in the matter of names.

" I will bake some bread, Doctor, for my babies;"

and the Prince threw off his coat and rolled up his sleeves, and went to work. He opened the mouth of his burden on the bunk, thrust in his hand, drew out the yellow flour in the gold pan, poured in cold water from the bucket, and soon had a luscious cake baking before the fire in the frying-pan.

Bread for my babies! Poor brave devil! When had he tasted bread?

Little Klamat retreated to his club, and stood with his back to the corner, with his head down, but at the same time watching the Doctor from under his hair, as a cat watches a mouse; only he was not the cat in this case, by a great deal.

The Doctor talked but little, and then only in an enigmatical sort of a way with the Prince. He did not notice me, and that contributed to my instinctive dislike. Soon he took leave, and we four ate bread together.

A wind came up the Klamat from the sea, soft and warm enough to drip the icicles from the cabin eaves, and make the drooping trees along the river bank raise their heads from the snow as if with hope.

The Doctor came frequently and spent the evening as the weeks went by. The butchers' mules came braying down the trail ere long, and we needed bread and meat no more.

The thunder boomed away to the west one night as if it had been the trump of resurrection; a rain set in, and the next morning, Humbug Creek, as if it had heard a Gabriel blow, had risen and was rushing toward the Klamat and calling to the sea.

Some birds were out, squirrels had left the rocks and were running up and down the pines, and places where the snow had melted off and left brown burrs and quills, and little shells. The back-bone of the winter storm was broken.

To return once more to the Doctor: I can hardly say why I disliked him at first, or at all. One thing is certain, however, he was bald on the top or rather on the back of his head; and from childhood, I have always had a prejudice against men who first become bald on the back instead of the front of the head.

It looks to me as if they had been running away, trying to escape from somewhere or something, when old Time caught them by the back of the hair as they fled, and scalped them on the spot.

CHAPTER X

HE sunshine follows the rain. There was a sort of general joyousness. The Prince was now a king, it seemed to me. He had fought a battle with himself, with fate against him; fought it silent, patient and alone; he had conquered, and he was glad.

The great hero is born of the bitter struggle. Who cannot go down to battle with banners, with trumps and the tramp of horses? Who cannot fight for a day in a line of a thousand strong with the eyes of the world upon him? But the man who fights a moral battle coolly, quietly, patiently and alone, with no one to applaud or approve, as the strife goes on through all the weary year, and after all to have no reward but that of his own conscience, the calm delight of a duty well performed, is God's own hero.

He is knighted and ennobled there, when the fight is won, and he wears thenceforth the spurs of gold and an armour of invulnerable steel.

We went down again among the boulders in the bed of the creek. The Prince swung his pick, I shovelled the thrown-out earth, and the little Indians would come and look on and wonder, and lend a hand in an awkward sort of a way for a few minutes at a time, then go back to the cabin or high up on the hills in the sun, following whatever pursuit they chose.

The Prince did not take it upon himself to direct or dictate what they should do, but watched their natural inclinations and actions with the keenest interest.

He loved freedom too well himself to attempt to fetter these little unfortunates with rules and forms that he himself did not hold in too great respect; and as for taxing them to labour, they were yet weak, and but poorly recovered from the effects of the famine on the Klamat.

Besides, he had no disposition to reduce them to the Christian slavery that was then being introduced, and still obtains, up about Mount Shasta, wherever any of the Indian children survive.

The girl developed an amiable and gentle nature, but the boy showed anything but that from the first. He always went out of the cabin whenever strangers entered, would often spend days alone, out of sight of everyone, and stubbornly refused to speak a word of English. At the end of weeks he was untamed as ever, and evidently untamable. The Prince had procured him a cheap suit of clothes, something after the fashion of the miner's dress; but he despised it, and would only wear his shirt with the right arm free and naked, the red sleeve tucked in or swinging about his body. He submitted to have his hair trimmed, but refused to wear a hat.

His chief delight was, in pointing and making faces at the Doctor's bald head, whenever that individual entered, as he stood in the corner by his club; but I never knew him to laugh, not even to smile. The first great epoch of his civilized life was the receipt of a knife as a gift from the Prince. It was more to him than diamonds to a bride. He kept it with him everywhere; slept with it always. It was to him as a host of companions.

Sometimes he talked in the Indian tongue to the girl, but only when he thought no one noticed or heard him.

The girl was quite the other way. She took to domestic matters eagerly, learned to talk in a few weeks, after a fashion, and was most anxious to be useful, and as near like an American as possible. She had a singular talent for drawing. One day she made an excellent charcoal picture of Mount Shasta, on the cabin door, and was delighted when she saw the Prince take pride in her work. She was eager to do everything, and insisted on doing all the cooking.

She had a great idea of the use of salt, and often an erroneous one. For instance, one morning she put salt in the coffee as well as in the beef and beans. I think it was an experiment of hers—that she was so anxious to please and make things palatable, she put it in to improve the taste. I can very well understand how she thought it all over, and said to herself, "Now if a little pinch of this white substance adds to the beans, why will it not contribute to the flavour of the coffee?" Once she put sugar on the meat instead of salt, but the same mistake never happened twice.

I must admit that she was deceitful, somewhat. Not wilfully, but innocently so. In fact, had anything of importance been involved, she would have stood up and told the whole simple truth with a perfect indifference to results. She did this once I know, when she had done an improper thing, in a way that made us trust and respect her. But she did so much like to seem wise about things of which she was wholly ignorant. When she had learned to talk she one day pretended to Klamat to also be able to read and understand what was written on the bills of the butchers. Her ambition seemed to be to appear learned in that she knew the least about. That is so much like many people you meet, that I know you are prepared to call her half-civilized, even in these few weeks.

This sort of innocent deceit is no new thing, particularly in women. And I rather like it. Go on to one of our fashionable streets to-day in America, and there you will find that the lady who has the least amount of natural hair has invariably the largest amount of artificial fix-ups on her head. This rule is almost infallible; it has hardly the traditional exception to testify to its truth.

In fact, does not this weakness extend even to man? You can nearly always detect a bald-headed man, even while his hat is on his head, by the display and luxuriance of the hair peeping out from under his hat. With the bald-headed man every hair is brought into requisition, every hair is brushed and bristled up into a sort of barricade against the eyes of the curious. The few hairs seem to be marshalled up for a fierce bayonet charge against any one who dares suspect that the head which they keep sentry round is bald. That man is bald and he feels it. Only bald-headed men make this display of what hair they have left.

And I am not sure but that nature herself is a little deceitful. The dead and leafless oaks have the richest growth of ivy, as if to make the world believe that the trees were thriving like the bay. All about the mouths of caves, all openings in the earth, old wells and pits, the rankest growths abound, as if to say, here is no wound in the breast of earth! here is even the richest and the choicest spot upon her surface.

To go further into a new field. If a true woman loves you truly she fortifies against it in every possible way as a weak place in her nature. She tries to deceive, not only the world, but herself. To keep out the eyes of the inquisitive she would build a barricade to the moon. She would not be seen to whisper with you for the world. Yet if she loved you less, she would laugh and talk and whisper by the hour, and think nothing of it. I like such deceit as that. It is natural.

The miners were at work like beavers. Up the stream and down the stream the pick and shovel clanged against the rock and gravel from dawn until darkness came down out of the forests above them and took possession of the place.

The Prince worked on patiently, industriously with the rest, with reasonable success and first-rate promise of fortune. The pent-up energies of the camp were turned loose, and the stream ran thick and yellow with sediment from pans, rockers, toms, sluices and flumes. Never was such industry, such energy, such ambition to get hold of the object of pursuit and escape from the cañon before another winter set up an impassable wall to the civilized world.

Spring came sudden and full-grown from the south. She blew up in a fleet of sultry clouds from the Mexican seas, along the Californian coast, and drew up to us between the rocky, pine-topped walls of the Klamat.

At first she hardly set foot in the cañon. The sun came down to us only about noon-tide, and then only tarried long enough to shoot a few bright shafts through the dusk and dense pine-tops at the banks of snow beneath, and spring did not like the place as well as the open, sunny plains over by the city, and toward the Klamat lakes. But at last she came to take possession. She planted her banners on places the sun made bare, and put up signs and land-marks not to be misunderstood.

The balm and alder burst in leaf, and catkins drooped and dropped from willows in the water, till you had thought a legion of woolly caterpillars were drifting to the sea. Still the place was not to be surrendered without a struggle. It was one of winter's struggles. He had been driven, day after day, in a march of many a thousand miles. He had retreated from Mexico to within sight of Mount Shasta, and here he turned on his pursuer. One night he came boldly down and laid hands on the muddy little stream, and stretched a border of ice all up and down its edges; spread frost-work, white and beautiful, on pick, and tom, and sluice, and flume and cradle, and made the miners curse him to his beard. He cut down the banners of the spring that night, lamb-tongue, Indian turnip and catella, and took possession as completely as of old.

The sun came up at last and he let go his hold upon the stream, took off his stamp from pick and pan, and tom, and sluice and cradle, and crept in silence into the shade of trees and up the mountain side against the snow.

And now the spring came back with a double force and strength. She planted California lilies, fair and bright as stars, tall as little flag-staffs, along the mountain side, and up against the winter's barricade of snow, and proclaimed possession absolute through her messengers, the birds, and we were very glad.

Paquita gathered blossoms in the sun, threw her long hair back, and bounded like a fawn along the hills. Klamat took his club and knife, drew his robe only the closer about him in the sun, and went out gloomy and sombre in the mountains. Sometimes he would be gone all night.

At last the baffled winter abandoned even the wall that lay between us and the outer world, and drew off all his forces to Mount Shasta. He retreated above the timber line, but he retreated not an inch beyond. There he sat down with all his strength. He planted his white and snowy tent upon this everlasting fortress, and laughed at the world below him. Sometimes he would send a foray down, and even in mid-summer, to this day, he plucks an ear of corn, a peach, or apricot, for a hundred miles around his battlement, whenever he may choose.

Now that the way was clear, immigrants and new arrivals of all kinds began to pour into the camp. The most noticeable was that of the new Alcalde.

This Alcalde was appointed by the new commissioners of the new county, and as might have been expected, since the place brought neither profit nor honour, was only a broad-cloth sort of a man. A new arrival from the States, looking about for a place where he could sit down and eat his bread exempt from the primal curse. No doubt this little egotist said to himself, "If there is a spot on earth where God's great tribute-taker will not find me, it is over at The Forks, on Humbug, and there will I pitch my tent and abide."

He had read just enough law to drive every bit of common sense out of his head, and yet not enough to get a bit of common law into it; except, perhaps, the line which says that "Law is a rule of action prescribed by the superior, which the inferior is bound to obey."

Being austere in his tastes, and feeling that he had a dignity to sustain, he made friends with the Doctor, and took up quarters in the Doctor's cabin.

As is the case with all small creatures, the Judge came into camp with a great flourish of trumpets, and what was most remarkable, he wore a "stovepipe" hat and a "boiled shirt;" the first that had ever been seen in the camp. This was a daring thing to undertake. The Judge, of course, had not the least idea of his achievement and the risk he incurred.

These men of the mountains always have despised and perhaps always will despise a beaver hat. Why? Here is food for reflection. Here is a healthy, well-seated antipathy to an innocent article of dress, without any discovered reason. Let the profound look into this.

As for myself, I have looked into this thing, but am not satisfied. The only reason I can give for this enmity to the " tile " in the mountains of California, is not that the miners hold that there is anything wrong in the act or fact of a man wearing a beaver, but because it invests the man with a dignity—an artificial dignity, it is true, but none the less a dignity—too far above that of the man who wears a slouch or felt. The beaver hat is the minority, the slouch hat is the majority; and, like all great majorities, is a mob—a cruel, heartless, arrogant, insolent mob, ignorant and presumptive. The beaver hat is a missionary among cannibals in the California mines. And the saddest part of it all is, that there is no hope of reform. Tracts on this subject would be useless. Fancy a beaver hat in a dripping tunnel, or by the splashing flume or dumping derrick!

Born of a low element in our nature is this antagonism to the beaver hat; cruel as it is curious, selfish, but natural.

The Englishman knows well the power and dignity of a beaver hat. Go into the streets of London and look about you. Surely some power has issued an order not much unlike that of the famous one-armed Sailor—" England expects every man to wear a beaver hat."

But to return to this particular hat before us, it is safe to say that no other man than the Judge in all California could have brought into camp and worn with impunity this hat.

It is true there was a universal giggle through the

camp, and it is likewise true that the Howlin' Wilderness called out, " Oh, what a hat! Set 'em up! Chuck 'em in the gutter! Saw my leg off!" and so on, as the Judge passed that way the morning after his arrival. But shrewd men at once took his measure; saw that he was a harmless little egotist, and in their hearts took his part in the hat question, and set him up as a sort of wooden idol of the camp.

It is not best to always seem too strong in the presence of strong, good men. Man likes to pet and patronize his fellow when he is weak. A strong man will throw his arms around a helpless man and protect him. Strength challenges strength. The combat of bulls on the plain! Possibly man inclines to uphold the weak because there is no suggestion of rivalry, but I do not think that. Here is room for thought.

" It's all right, boys," said six-foot Sandy, as he stood at the bar of the Howlin' Wilderness, and held out his glass for a little peppermint: " It's all right, I tell you! He shall run a hat as tall as Shasta if he likes, and let me set eyes on the shyster that interferes. It's a poor camp that can't afford one gentleman, anyhow." And here he hitched up his duck breeches, threw the gin and peppermint down his throat, and wiping his hairy mouth on his red sleeve, turned to the crowd, ready to "chaw up and spit out," as he called it, the first man who raised a voice against the Judge and his beaver hat in all The Forks.

Six-foot Sandy was an authority at The Forks. A brawny and reckless miner—a sort of cross between a first-class miner and a second-class gambler; a man who vibrated between his claim up the creek and the Howlin' Wilderness saloon. But he was a shrewd, brave man, of the half-horse, half-alligator kind, and was both feared and respected. After that the beaver hat was safe at The Forks, and a fixture.

To illustrate the power and dignity of the beaver hat even here, where reverence and respect for anything that smells of civilization is not to be thought of, I may mention that a month or two after the event described above, another beaver hat put in an appearance at The Forks. There was not even a protest. The man had sense enough to keep silent, took a quiet game of " draw " with the boys at the Howlin' Wilderness, and won at once the title of Judge.

After dark the quiet game went on in the corner, and Sandy came down from the claim.

" Who's that?" said Sandy to the bar-keeper, as he threw his left thumb over his shoulder, and with his right hand lifted his gin and peppermint.

" That? why that's Judge—Judge—why, the new Judge."

" Judge hell!" said Sandy, wiping his beard and looking sharply under the hat rim. " I know him, I do. He's a waiter over in a Yreka restaurant. I'll go for him, I will. He is a fraud on the public."

And he went up behind the man, as he sat there on a three-legged stool, serenely leading out his ace for his opponent's Jack.

" Come down!" said the new Judge, gaily; "come down! I have you now! Come down!"

Sandy raised his hands, his great broad hands, like slabs of pine, and brought them down on top of the beaver hat like an avalanche. The hat shot down and the head shot up, till it was buried out of sight in the wrecked and ruined beaver.

The man sprung to his feet, thrust out his hands, and jumped about like a boy in " Blind-man's-buff," and Sandy walked back to the bar, cool and unconcerned, and ordered gin and peppermint.

The man at last excavated his nose, and took a bee-line for the door, amid howls of delight from the patrons of the Howlin' Wilderness. That is the usual fate of beavers in the mines. They may be respected, but they perish for all that.

Let a member of Congress, or even of the Cabinet, go up into the mountains with a beaver, and ten to one he would have it driven down over his nose. He would have to stand it too; he would have to laugh, call it a good joke, and treat " the boys" in the bargain. After that they would call him a good fellow, give him "feet" in an extension of the " Jenny Lind" ledge, " Midnight Assassin," or " Roaring Lion," and vote for him, if he should be a candidate for office, to the last man.

I leave this question of the hat now to those wise

men of America who have rushed out upon the
frontier a pen in one hand, a telescope in the other,
and, viewing the Indian from afar off, decided in a
day that he was a bad and a bloody character.

I leave this question to those teachers, with every
confidence that their capacities will prove equal to
the task. The subject is worthy such men, and the
men worthy such a subject.

CHAPTER XI

OW that we have got a Judge," said Sandy one day, " why not put him to work?"

There had been a pretty general feeling against those who took part in the murder of the Indians the last winter kept alive by the miners, and Sandy, who was always boiling over on some subject, and was brimfull of energy, went and laid the case before the Judge and instituted a prosecution. Here was a sensation! The Court sent a constable to arrest a prisoner with a verbal warrant, and the man came into Court; the Howlin' Wilderness, followed by half the town, gave verbal bonds for his appearance next Saturday, and the Court adjourned to that day.

Sides were taken at once. The idlers of course all taking sides with the prisoner ; the miners mostly going the other way. Sandy took it upon himself to prosecute. He could hardly have been in earnest, yet he seemed to be terribly so. The assassins were active in getting evidence out of the way, making friends with the Judge, and intimidating all who dared express sympathy with the Indians. The miners, with the exception of Sandy, were rather indifferent. They knew very well that this weak little egotist would only make a farce of the affair, even though he had capacity to enter a legal committal. The giant Sandy, however, held his own against all the town and promised a lively time.

The Indian boy came home that night beaming with delight. His black eyes flashed like the eyes of a cat in the dark. I had thought him incapable of excitement. He had always seemed so passive and sullen that we had come to believe he had no life or passion in him.

He talked to Paquita eagerly, and made all kinds of gestures; put his fingers about his neck, stabbed himself with an imaginary knife, threw himself towards the fire, and shot with an imaginary gun at an imaginary prisoner. Would he be hung, stabbed, burnt or shot? The boy was so eager and excited, that once or twice he broke out into pretty fair English at some length, the first I had ever heard him utter.

The Doctor, as I said, was unpopular. In fact, doctors usually are in the mines. Whether this is because nine-tenths of those who are there are frauds and impostors, or whether it is because miners give open expression to a natural dislike that all men feel for the man to whose ministry we all have to submit ourselves some day, I do not pretend to say.

Even the Indian boy disliked the Doctor bitterly, and one day flew at him, without any cause, and clutched a handful of hair from his thin and half-bald head. The Judge, too, disliked the Doctor, and only the evening before the trial some one, passing the cabin, heard the Judge call the Doctor a fool to his teeth.

That was a feather in the Judge's hat, in the eyes of The Forks, but a bad sign for the Doctor. The Doctor should have knocked him down, said The Forks.

The day of trial came, and Sandy, in respect for the Court and the occasion, buttoned up his flannel shirt, hid his hairy bosom, and gave over his gin and peppermint during all the examination.

The prisoner was named "Spades." Whether it was because he looked so like the black, squatty Jack of Spades I do not know; but I should say he was indebted to his likeness to that right or left bower for his name.

There was not the slightest doubt that he had deliberately murdered two or three Indian children, butchered them, as they crouched on the ground and tried to hide under the lodges, with his knife, on the day of the massacre; but there were grave doubts as to what the Judge would do in the case, for he had been pretty plainly told that he must not hold the man to answer.

A low, wretched man was this—the lowest in the camp; but he stood between others of a more respectable character and danger. His fortune in the matter was a prophecy of theirs. The prisoner was nearly drunk as he took his seat on a three-legged stool before the Judge in the Howlin' Wilderness. He sat with his hat on. In fact, miners, in the matter of wearing hats, would make first-class Israelites.

" Ef I ain't out o' this by dark," said Spades, as he jerked his head over his shoulder and spirted a stream of amber at the back-log, " I'll sun somebody's moccasins, see if I don't." And he looked straight at the Judge, who settled down uneasily in his seat, and placed his beaver hat on the table between himself and the prisoner as a sort of barricade.

Two or three gamblers, good enough men in their way, acted as attorneys for Spades. They at once turned themselves loose in plausible, if not eloquent, speeches against the treacherous savage. Sandy now introduced his witness for the prosecution. This man told how Spades had butchered the babes down on the Klamat, in detail; and then others were called and did the same. It was a clear case, and Sandy was delighted with his prosecution.

The other side did not ask any questions. The attorneys whispered a moment among themselves, and then one of them got up, took the stand, and gravely asserted that on that day, and at the very moment described, he was playing poker with Spades at two bits a corner in the Howlin' Wilderness. Then another arose with the same account; and then another. It was the clearest *alibi* possible.

Sandy said nothing, and the case was closed. He looked black across the table at the defence, and then went up to the bar, and called for gin and peppermint, alone.

This was the first attempt to introduce law practice at The Forks, and no wonder that it did not work well, and that some things were forgotten. All were new hands—Court, counsel, and nearly all present, here witnessed their first trial.

Poor Sandy had forgotten to have his witnesses sworn, and the Court had not thought of it.

The testimony being all in, the Court proceeded solemnly to sum up the case. In conclusion, it said, " You will observe that, as a rule, the further we go from the surface of things the nearer we get to the bottom." This brought cheers and waving of hats from the Howlin' Wilderness, and the Court repeated, " I am free to say that the Court has gone diligently into the depths of this case, and that, as a rule, the further you get from the surface of things the nearer you get to the bottom. The case looked dark indeed against the prisoner at first; but the Court has gone to the bottom of the matter, and he is now white as snow."

"Hear! hear! hear!" shouted a man from Sydney, who always hobbled a little as if he dragged a chain when he walked.

" Snow is good ! " said a miner between his

teeth, as he looked at the black visage of the prisoner.

"You see," continued the Judge, "that things are often not so black as they first appear, particularly if they are only fairly washed."

"Particularly if they are whitewashed!" said Sandy, as he swallowed his gin and peppermint and left the saloon in disgust.

All this time a tawny little figure had stood back in the corner unseen, perhaps, by any one. It was Klamat with his club. He had watched with the eyes of a hawk the whole proceeding. He had drank in every sentence, and had never once taken his eyes from the Court or the prisoner.

At last, when the Judge decreed the prisoner free, and the Court adjourned, and all ranged themselves in a long, single file before the bar, calling out "Cocktail," "Tom-and-Jerry," "Brandy-smash," "Gin-sling," "Lightning straight," "Forty rod," and so on, he slipped out, looking back over his shoulders, with his thin lips set, and his hand clutching a knife under his robe.

That evening the Judge was again belabouring the Doctor with his tongue, which had been made more than ordinarily loose and abusive by the single-file drilling process that had been repeated at the Howlin' Wilderness in the celebration of Spades' acquittal.

"That little Doctor 'll put a bug in his soup for him yet, see 'f he don't," said some one that evening at the saloon, when the man who had heard the Judge's abuse had finished reciting it.

" All right, let him," said a man, who stood stirring his liquor with a spoon, in gum-boots and with a gold-pan under his left arm. " All right, let him;" said the bearded sovereign, as he threw back his head and opened his mouth. " It's not my circus, nor won't be my funeral;" and he wiped his beard and went out saying to himself:—

> " Fight dog, and fight bar,
> Thar's no dog of mine thar."

The Prince, with that clear common-sense which always came to the surface, had foreseen the whole affair so far as the trial was concerned, and had remained at home hard at work in the claim; I told him all that had happened, and he only shrugged his shoulders.

The next morning the butcher shouted down from the cabin as he weighed out the steaks: " A man for breakfast up in town, I say! a man for breakfast up in town, and I'll bet you can't guess who it is."

" Who?".

" The Judge!"

The man had been stabbed to death not far from his own door, some time in the night, perhaps just before retiring. There were three distinct mortal wounds in the breast. There had evidently been a short, hard struggle for life, for in one hand he clutched a lock of somebody's hair. There was no mistake about the hair. That long, soft, silken, half curling, yellow German hair of the Doctor's, that grew on the sides of his naked head—there was not to be found another lock of hair like this in the mountains.

The dead man had not been robbed. That was a point in the Doctor's favour. He had been met in the front, had not been poisoned, or stabbed or shot in the back; that was another very strong point in the Doctor's favour.

In some of the northern states of Mexico, particularly at Guadalajara, I remember some years ago it was a pretty good defence for a man charged with murder, if he could prove that he had not plundered the dead, and that he had met him from the face like a man. These Mexicans held that man is not naturally vicious or bloodthirsty, and will not take life without cause: that if he did not murder a man to rob him, he had some secret and perhaps sufficient wrong to redress, to at least give some show of right; then if, added to these, he met his man like a man and he came off victor, although he slew the man, the law for that would hardly take his life.

There was something of this feeling in the camp now. However, if there had been an alcalde at The Forks, there is no doubt the Doctor had been at once arrested; but as there was nothing of the kind nearer than a day's ride, nothing was done. Besides, the Judge had made himself particularly odious to the miners, and gamblers are the last men in the world to meddle with the law. They settled their suits with steel across a table, or with little bull-dog deringers around a corner. Sometimes they have a six-shooter war dance in the streets, if the misunderstanding is one in which many parties are concerned.

As a rule, a funeral in the mines is a mournful thing. It is the saddest and most pitiful spectacle I have ever seen. The contrast of strength and weakness is brought out here in such a way that you must turn aside or weep when you behold it. To see those strong, rough men, long-haired, bearded and brown, rugged and homely-looking, with something of the grizzly in their great, awkward movements, now take up one of their number, straightened in the rough pine box, in his miner's dress, and carry him up, up on the hill in silence—it is sad beyond expression.

He has come a long way, he has journeyed by land or sea for a year, he has toiled and endured, and denied himself all things for some dear object at home, and now after all, he must lie down in the forests of the Sierras, and turn on his side and die. No one to kiss him, no one to bless him, and say " good-bye," only as a woman can, and close the weary eyes, and fold the hands in their final rest: and then at the grave, how awkward— how silent! How they would like to look at each other and say something, yet how they hold down their heads, or look away to the horizon, lest they should meet each other's eyes. Lest some strong man should see the tears that went silently down from the eyes of another over his beard and on to the leaves.

But the Judge had no such burial as this. Sandy was on a spree, and the gamblers placed Spades at the head of the funeral. They had no respect for the man and kept away. Spades was chief mourner, and the poor little man was laid alone on the hillside, with hardly enough in attendance to do the last offices for the dead.

That night Spades entered the Howlin' Wilderness wearing a beaver hat. Sandy saw this, set down the glass of gin and peppermint untouched, and went straight up to the man. He seized him by the throat and shook him till his teeth smote and ground together like quartz rocks in a feeder. Then he picked up the hat reverently and respectfully as his condition would allow, and laid it gently on the roaring pine-log fire. That was the last of the first beaver hat of Humbug.

The Doctor appeared out of place in this camp from the first. Every one seemed to feel that—perhaps no one felt it more keenly than himself.

There are people, it seems to me, who go all through life looking for the place where they belong and never finding it. This to me is a very sad sight. They seem to fit in no place on top of the earth.

The general feeling of dislike that had always been observed, now became one of contempt. No one noticed or spoke to him now. He came to hold down his head very soon, and to shun people instinctively since they seemed to wish to shun him.

I am bound to confess, right here, that after this murder, when the whole camp seemed turned against this shy, shrinking, silent man, when he was despised by all, when no one would share the path with him, but would make him stand aside and leave the trail as if he had been an Indian or a Chinaman, I began to sympathize with him. When the world pointed its finger and set the mark of Cain upon the man, I began to like him.

This, you say, seems to you remarkable. It is certainly remarkable, or I should not trouble myself to mention it.

There was now an expression in this man's face that I had not seen before. A sort of weary, tired look it was, that was pitiful. An idea took possession of me that he had grown tired in his journey from place to place in the world, looking for the place where he belonged, for a sort of niche where he would fit in, and which he had never yet found.

There are men who sit in a community like a centre gem in a cluster of diamonds, and who cannot be taken away without deranging and marring the whole. The place of such a man is vacant till the last one of the cluster of which he forms the centre goes down in the dust.

There are others, again, who grow on the side or even in the centre of a community, like a great wart or wen. They sap its strength, they stop its growth, they poison it thoroughly, and it dies : a miserable, contemptible community, all through that one bad man.

But the Doctor was neither of these. He had never yet found his place, had never yet taken root or hold anywhere, but had been blown or rolled or thrown or pitched or shuttle-cocked about, it seemed to me, from the beginning of his life; whenever that may have been. A sort of sour, dried-up apple, that no one would eat, yet an apple that no one would care to pitch out of the window.

I had always hated and feared the man till now. The universal dislike, however, aroused a sort of antagonism in my nature, that always has, and I expect always will, come to the surface on such occasions on the side of the poor or much despised, perfectly regardless of propriety, self-interest, or any consideration whatever.

If a man has succeeded and is glad, let him go his way. What should I have to do with him? My lot and my life thus far have been with the poor and the lonely, and so shall be to the end. They can understand me.

And maybe, often, there is a kind of subtle wisdom in this view of men. I think it is born of the fact that your ostentatious, prosperous man, your showy rich man of America, is so very, very poor, that you do not care to call him your neighbour. It is true he has horses and houses, and land and gold, but these horses and houses, and

lands and coins, are all in the world he has. When
he dies these will all remain and the world will
lose nothing whatever. His death will not make
even a ripple in the tide of life. His family, whom
he has taught to worship gold, will forget him in
their new estates. In their hearts they will be glad
that he is gone. They will barter and haggle with
the stone-cutter toiling for his bread, and for a
starve-to-death price they will lift a marble shaft
above his head with an iron fence around it—typical,
cold, and soulless!

Poor man, since he took nothing away that one
could miss, what a beggar he must have been! The
poor and unhappy never heard of him: the world has
not lost a thought. Not a note missed, not a word
was lost in the grand, sweet song of the universe
when he died.

Save us from such men. America is full of them.
She boils over with them in a sort of annual eruption.
She throws them over the sea into abbeys, and
sacred places, with their hats on; they are howling,
hoarser than jackals, up and down the Nile and
over and away towards Jerusalem.

It was remarkable how suddenly the Indian
children sprung up with the summer. No one could
have recognized in this neat, modest, sensitive girl,
and this silent, savage-looking boy, who sometimes
looked almost a man, the two starved, naked little
creatures of half a year before.

There was a little lake belted by wild red roses

and salmon berries, and fretted by overhanging ferns under the great firs that shut out the sun save in little spars and bars of light that fell through upon a bench of the hills; a sort of lily pond, only half a pistol shot across, at the bottom of a waterfall, and clear as sunshine itself. Here Paquita would go often and alone to pass her idle hours. I chanced to see her there on the rim, walking against the sun and looking into the water as she moved forward, now and then back, across her shoulder, as a maiden in a glass preparing for a ball. She had first been made glad with her first new dress—red, and decorated with ribbons, made gay and of many colours. The poor child was studying herself in the waters.

This was not vanity; no doubt there was a deal of satisfaction, a sort of quiet pride, in this, but it was something higher, also. A desire to study grace, to criticize her movements in this strange and to her lovely dress, and learn to move with the most perfect propriety. She practised this often. The finger lifted sometimes, the head bowed, then the hands in rest and the head thrown back, she would walk back and forth for hours, contemplating herself and catching the most graceful motion from the water.

What a rich, full, and generous mouth was hers— frank as the noon-day! Beware of people with small mouths, they are not generous. A full, rich mouth, impulsive and passionate, is the kind of mouth to trust, to believe in, to ask a favour of, and to give kind words.

There are as many kinds of mouths as there are crimes in the catalogue of sins. There is the mouth for hash!—thick-lipped, coarse, and expressionless, a picket of teeth behind with bread about the roots. Bah! Then there is the thin-lipped, sour-apple mouth, sandwiched in between a sharp chin and thin nose. Look out!

There are mischievous mouths, ruddy and full of fun, that you would like to be on good terms with if you had time, and then there is the rich, full mouth, with dimples dallying and playing about it like ripples in a shade, half sad, half glad—a mouth to love. Such was Paquita's. A rose, but not yet opened; only a bud that in another summer would unfold itself wide to the sun.

CHAPTER XII

STILL we wrought, the Prince and I, patiently and industriously. So did thousands above us and below us; there was a clang of picks and shovels, the smiting of steel on the granite, a sound through the sable forests, an echoing up the far hill-sides like the march of an army to battle, clashing the sword and buckler.

Every man that wrought there worked for an object. There was a payment to be met at home; a mortgage to be lifted. The ambition of one I knew was to buy a little home for his parents; another had orphan sisters to provide for; this had an invalid mother. This had a bride, and that one the promise of a bride. Every man there had a history, a plan, a purpose.

Every man there who bent above the boulders, and toiled on silently under the dark-plumed pines and the shadows of the steep and stupendous mountains, was a giant in body and soul.

Never since the days of Cortez has there been
gathered together such a hardy and brave body of
men as these first men of the Pacific. When it took
six months' voyaging round the Horn, and imminent
perils, with like dangers and delays, to cross the
isthmus or the continent, then the weak of heart
did not attempt it and the weak of body died on the
way. The result was a race of men worthy of the
land. The world's great men were thus drawn out,
separated and set apart to themselves out here on the
Pacific. There was another segregation and sifting
out after the Pacific was reached. There lay the
mines open to all who would work; no capital but a
pick and pan required. The most manly and independent life on earth. At night you had your pay
in your hand, your reward weighed out in virgin
gold. If you made five, ten, fifty, or a thousand
dollars that day, you made it from the fall of no man;
no decline of stocks or turn in trade which carried some
man to the bottom brought you to the top; no speculation, no office, no favour, only your own two hands
and your strong, true heart, without favour from any
man. You had contributed that much to the commerce of the world. If there is any good in gold, you
had done that much good to the world, besides the
good to yourself. What men took this line of life!
But some preferred to trade, build towns, hang about
them, and practise their wits on their fellow-men.

You see at once that the miners were the cream
of the milk in this second separation.

The summer wore on, and Paquita remained with us, an industrious, lovely little girl. She was the pet of the camp. She dressed with taste, and was modest, sensitive, intelligent, and beautiful. It was noticeable that men who lived in that vicinity dressed much more neatly than in any other part of the camp, and even men who had to pass that way to reach The Forks kept their shaggy beards in shape, and their shirt bosoms buttoned up when they passed. Such is the influence of even the presence of woman.

Klamat was wild as ever. The miners would suppose him spending his nights with us, and we would suppose him still with them, and thus he had it all his own way, wandered off with his club and knife into the hills, down to the river, and slept Heaven knows where.

At last one Sunday the Prince taught him the use of the rifle. This was to him perhaps the greatest event of his life. He danced with delight, made all sorts of signs about the game he would kill, and how much he would do for the Prince. He was faithful to his word. He began to repay something of his trouble. He brought game to the Prince and to us in abundance, but refused to let any one else have so much as a quail.

Once the Prince gave a shoulder of venison to some neighbour boys below us. Klamat went down when the men were at work, took the axe, broke open the door, and took and threw the meat over the bank into the claim. This made him natural enemies, and it took great caution on the part of the Prince to save his life.

He never talked, never smiled; a sour, bitter-looking face was his, and he had no friends in the camp outside our own cabin. He stood his club in the corner now, and used the rifle instead. In a few days he had polished the barrel and all the brass ornaments till they shone like silver and gold.

Once a travelling missionary, as he called himself, gave him a tract. He took it to Paquita, who held it up and pretended to him that she could read it all as readily as the white men. This was one of her little deceits. Poor children! No one had time to teach them to read, or to set them much of an example. How they wondered at the endless toil of the men.

The Doctor in the meantime ranged around the hill sides, wrote some, gathered some plants, and seemed altogether the most listless, wretched, miserable man you could conceive. He made his home in our cabin now, and rarely went to town; for when he did, so sure one of the hangers-on about the saloons was sure to insult him. Sometimes, however, he would be obliged to go, such as when some accident or severe illness would compel the miners to send for him, and he never refused to attend. On one of these occasions, Spades, half drunk and wholly vicious, caught the Doctor by the throat as he met him in the trail near town, and shook him much as he had been shaken by Sandy some months before.

Spades boasted he had made his old teeth rattle like rocks in a rocker. The Doctor said nothing, but got off as best he could and came home. He did not even mention the matter to any one.

Shortly after this Spades was found dead. He was found just as the Judge had been found, close to his cabin door, with the three mortal stabs in the breast, only he did not have the lock of hair in his hands from the Doctor's head.

There was talk of a mob. This thing of killing people in the night, even though they were the most worthless men of the camp, and even though they were killed in a way that suggested something like fair play, and revenge rather than robbery, was not to be indulged in, even at Humbug, with impunity. Some of the idlers got together at the Howlin' Wilderness to pass resolutions, and take some steps in the matter, as Spades lay stretched out under the old blue soldier coat on a pine slab that had many dark stains across and along its rugged surface, but they fell into an exciting game of poker, at ten dollars a corner, and the matter for the time was left to rest. No Antony came to hold up the dead Cæsar's mantle, and poor Spades was buried much as he had buried the Judge a short time before.

Some one consulted Sandy on the subject, about the time of the funeral, as he stood at the bar of the Howlin' Wilderness for his gin and peppermint. Sandy was something of a mouth-piece for the miners, not that he was a recognized leader; miners, as a rule, decline to be led, but rather that he knew what they thought on most subjects, and preferred to act with them and express their thoughts, rather than incline to the idlers about The Forks. He drank his gin in silence, set down his glass, and said in an oracular sort of way, as if to himself, when passing out of the door:

" Well, let 'em rip; it 's dog eat dog, anyhow ! "

But it was evident that this matter would not blow over as easily as did the death of the Judge. True, there was no magistrate in camp yet, but there was a live Sheriff in the city.

The Doctor went on as usual, avoiding men a little more than before, but other than this I could see no change in the man or his manner of life.

He and the Prince had many strange theories. Men in the mines think out some great things, as they dig for gold all day, with no sound save the ripple of the mountain stream and the sharp quick call of the quail in the chapparal, to disturb them, through all the days of summer. They come upon new thoughts as upon nuggets of gold.

Sometimes they talked in bitter terms about the treatment of the Indians. They had humane and I think just and possible theories on this subject, which I remember very well, and may sometime submit to the Government, if I can only get a hearing within the next ten years. It will hardly be worth while after that time, although, after the Indians are all dead, no doubt we will have some very humane and Christian plans advanced by which they may be made a prosperous and contented people.

I am constantly asked: " Does not the Government interfere? Does not the Government take charge of these Indians after having taken their lands, and lakes, and rivers?" Nonsense! The Government! The Indian Bureau, Indian Agent, or whatever you choose to call that part of the North American Republic deputed to distribute red blankets and glass beads to the North-American Indian, had not yet put in an appearance on the Klamat. I doubt if he has reached that portion of the interior to this day.

When he does arrive he will find now only falling lodges with grass growing rank about the doorways; he will find mounds all up and down the river that were made by a continual round of encampments reaching back to a time when the Chaldeans named the stars; he will find perhaps an old woman or two, or a bent old warrior, sitting in rags and wretchedness, lamenting, looking back with dimmed eyes to another age, and that is all.

Twenty years ago the Indians of the Forks of the Willamette, rode by my father's cabin in bands, single file, a mile or two in length. They rode spotted horses, had gay clothes and garments of many colours. The squaws chanted songs of a monotonous kind, not without some melody, as they rode by astride, with papooses swinging on boards from the saddle-bow, and were very happy.

They saw the country settling up day by day, but never raised a hand against the whites.

The whites were insolent, it is true, for had not Government given them the land, and had they not journeyed a long way to possess it?

Then the country was fenced up and their ponies could not get pasture; the lands were ploughed and the squaws could not get roots and acorns. But worst of all, the whites killed and frightened off the game, and the Indians began to starve and die. Once or twice they undertook to beg, about the Forks of the Willamette, but the settlers set dogs on them, and they went back to their lodges and died off in a few years by thousands. The world wondered why the Indians died. "They are passing away," said the substantial idiot who edited the "Star of the West." "They are a doomed race," said the minister. I think they were.

Less than six months ago I visited this spot. How many Indians do you suppose I found there of the permanent old settlers? Two! Captain Jim and his squaw. All along the silver river, where it makes its flashing course against the sun, the banks are black and mellow, and the grass grows tall and strong from the bones and ashes of the "doomed race."

Captain Jim declines to surrender to the Reservation. They caught him once, him and his squaw, but he got away after a year or two, and not only brought back his own squaw, but one of a neighbouring tribe, and has ever since been dodging about through the hills overlooking the great valley where his fathers were once the lords and masters, with only the Great Spirit to say yea or nay to them.

Captain Jim is a harmless fellow, and a good hunter. Sometimes in harvest he goes down in the fields and binds wheat, and gets pay like a white man. His squaws gather berries and sell them to the whites. Sometimes they take a great fancy to children, and give them all the berries they have, and will take nothing for them. Captain Jim says that is not good management. One day some one asked him why he had two squaws. He studied awhile, and said he had two squaws so that they could bury him when he died. He wears a stiff-brimmed beaver hat with feathers in it; clothes like a white man, even to the white shirt; smokes and chews tobacco, swears, and sometimes gets drunk. In fact, he is so nearly civilized, that no great efforts are now made to return him to the Reservation. Some day soon the two wives of Captain Jim will be permitted to lay the last of the Willamette Indians to sleep on the banks of that sunny river.

What would I do? It would be long to tell. But I would blow the Indian Bureau to the moon. I would put good men, and plenty of them, to look into the Indians' interest. I would set apart good tracts of land for each tribe. I would pay these men so well that they would not steal from the Indians, if I could not get honest men otherwise. I would make their office perpetual, and I would make it one of honour and of trust.

But what do we do instead? We change the man in charge every few years, before he has even got a glimpse at the inner life of an Indian. We send out some red-mouthed politician, who gets the place because he happens to have a great influence with the Irish vote of New York, or the German vote of Pennsylvania. We wait, nine cases out of ten, till the matter adjusts itself between the whites and the reds. If the Indians are peaceful, as in the case of the Willamette, why interfere? If they go to war they must be made peaceful. This is the way it has gone and still goes on, to the eternal disgrace of the country. If a trouble comes of this clashing together of the whites and the reds, we hear but one side of the story. The Indian daily papers are not read.

CHAPTER XIII

IRGIN gold, like truth, lies at the bottom. It is a great task in the placer mines, as a rule, particularly in the streams, to get on the bed-rock to open a claim and strike the lead. When this is done the rest is simple enough. You have only to keep your claim open, to see that the drain is not clogged, the tail race kept open, and that the water does not break in and fill up your excavation by which you have reached the bed rock. All this the Prince and I had accomplished. The summer was sufficiently cool to be tolerable in toil; the season was unusually healthy, and all was well.

At night, when the flush of the sun would be blown from the tree tops to the clouds, we two would sit at the cabin door in the gloaming, and look across and up, far up, into the steep and sable skirting forest of firs, and listen to the calls of the cat-bird, or the coyote lifting his voice in a plaintive murmur for his mate on the other side.

The Doctor would sit there too, in silence, close at hand, and dream and forget the ways of man; and, perhaps, think sadly, but certainly enough, there was one place, one narrow place, at last, where he would fit in and no one would come to disturb him.

Klamat would come in with a string of quails, sometimes, at dusk, or a venison saddle, a red fox or a badger, stand his gun in the corner with his club, and turn himself to rest close at hand.

Paquita would drop down from the woods on the hill above the cabin, the little belle and beauty of the camp. But she never spoke to the miners or any one, save to only answer them in the briefest way possible.

They hardly liked this; and they hardly liked the Prince from the start, I think, anyhow. He was, as an expression of the time went, a little too "fine-haired." He spoke too properly; he never "got on any glorious benders," with the western men, nor could he eat codfish, or talk about Boston, with the eastern. He took hold of no man's hand hastily.

I like that.

Paquita had a great deal to tell about Mount Shasta. She had been on the side beyond. In fact her home was there, she said, and she described the whole land in detail. A country sloping off gradually toward the east and south; densely timbered, save little dimples of green prairies, alive with game, dotted down here and there, buried in the dark and splendid forests on the little trout streams that wound still and crooked through wood and meadow.

She had been out here on the Klamat on a visit, with her mother and others, the fall and winter before. She said they had come down from the lakes in canoes. She also insisted strongly that her father was a great chief of the Modocs and mountain Shastas.

Indians are great travellers, far greater than is generally believed, and it was quite reasonable to take that part of the young lady's story as literally true; but the part about her father being a great chief was set down as one of her innocent fictions by which she wished to dignify herself, and appear of some importance in the eyes of the Prince.

Still as there had been quite a sensation in camp about new mines in that direction, it was interesting to talk to one who had been through the country, and could give us some accurate account of it. After that, finding the Prince was interested enough to listen, she would take great pleasure in describing the country, character, and habits of the Indians, and the kind of game with which the forest abounded.

She would map out on the ground with a stick the whole country, as you would draw a chart on the black board.

The feeling against the Doctor had not yet blown over. It was pretty generally understood that the sheriff or a deputy from across the mountain would soon be over with a warrant for his apprehension.

Why not escape? There are some popular errors of opinion that are amusing. Men suppose that if a man is in the mountains he is safe, hid away, and secure; that he has only to step aside in the brush and be seen no more.

As a rule, it is infinitely better to be in the heart of a city. Here was a camp of three thousand men. Each man knew the face of his neighbour. There was but one way to enter this camp, but one way to go out; that way led to the city. We were in a sac, the further end of a cave, as it were. You could not go this way, or that, through the mountains above. There were no trails; there was no food. You would get lost; you would starve.

Besides, there were wild beasts, and wilder men, ready to revenge the hundred massacres up and down the country, not unlike the one described. Here, in that day at least, if a man did wrong he could not hide. The finger of God pointed him out to all.

Late one September day it grew intensely sultry; there was a haze in the sky and a circle about the sun. There was not a breath. The perspiration came out and stood on the brow, even as we rested in the shadow of the pines. A singular haze; such a day, it is said, as precedes earthquakes.

The black crickets ceased to sing; the striped lizards slid quick as ripples across the rocks, and birds went swift as arrows overhead, but uttered no cry. There was not a sound in the air nor on the earth.

Paquita came rushing down to the claim, pale and excited. She lifted her two hands above her head as she stood on the bank, and called to us to come up from the mine. " Come," she cried, "there will be a storm. The trees will blow and break against each other. There will be a flood, a sea, a river in the mountains. Come!" She swayed her body to and fro, and the trees began to sway above her on the hills, but not a breath had touched the mines.

Then it grew almost dark; we fairly had to feel our way up the ladder. A big drop sank in the water close at hand, splashing audibly; the trees surged above us and began to snap like reeds.

There was a roar like the sea—loud, louder. Nearer now the trees began to bend and turn and lick their limbs and trunks, interweave and smite and crush, until their tops were like one black and boiling sea.

Fast, faster, the rain in great warm drops began to strike us in the face, as we miners hastened up the hill to the shelter of the cabin. At the door we turned to look. The darkness of death was upon us; we could hear the groans and the battling of the trees, the howling of the tempest, but all was darkness, blackness, desolation. Lightning cleft the heavens.

A sheet of flame—as if the hand of God had thrust out through the dark and smote the mountain side with a sword of fire.

And then the thunder shook the earth till it trembled, as if Shasta had been shaken loose and broken from its foundation. No one spoke. The lightning lit the cabin like a bonfire. Klamat stood there in the cabin by his club and gun. There was in his face a grim delight. The Doctor lay on his face in his bunk, hiding his eyes in his two hands.

No one undressed that night in the camp.

The next morning the fury of the storm was over, but it was not yet settled. We ventured out and looked down into the stream. It was nearly large enough to float a steamer. The claim was filled up as perfectly as when we first took it from the hands of the Creator. Ten feet of water flowed swift and muddy over it towards the Klamat and the sea.

Logs, boards, shingles, rockers, toms, sluices, flumes, pans, riffles, aprons went drifting, bobbing, dodging down the angry river like a thousand eager swimmers.

The storm had stolen everything, and was rushing with his plunder straight as could be to the sea, as if he feared that dawn should catch him in the camp, and the miners come upon him to reclaim their goods.

Every man in the camp was ruined. No man had dreamed of this. Maybe a few had saved up a little fortune, but, as a rule, all their fortunes lay in the folds of the next few months. Every man had his burden now to bear. The mortgage on the farm, the home for the old, the orphans, the invalid sister !

Brave men! they said nothing; they set their teeth, looked things squarely in the face, but did not complain. One man, however, who watched the flood from a point on the other side and saw his flume swept away, swung his old slouched hat, danced a sort of savage hokee-pokee, and sang:

> " O, everything is lovely,
> And the goose hangs high!"

A strange song, indeed!

To them this disaster meant another weary winter in the mines—disease, scurvy, death. Many could not endure it. They understood their claims could not be opened till another year, and set their faces for other mines which they had heard of, further on. Mining life is not unlike life at large.

We two had not saved much money. And what portion of that had I earned? I could not well claim a great deal, surely. How much would be left when the debts were paid—the butcher and the others? True, the claim was valuable, but it had no value now—not so much as a sack of flour. There were too many wanting to get away, and men had not yet learned the worth of a mine. Sometimes in these days new excitements, new diversions, would tap a camp, drain it dry, and not leave a soul to keep the coyotes from taking possession of the cabins.

"What will you do?" said the Prince to me one day, as we sat on the bank, wishing in vain for the water to subside.

" We cannot reach the bed-rock again till far into the next year. What will you do?"

" May I stay with you?"

The strong man reached me his two hands—" As long as I live and you live, my little one, and there is a blanket to my name we will sleep under it together.

" We will leave this camp. I have hated it from the first. I have grown old here in a year. I cannot breathe in this narrow cañon with its great walls against the clouds. We will go."

CHAPTER XIV

HAT night the Prince talked a long time with Paquita about the new country on the other side of the Shasta, and putting her account and my brief knowledge of the country together, we resolved to go there, where gold, according to her story, was to be had almost for the picking up, if the Indians did not interfere.

A new trouble arose. What was to be done with the two little savages? What would any other man have done? Gone about his business and left them to shift for themselves! Had he not saved their lives? Had he not fed them through all that dreadful winter? What more should he do?"

One morning this man rested his elbows on the table, and with his face buried in his hands was a long time silent.

"Pack up," said the Prince, at last, to the little girl. In a few moments she stood by his side with a red calico dress and some ribbons tied up in a handkerchief in one hand, and a pair of moccasins in the other.

The Doctor was anxious to get away—more anxious, perhaps, than any one. For what had the camp been to him? If I could have had my way or say, I would have left this mysterious, sad-faced, silent man behind.

I think the Prince would have done the same. We cannot always have our own way, even with ourselves.

Why does the man not do thus and so, we say? What is there to hinder him? Who shall say yea or nay? Is he not his own master? No. No man is his own master who has a conscience.

If this man had been of stronger will, had he not been so utterly helpless and friendless, we could have left him, and would have left him gladly; as it was, it was not a matter of choice at all.

Ponies were scarce, and mules were high-priced and hard to get, but the Doctor was not so poor as we, and he put his money all in the Prince's hands. So we had a tolerable outfit.

A very little pony would answer for me, the commonest kind could bear Paquita and her extra dress, while Klamat could walk and make his own way through the woods, like a greyhound.

The Prince procured a great double-barrelled shot gun, throwing buck-shot by the hand-full, for himself, and pistols for all, for we were going into the heart of a hostile country.

An officer, it was rumoured, was on the watch for the Doctor, and Klamat prepared to lead us by way of a blind trail, up the mountain side, without passing out by way of the Howlin' Wilderness at The Forks.

One of the most interesting studies, as well as one of the rarest, is that of man in a state of nature. Next to that is the state of man removed from, or above the reach of, all human law, utterly away from what is still more potent to control the actions of men, public opinion—the good or ill-will of the world.

As far as my observation has gone I am bound to say, that any expression on the subject would be highly laudatory of the native goodness of man. I should say, as a rule, he, in that state, is brave, generous, and just.

But in civilization I find that the truly just and good man is rarely prominent, he is hardly heard of, while some little sharp-faced commercial meddler, who never spends or bestows a farthing without first balancing it on his finger, and reckoning how much it will bring him by way of honour in return, is often counted the noblest man among you.

Therefore, I say that the truest men are those who are men for the sake of their manhood. A true man does a good deed for the sake of doing good, for the satisfaction of it, for the dignity that it gives him in his own eyes, and not the eyes of the world.

You see some noble and interesting things when

the winds have blown men away from the shore to where there is no law to punish crime, no public opinion to reward merit, where men act from within and not from without.

That aristocratic and highly respectable gentleman, the Hon. Mr. Perkins, of Perkinsville, who gave the thousand dollars to the Sanitary Commission, and a like sum to the church, and had it published over all the land, received offices and posts of honour for the same, and always cherished a fond hope that the facts would be appropriately set forth on his tombstone, for which he had just contracted with a dealer, in finest Italian marble, and at a splendid bargain, too, as the man was about to fail and compelled to have the money,—would probably have acted quite otherwise here.

Similar deeds done under the eyes of an approving world might not take place in the mountains where there is no public opinion, no press to pronounce a man a benefactor, no responding public to build a monument. Such gifts have their reward on earth. In fact, they are more than repaid. The glory is worth more than the gold ; and the poor are under no obligations whatever. " Let not thy left hand know what thy right hand doeth " means very much more than is expressed.

With his moccasins bound tight about his feet and reaching up so as to embrace the legs of his buckskin pantaloons, his right arm freed from the hateful red-shirt sleeve which hung in freedom at his side, some eagle feathers in his hair, and his rifle on his shoulder, Klamat, with a beaming countenance, led the way from the cabin.

The Prince had assigned him the post of honour, and he was carried away with delight. He seemed to forget that he was the only one on foot. No doubt he would gladly have given up the red shirt and buckskins, all but his rifle, with pleasure, at this supreme moment, had they been required, to insure his position as leader.

Alexander gave away to his friends the last of the spoils after a great battle. " And what have you kept for yourself?" said one. " Hope and glory," he answered.

Klamat was an infant Alexander.

I followed, then Paquita, the Doctor next. The Prince took up a piece of charcoal from the heap of ashes outside the cabin, and wrote in great bold letters on the door :

" To Let."

We crossed the stream at a cabin below, just as the men were beginning to stir.

They seemed to know that something unusual was taking place. They straightened themselves in the fresh light and air, washed their hands and hairy faces in the gold-pans on the low pine stump by the door, but tried, or seemed to try, not to observe.

Once across the stream, Klamat led steeply up the hill for a time, then he would chop and cut to right and left in a zigzag route until we had reached the rim of a bench in the mountain. Here he stopped and motioned the Prince to approach, after he had looked back intently into the camp and taken sight by some pines that stood before him.

The Prince rode up to the boy and dismounted; when he had done so, the little fellow lifted three fingers, looked excited, and pointed down upon the old cabin. It was more than a mile away, nearly a mile below; but the sun was pitching directly down upon it, and all things stood out clear and large as life.

Three men rode quickly up to the cabin, leaned from their mules and read the inscription. The leader now dismounted, kicked open the door and entered. It does not take long to search a cabin, without a loft or even a bed to hide under, and the man did not remain a great while within.

Without even taking pains to close the door, to keep out coyotes and other things, as miners do, so that cabins may be habitable for some way-farer, or fortune-hunters who may not have a house of their own, he hastily mounted and led the party down to the next cabin below.

The miners were evidently at breakfast, for the man leaned from his saddle and shouted two or three times before any one came out.

The door opened, and a very tall, black-bearded hairy man came forth, and walked up before the man leaning from his mule.

What was said I do not know, but the bare-headed, hairy man pointed with his long arm up the mountain on the other side, exactly the opposite course from the one that had been taken by the fugitives.

Here the officer said something very loud, pushed back his broad-brimmed hat, and pointed down the stream. The long-armed, bare-headed, hairy man again pointed emphatically up the mountain on the other side, and then wheeled on his heel, entered, and closed the door.

The interview had evidently not been a satisfactory one, or a friendly one to the officer, and he led his men slowly down the creek with their heads bent down intently to the trail. They did not go far. There were no fresh tracks in the way. The recent great rain had made the ground soft, and there was no mistaking the absence of the signs.

There was a consultation: three heads in broad hats close together as they could get sitting on their mules. Now a hat would be pushed back, and a face lifted up exactly in our direction. We had sheltered behind the pines. Klamat was holding the Prince's mule's nose to keep it from braying to those below. Paquita had dismounted a little way off, behind a clump of pines, and was plucking some leaves and grasses for her pony and the pack-mule to keep them still. The Doctor never seemed more stupid and helpless than now; but, at a sign from Klamat, stole out to the shelter where Paquita stood, dismounted, and began to gather grasses, too, for his mule.

A poor, crooked, imitative little monkey he looked as he bent to pluck the grass; at the same time watching Paquita, as if he wished to forget that there was any graver task on hand than to pluck grass and feed the little mules.

Mules are noisy of a morning when they first set out. The utmost care was necessary now to insure silence.

Had the wind blown in our direction, or even a mule brayed below, these mules in the midst of our party would have turned their heads down hill, pointed their opera-glasses sharply for a moment or two at the sounds below, and then, in spite of kicks or clubs, have brayed like trumpets, and betrayed us where we stood.

There was no excitement in the face of the Prince, not much concern. His foot played and patted in the great wooden stirrup, and shook and jingled the bells of steel on his Spanish spur, but he said nothing.

Sometimes the men below would point in this direction and then in that with their long yellow gauntlets, then they would prick and spur their mules till they spun round like tops.

When a man pricks and spurs his mule, you may be sure that he is bothered.

A Yankee would scratch his head, pull at his ear, or rub his chin ; an Englishman would take snuff; a Missourian would take a chew of tobacco, and perhaps swear ; but a Californian in the mountains disdains to do anything so stupid and inexpressive. He kicks and cuffs and spurs his mule.

At length the leader set his spurs in the broad hair-sinch, with the long steel points of the rowels, and rode down to the water's edge. A twig was broken there. The Doctor had done that as we crossed, to get a switch for his mule, and brought down the wrath of Klamat, expressed, however, only in frightful grimaces, signs, and the flashing of his eyes. The officer dismounted, leaned over, brushed the burs aside, took some of them up, and examined them closely.

An arm was now lifted and waved authoritatively to the two men sitting on their mules in the trail, and they instantly struck the spurs in the broad sinch, and through into the tough skins of their mules, I think, for they ambled down toward the officer at a rapid pace and—consternation! One of them threw up his head and brayed as if for life.

The Prince's mule pointed his opera-glasses, set out his legs, took in a long breath, and was just about to make the forest ring, when his master sprung to the ground, caught him by the nose, and wrenched him around till he fell upon his haunches.

Here Klamat made a sign, threw the Doctor on his mule, left Paquita to take care of herself, and led off up the hill. We mounted, and followed as fast as possible; but the Prince's mule, as if in revenge, now stopped short, set out his legs, lifted his nose, and brayed till the very pine-quills quivered overhead.

After he had brayed to his satisfaction, he gave a sort of grunt, as if to say, " We are even now," and shot ahead. The little pack-mule was no trouble. He had but a light load, and, as if in gratitude, faithfully kept his place.

A pony or horse must be led. Anything but a mule will roam and run against trees, will lodge his pack in the boughs that hang low overhead, or, worse still, stop to eat of the branches or weeds, and grasses under foot. The patient, cunning little Mexican mule will do nothing of the sort. He would starve rather than stop to eat when on duty; and would as soon think of throwing himself down over one of the cliffs that he is familiar with as to injure or imperil the pack that has been trusted to his care, by butting against trees, or lodging under the boughs that hang above the trail. He stops the instant the pack is loose, or anything falls to the ground, and refuses to move till all is made right.

We could not keep pace with Klamat, hasten as we might, through the pines. Like a spirit, he darted here and there through the trees, urging and beckoning all the time for us to follow faster.

We could not see our pursuers now, yet we knew too well that they were climbing fast as their strong-limbed sturdy mules would serve them, the hill that we had climbed an hour before. The advantage, on one hand, was theirs; on the other, we had things somewhat our own way. The chances were about evenly balanced for escape without blood.

Any one who frequents the mountains of the north will soon notice that on all the hill-sides facing the sun there is no undergrowth. You may ride there, provided you do not wedge in between the trees that grow too close together to let you pass, or go under a hanging bough, the same as in a park. But if you get on the north side of the hill, you find an undergrowth that is almost impassable for man or beast. Chaparral, manzanita, madroño, plum, white thorn, and many other kinds of shrubs and trees, contribute to make a perfectly safe retreat from men for the wild beasts of those regions. In a flight, this is the chief thing to do. Keep your eye on the lay of the hills, so that you may always be on the south side, or you will find yourself in a net.

CHAPTER XV

NOTHER danger lies in getting too low down on the hillside to the sea. On that side, where only grass has grown and pine-quills fallen without any undergrowth to hold them there, and contribute its own decaying and cast-off clothes to the soil, the ground is often broken, and, unlike the north side of the hills, shows here and there steep bluffs and impassable, basaltic blocks, or slides of slate or shale on which it would be madness to venture.

The only safe thing to do is to find the summit, and keep along the backbone of the mountain, and thus escape the chapparal nets of the north and the precipices of the south.

Great skill consists in being able to reach the summit successfully, and still greater in keeping along the backbone when it is once reached, and not follow off on one of the spurs that often shoot up higher than the back of the main ridge. There are many trails here, made by game going to and fro in the warm summer days, or in crossing the ridges in their semi-annual migrations down to the rivers and back again to the mountains.

The temptations to take one of these trails and abandon the proper one, which is often dim and sometimes wholly indistinct, are many. It takes the shrewdest mountaineer to keep even so much as for one day's journey along the backbone without once being led aside down the spurs into the nets of chapparal, or above the impassable' crags and precipices. Of course, when you can retrace your steps it is a matter of no great moment; you will only lose your time. But with us there was no going back.

When we had reached the second bench we turned to look. Soon the heads of the men were seen to shoot above the rim of the bench below; perhaps less than a mile away. No doubt they caught sight of us now, for the hand of the officer lifted, pointed in this direction, and he settled his spurs in his sinch, and led his men in pursuit.

Deliberately the Prince dismounted, set his saddle well forward, and drew the sinch tight as possible. We all did the same; mounted then, and followed little Klamat, who had by this time set both arms free from the odious red shirt which was now belted about the waist, up the hill as fast as we could follow.

We reached the summit of the ridge. Scintillations from the flashing snows of Mount Shasta shimmered through the trees, and a breath of air came across from the Klamat lakes and the Modoc land beyond, as if to welcome us from the dark, deep cañon with its leaden fringe, and lining of dark and eternal green.

The Doctor pushed his hat back from his brow and faintly smiled. He was about to kiss his hand to the splendid and majestic mountain showing in bars and sections through the trees, but looked around, caught the eye of Klamat, and his hand fell timidly to his side.

As for Paquita, she leaped from her pony and put out her arms. Her face was radiant with delight. Beautiful with divine beauty, she arched her hand above her brow, looked long and earnestly at the mountain, and then, in a wild and unaccountable sort of ecstasy, turned suddenly, threw her arms about her pony's neck, embraced him passionately and kissed his tawny nose.

We had been buried in that cañon for so long. We were like men who had issued from a dungeon. As for myself, I was much as usual; I clasped and twisted my hands together as I let my reins fall on my horse's neck, and said nothing.

Our animals were mute now, too; no mule of the party could have been induced to bray. They were tired, dripping with sweat, and held their brown noses low and close to the ground, without attempting to touch the weeds or grasses.

Klamat threw up his hand. The men had appeared on the bench below. We had evidently gained on them considerably, for here we had ten minutes' rest before they broke over the mountain bench beneath. This was encouraging. No doubt a saddle had slipped off back over a mule's rump in some steep place they had just mounted, and thus caused the delay, for they had neglected to sinch their saddles in their great haste.

They dismounted now, and settled their saddles. We tightened our saddles also. This was the summit, and now came the demand for skill.

When the officer threw his leg over the macheers of his saddle below, Klamat set forward. His skill was as wonderful as his endurance. Being now on the summit, he could travel without halting to breathe; this, of course would be required if he hoped to keep ahead. And even then, where would it all end? It is most likely no one had thought of that. For my part, I kept watching the sun and wishing for night.

This is an instinctive desire of all things rational or irrational, I think, that are compelled to fly—

"O that night or Blucher would come."

It was hardly possible to keep ahead of our pursuers all day, well mounted as they were, and one of our party on foot, yet that seemed to be the only hope. There yet was an alternative, if the worst came to the worst. We could ambush and shoot them down. I saw that Klamat kept an eye constantly on his rifle when not foxing the trail and eyeing the pursuers.

The Prince was well armed. He carried his double-barrelled piece before him in the saddle-bow. The rest of us were not defenceless. The deed was more than possible.

These men wanted the Doctor: him only, so far as we knew. The Doctor was accused of murder. The officer, no doubt, had due process, and the legal authority to take him. To the Prince he was nothing much. He was no equal in physical or mental capacity. He was failing in health and in strength, and could surely be of no future possible use to us. Why should the Prince take life, or even imperil ours for his sake?

The answer, no doubt, would be very unsatisfactory to the civilized world, but it was enough for the Prince. The man needed his help. The man was almost helpless. This, perhaps, was the first and strongest reason for his course. There is a great deal in this chivalrous disposition to shield the weak.

When woman arises and asserts herself, as the sharp-tongued, thin-lipped puritaness proposes, and is no longer dependent, man's arm will no longer be reached as a shield, but as a sword.

Whenever woman succeeds in making herself a soldier she must fight. The beasts of the field will fight to the death for the young while they are helpless; but when they grow strong and swift the beasts of the field will run away and leave them to their fate, or even fight against them when they are strong, as bravely as they did for them when they were weak.

At the bottom of all other reasons for taking care of this man, who seemed to become every day less capable of taking care of himself, was a little poetical fact not forgotten. This man furnished bread when we were hungry—when the snow was deep, when the earth lay in a lock-jaw, as it were, and could not open her mouth to us.

Now and then Klamat would turn his eyes over his shoulder, toss his head, and urge on. The eagle-feathers in his black hair, as if glad to get back again in the winds of Shasta, floated and flew back at us, and we followed as if we followed a banner. A black banner, this we followed, made of the feathers of a fierce and bloody bird. Where would it lead us? No buccaneers of the sea were freer, wilder, braver at heart than we. Where would it lead us?

One thing was fearfully against us. The recent rains had made the ground soft and spongy. The four horses made a trail that could be followed on the run. Even where the pine-quills lay thickest, the ground would be broken here and there so as to leave little doubt or difficulty to our pursuers.

Had it been a dry autumn the ground would have been hard as an adobe, and we might have dodged to one side almost anywhere, and, providing our mules did not smell and hail the passing party, escaped with impunity. As it was, nothing seemed left but to persist in flight to the uttermost. And this we did.

We did not taste food. We had not tasted water since sunrise, and it was now far in the afternoon. The Doctor began to sit with an unsteady motion in his saddle. The mules were beginning to bray; this time from distress, and not excess of spirits. The Prince's mule had his tongue hanging out between his teeth, and, what was worse, his ears began to flop to and fro as if they had wilted in the sun. Some mules put their tongues out through their teeth and go very well for days after; but when a mule lets his ears swing, he has lost his ambition, and is not to be depended on much longer.

A good mountain mule should not tire short of a week, but there is human nature wherever there is a bargain to be made, and there are mule jockeys as well as horse jockeys even in the mountains; and you cannot pick up good mules when you like, either for love or money. The men who followed had, no doubt, a tried and trusty stock. Things began to look critical.

The only thing that seemed unaffected was Klamat. Two or three times through the day he had stood his rifle against a pine, drew his belt a knot or two tighter, fastened his moccasin-strings over, and then dashed ahead without a word. Our banner of eagle feathers still floated defiantly, and promised to lead even further than we could follow. Closer and closer came the pursuers. We could see them striking their steel spurs in their sinches as if they would lift their tired mules along with their heels.

Once they were almost within hail; but a saddle slipped, and they lost at least ten minutes with a fractious mule, that for a time concluded not to be sinched again till it had taken rest.

The sugar-pines dropped their rich and delicate nuts as we rode by, from pyramid cones as long as your arm, and little foxy-looking pine squirrels with pink eyes, stopped from their work of hoarding them for winter, to look or chatter at us as we hurried breathless and wearily past.

Mount Shasta still flashed down upon us through the dark rich boughs of fir and pine, but did not thrill us now.

When the body is tired, the mind is tired too. You get surfeited with grandeur at such a time. No doubt the presence tames you somewhat, tones down the rugged points in you that would like to find expression; that would find expression in fretful words but for this greatness which shows you how small you are; but you are subdued rather than elevated.

Suddenly Klamat led off to the right as if forsaking the main summit for a spur. This seemed a bad sign. The Prince said nothing. At any other time I dare say he would have protested.

We had no time to dispute now; besides, almost any change from this toilsome and eternal run was a relief. What made things seem worse, however, this boy seemed to be leading us back again to The Forks. We were edging around at right angles with our pursuers. They could cut across if we kept on, and head us off. We were making more than a crescent; the boy was leading us right back to the men we wished to escape.

Soon he went out on a point and stopped. He beckoned us to ride up. We did so. It seemed less than half a mile to a point we had passed less than an hour since, and, as far as we could see, there was only a slight depression between. The officer and his party soon came in sight. As they did so he raised his arm. We were not unobserved.

Klamat sat down to rest, and made signs that we should dismount. I looked at the Prince to see what he would do. He swung himself to the ground, looking tired and impatient, and we all did the same. The Doctor could not keep his feet, but lay down, helpless, on the brown bed of quills from the sugar-pines that clustered around and crowned the point where we had stopped to rest.

The officer and his men looked to their catenas; each drew out a pistol, revolved the cylinder, settled the powder back in the tubes by striking the ivory handles gently on the saddle pommels, saw that each nipple still held its cap, and then spurred their mules down the hillside as if to cross the depression that lay between, and head us off at once. They were almost within hail, and I thought I could hear the clean sharp click of the steel bells on their Spanish spurs as they descended and disappeared among the tree-tops as if going down into a sea.

Klamat had learned some comic things in camp, even though he had not learned, or pretended he had not learned, to talk. When the men had disappeared among the branches of the trees, he turned to the Prince and gravely lifted his thumb to his nose, elevated his fingers in the air, and wriggled them in the direction of the place where the officer was seen to descend.

Every moment I expected to see the muzzles of those pistols thrust up through the pines as the three men turned the brow of the hill. They did not appear, however, and as we arose to adjust our saddles after some time, I stepped to the rim of the hill and looked over to the north side. The hill was steep and rugged, with a ledge, and lined with chapparral. A white-tailed rabbit came through, sat down, and looked back into the cañon. Some quails started and flew to one side, but that was all I saw or heard.

The Doctor had to be assisted to his saddle. He was pale, and his lips were parched and swollen. Slowly now Klamat walked ahead; he, too, was tired. We had rested too long, perhaps. You cannot get an Indian to sit down when on a long and severe journey, unless compelled to, to rest others. The cold and damp creeps into the joints, and you get stiff and tenfold more tired than before. Great as the temptation is to rest, you should first finish your race, the whole day's journey, before you let your nerves relax.

Slowly as we moved, however, our pursuers did not reappear. We were still on the ridge, in spite of the sharp and eccentric turn it had taken around the head of the river.

As the sun went down, broad, blood-red banners ran up to the top of Shasta, and streamed away to the south in hues of gold; streamed and streamed as if to embrace the universe in one great union beneath one banner. Then the night came down as suddenly on the world as the swoop of an eagle.

The Doctor, who had all the afternoon kept an uncertain seat, now leaned over on his mule's mane, and had fallen, but for the Prince who was riding at his side.

Klamat came back and set his rifle against a pine. We laid the feeble man on the bed of quills, loosened the sinches as the mules and ponies let their noses droop almost to the ground, and prepared to spend the night. This was imperative. It was impossible to go farther. That would have been the death of the man we wished to save.

A severe ride in the mountains at any time is a task. Your neck is wrenched, and your limbs are weary as you leap this log or tumble and stumble your tired animal over this pile of rocks or through that sink of mud, until you are tired enough by night;

but when you ride an awkward and untrained mule, when you have not sat a horse for a year, and have an old saddle that fits you like an umbrella or a barrel, you get tired, stiff-limbed, and used up in a way that is indescribable. As for poor Paquita she was literally crucified, but went about picking up quills for beds for all, and never once murmured.

The Doctor was very ill. Klamat went down the hill-side and found some water to wet his lips, but this did not revive him. It was a cold evening. The autumn wind came pitching down from the Shasta, sharp and sudden. The old Frost King, who had been driven to the mountain-top in the early summer, was descending now by degrees to reclaim his original kingdom.

We unpacked the little mule and spread a bed for the suffering man, but still he shivered and shook, and we could not get him warm. We, too, were suffering from the cold. We could hardly move when we had rested a moment and let the cold drive back the perspiration, and drive the chill to the marrow.

" A fire," said the Prince.

Klamat protested against it. The sick man grew worse. Something warm would restore him.

We must have a fire. Paquita gathered up some pine knots from the hill side. A match was struck in the quills. The mules started, lifted their noses, but hardly moved as the fire sprung up like a giant full-grown, and reached for the cones of the sugar-pines overhead. There was comfort and companionship in the fire. We could see each other now,— our little colony of pilgrims. We looked at each other and were revived.

We had a little coffee-pot, black and battered it is true, but the water boiled just the same, and as soon as if it had been silver.

This revived the Doctor. Hunger had much to do with his faintness. He now sat up and talked, in his low quiet way, looking into the fire and brushing the little mites of dust and pine-quills from his shirt, as if still to retain his great respectability of dress; and by the time we all had finished our coffee, he was almost as cheerful as we had ever seen him before.

The moon came out clear and cold, and we spread our damp and dusty blankets on the quills between the pines, with the snowy front of the Shasta lifting, lifting like a bank of clouds away to the left, and the heads of many mining streams dipping away in so many wild and dubious directions that no one but our little leader, perhaps, could have found the way to the settlements without the gravest embarrassment.

Klamat had gone down the hill for water, this time leaving his rifle leaned against a pine, though not without casting a glance back over his shoulder as if to say, " Look sharp! but I will be back at once." We all were still warming ourselves by the fire, I think, though there are some sudden things you cannot just recall.

A wave of fate strikes you so strong sometimes,

that you are swallowed up. Heads and ears you go under it and you see nothing, you remember nothing. It seems to take your breath.

Click! click! click! a tired mule started, snuffed, and then dropped his head, for it was over in an instant.

"Hands up, gentlemen! hands up! Don't trouble yourselves to move! There, that will do! You are the one we want. Pass in your checks!"

The Doctor hid his face in his hands, and let them take his arms without a word.

The fire had done the mischief. Klamat did not come back; at least, he did not let it be known if he did. Paquita opened her large eyes very wide, pushed back her hair, and rested her hands in her lap as she sat looking at the three strange men in elegant top boots and broad-brimmed hats.

"A pretty man you are, Mr. Prince, to run with this fellow," said the officer, "to give me this race. For a coon skin I would take you in charge too."

Here he arose, went over, and looked at the animals in the firelight, as if looking for some cause to lay hands on the Prince, took general charge of the camp as if it were his own, lit his pipe, had one of the men make coffee, and seemed quite at home.

If the Prince uttered a word all this time I do not remember it.

"Where's your other Ingin, Prince?" said the officer, looking about and seeing but the four saddles. "Put him in the bush, or left him in the camp? Rather a good-looking piece you got here now, ain't she?" He pointed his pipe-stem at Paquita.

For the first time the Prince showed colour.

The officer and his men, toward midnight, spread their blankets on the other side of the fire. They were scarce of blankets, and the night was cold.

This may be the reason they all spread down together. But there is nothing that will excuse such a stupid thing in the mountains. Sleep apart. Wide apart, rods apart: never two together, unless you wish to make a broad target of yourselves where the muzzle of one gun can do the work of many.

Before lying down the men did what they could for their tired beasts; and then the officer came up to the Doctor, who still gazed and gazed into the fire, and, drawing something from his pockets that chinked like chains, said—

" Your hands !"

" He is ill," said the Prince, " very ill. I will answer for him. Iron me instead; but that man is a nervous, sensitive man that cannot bear to be chained."

The officer laughed a little and, without answering, took the Doctor's unresisting hands and linked them together with a snap that made one shudder; then, laying him back in his blankets, looked to his pistol, and saying—

" Don't move! Don't you attempt to move !" walked over to the other side of the pine-knot fire, and, pistol in hand, lay down by his companions, looking all the time across the fire at his prisoner.

The Prince arose, went and gathered up pine-knots by the light of the moon, and laid them on the fire. Paquita looked inquiringly at him, and then went and did the same. When the fire loomed up, he lifted the blankets from the Doctor's feet, drew off his boots, and let the warm, cheerful fire fall on the wretched man.

The officer lay like a fox watching every move and motion, with his head on his saddle, and his nose just above the blankets. His pistol hand was at his side clutching the revolver. The other men were equally wide awake and watchful at his side.

" Lie down, Paquita," said the Prince, " lie down and rest with your moccasins to the fire; you have had a hard and bitter day of it. I will keep the fire."

The child obeyed. He waved his hand at me to do the same, and I was soon sound asleep.

The last I saw of the Prince before falling asleep—he was resting on his side with his hand on his head, and elbow on his blankets. In the mountains, when you spread your blankets, you put your arms—rifle or pistols—in between the blankets as carefully as if they were children. This is done, in the first place, to keep them dry, and, in the second place, to have them ready for use. They are laid close to your side. The heat of your body keeps out the damp.

I awoke soon. I was too bruised, and sore, and sick in mind and body, to sleep. There is a doleful, dreary bird that calls in this country in the night, in the most mournful tone you can imagine. It is a sort of white-headed owl; not large, but with a very hoarse and coarse note. One of these birds was calling at intervals down the gorge to the right, and another answered on the other side so faintly I could just hear it. An answer would come just as regularly as this one called, and that would sound even more doleful and dreary still, because so far and indistinct. The moon hung cold and crooked overhead, and fell in flakes through the trees like snow.

The Doctor put out his two hands, pushed back the blanket, and raised his head. He looked to the left in the gorge as if he contemplated a spring in that direction. I think that, at last, he had summoned up courage to make a desperate effort to escape.

He drew up his legs slowly, as if gathering his muscles for a leap. My heart stood still. All seemed clear. I could see the nerves of his face quiver in the moon.

He turned his head to the officer, not six feet away across the fire, and looked squarely into the ugly, sullen muzzles of three lifted pistols.

The Doctor sank back with a groan. His face was white as the moon that shone down upon it through the quills above his head.

The officer and his men exchanged glances, and lay down without a word. The Prince was possibly asleep. Still, ever and again, the doleful bird kept calling, and the woful answer came back like an echo of sorrow across the great black cañon below.

The moon kept settling and settling to the west among the yellow stars, as broad and spangled as California lilies, and the morning was not far away.

Again the Doctor drew in his naked feet. I could see the muscles gather and contract, and I knew he was again preparing for a spring. All was still. He raised his head, and three pistol muzzles raised and met the man half way. He crept back far down in the blankets, hid his head in the folds, and shuddered and shivered as with an ague.

Dawn was descending and settling around the head of Shasta in a splendour and a glory that words will never touch.

There are some things that are so far beyond the reach of words that it seems like desecration to attempt description. It was not the red of Pekin, not the purple of Tyre or the yellow of the Barbary coast; but merge all these, mixed and made mellow in a far and tender light—snow and sun, and sun and snow—and stars, and blue and purple skies all blended, all these in a splendid, confused, and indescribable glory, suffusing the hoary summit, centering there, gathering there, resting a moment—then radiating, going on to the sea, to broad and burning plains of the south, to the boundless forests of fir in the north, even to the mining camps of Cariboo, and you have a sunrise on the summit of Shasta.

The Prince lifted his head, rested on his elbow, rubbed his eyes as if he had surely slept, and then slowly and stiffly arose. The fire was low, almost out. He turned to gather pine-knots, laid them on the fire, and turned away as if to gather more. The Doctor seemed to sleep. The officer and his men were resting too. Perhaps they slept also.

" Click! click!"

I sprang to my feet.

" Don't trouble yourselves to move, gentlemen! Remain just where you are, gentlemen, just where you are!"

It was the Prince who spoke this time. He had approached the three heads from behind, and had the double-barrelled gun with its double handful of buck-shot levelled, as he spoke, against the tops of their heads as they lay there on their backs.

Approach a man lying down as if you meant to tread upon his scalp and pin him to the earth, and he is the most helpless of mortals. He cannot see you, he cannot turn around, he can do nothing. Here lay those men; they could see nothing but the black ugly muzzles of the double barrels. Their pistols were in their hands; they were plucky fellows, but they could not draw; they were as likely to shoot each other as an enemy or any one.

This coming upon a man when he is lying down on his back may not be the manliest way in the world, but it is the safest, certainly; and when the game is three to one, you have to take all the per-cent. you can, or, in mountain phrase, "just pass in your checks."

"Don't trouble yourselves to move, gentlemen; don't trouble to rise!"

The Prince said this with a mockery and irony in his tone that was bitter beyond expression ; as if all the poison and the venom of the cruel words and cruel treatment of the Doctor the night before had been rankling in his heart till it was ready to burst out of itself, and he now hissed it out between his teeth.

There was something in his words that told the three men that he would rather like it if they would only "trouble to move," move the least bit in the world. As if he would be particularly glad if even one of them would lift a finger, and give him even the least shadow of an excuse to blow them to the moon. They therefore "did not trouble to move."

Klamat came out here from the dark with the dawn. He approached the men like a shadow thrown by a pine from the far light, pulled down the blankets, and took the three pistols from their unresisting hands.

"You may sit up now," said the Prince, taking a seat across the fire by the side of the Doctor. "You may sit up now. You are my prisoners, but I will not handcuff you. I will give you back your arms if you obey me, and you shall return to your town.

"I will not ask you not to mention this little affair," said the Prince—raising the double barrels, as one of

the men seemed to be gathering his legs under him—
I will not ask you not to mention this little affair.
That is safe enough. You gents will be the last men
on earth to mention it. But I give you my word
that it shall never be mentioned by us, never, so long
as you do not attempt to molest this man. Make
the least attempt against him, or any one here, and
you shall be made the laughing-stock of your town."

The men looked at each other with hope. They
had expected to die on the spot.

" It's your pot, Prince, take it down. You hold
the papers, called us on a dead hand, you did, but this
was no bluff of mine. The only mislead made was
not to chain you down too, like a dog, as you deserve
to be."

The Prince coloured. " If you had not chained
this man," he said at last, quietly, " perhaps you
could have taken him with you. The only mistake
you made was to chain any man at all. Chain a man
that could not stand on his feet ! You deserve to
be shot; and if you repeat yourself, I will let Klamat
scalp you where you sit."

The Indian arose with his hand on his knife.
There was a fierce satisfaction in his face. He had
suffered too much through the night, through the
winter, through the year, to feel like trifling now.
The Indian boy had no other idea than the death of
the men. He certainly looked blank amazement
when, an hour later, the Prince, after discharging
their arms, and emptying their catenas of ammuni-

tion, returned them all again, and turned their faces to the city, civilly, almost politely.

The men rode sadly and silently away through the trees, now and then looking back over their shoulders.   The man-hunt was over.

CHAPTER XVI

PECULIARLY nervous man suffers from a mental ailment as distinctly as from a wound. He grows weak under the sense of mental distress the same as an ordinary man does from the loss of blood. Remove the cause of apprehension, and he recovers the same as the wounded man recovers. Free the mind, and you stop the flow of blood. He grows strong again.

We moved on a little way that day, slowly, to be sure, but fast enough and far enough to be able to pitch our camp in a place of our own choosing, with wood, water, and grass, the indispensable requisites of a mountain camp, all close at hand.

To the astonishment of all, the Doctor unsaddled his mule, gathered up wood, and was a full half-hand at supper. At night he spread his own blankets, looked to his pistols like an old mountaineer, and seemed to be at last getting in earnest with life.

The next day, as we rode through the trees, he whistled at the partridges as they ran in strings across the trails, and chirped at the squirrels over-head.

How delightful it was to ride through the grass and trees, hear the partridges whistle, pack and unpack the horses, pitch the tent by the water, and make a military camp, and talk of war ; imagine battles, shoot from behind the pines, and always, of course, making yourself a hero. Splendid! I was busy as a bee. I cooked, packed, stood guard, killed game, did everything. And so we journeyed on through the splendid forests, under the face of Shasta, and over peaceful little streams that wound silently through the grass, as if afraid, till we came to the head-waters of the Sacramento.

Sometimes we saw other camps. White tents pitched down by the shining river, among the scattered pines; brown mules and spotted ponies feeding, and half buried in the long grass; and the sound of the picks in the bar below us all made a picture in my life to love.

Once we fell in with an Indian party; pretty girls and lively unsuspicious boys along with their parents, fishing for salmon, and not altogether at war with the whites. They treated us with great kindness.

At last we branched off entirely to ourselves, cutting deep into the mountain as the winter approached, looking for a home. The weak condition of the Doctor made it necessary that we brought our journey to a close. We had taken a different route from others, for good and sufficient reasons. The trails and tracks of the hundreds of gold-hunters, who had mostly preceded us some months, lay considerably west of Mount Shasta, striking the head of the Sacramento river at its very source. They had found only a few bars with float gold, not in sufficient quantities to warrant the location of a camp, and pushed on to the mines farther south. Some, however, returned.

We sometimes met a party of ten or more, all well armed and mounted, ready to fight or fly as the case might require. The usual mountain civilities would be exchanged, brief and brusque enough, and each party would pass on its way, with a frequent glance thrown back suspiciously at our Indian boy with his rifle, the invalid Doctor leaning on his catenas, the Indian girl with her splendid hair and face as bright as the morning, and the majestic figure of the Prince. An odd-looking party was ours, I confess.

Paquita knew every dimple, bend or spur in these mountains now. The Prince entrusted her to select some suitable place to rest. One evening she drew rein and reached out her hand. Klamat stood his rifle against a pine, and began to unpack the tired little mule, and all dismounted without a word.

It was early sundown. A balm and a calm was on and in all things. The very atmosphere was still as a shadow and seemed to say, " Rest, rest!" We were on the edge of an opening; a little prairie of a thousand acres, inclining south, with tall, very tall grass, and a little stream straying from where we stood to wander through the meadow. A wall of pines stood thick and strong around our little Eden, and when we had unsaddled our tired. animals and taken the aparrajo from the little packer, we turned them loose in the little Paradise, without even so much as a lariat or hackamoor to restrain them.

The sun had just retired from the body of the mountain, but it was evident that all day long he rested here and made glad the earth; for crickets sang in the grass as they sing under the hearthstones in the cabins of the west, and little birds started up from the edge of the valley that were not to be found in the forest.

An elk came out from the fringe of the wood, threw his antlers back on his shoulders with his brown nose lifted, and blew a blast as he turned to fly that made the horses jerk their heads from the grass, and start and wheel around with fright. Brown deer came out, too, as if to take a walk in the meadow beneath the moon, but snuffed a breath from the intruders and turned away. Bears came out two by two in single file, but did not seem to notice us.

Some men say that the bear is deprived of the sense of smell in the wild state. A mistake. He relies as much on his nose as the deer; perhaps more, for his little black eyes are so small that they surely are not equal to the great liquid eyes of the buck, which

are so set in his head that he may see far and wide
at once. But the bear carries his nose close to the
ground, while that of the deer is lifted, and of course
can hardly smell an intruder in his dominions until
he comes upon his track. Then it is curious to observe him. ·He throws himself on his hind legs,
stands up tall as a man, thrusts out his nose, lifts it,
snuffs the air, turns all around in his tracks, and
looks and smells in every direction for his enemy.
If he is a cub, however, or even a cowardly grown
bear, he wheels about the moment he comes upon
the track, will not cross it under any circumstances,
and plunges again into the thicket.

We had a blazing fire soon, and at last, when
we had sat down to the mountain meal, spread on
a canvas mantaro on the ground, each man on his
saddle or a roll of blankets, with his knife in hand,
Klamat looked at our limited supply of provisions,
and then pointed to the game in the meadow.

He pictured sun-rise, the hunt, the deer, the
crack of his rifle, and how he would come into camp
laden with supplies. All this, he gave us to understand, would take place to-morrow, as he placed a
sandwich between his teeth, and threw his eyes
across his shoulder at the dark figures stealing
through the grass across the other side of our little
Eden.

The morning witnessed the fulfilment. Paquita
was more than busy all day in dressing venison, and
drying the meat for winter. The place was as full

of game as a park. No lonelier or more isolated place than this on earth. We walked about and viewed our new estates. The mules and ponies rolled in the rich grass, or rested in the sun with drooping heads and half-closed eyes.

Even the invalid Doctor seemed to revive in a most sudden and marvellous way. He saw that no white man's foot had ever trod the grasses of this valley; that there we might rest and rest and never rise up from fear. He could trust the wall of pine that environed us. It was impassable. He stood before an alder-tree that leaned across the silent, crooked little stream, and with his sheath-knife cut this one word:—HOME.

A little way from here Paquita showed us another opening in the forest. This was a wider valley, with warm sulphur and soda springs in a great crescent all around the upper rim. Here the elk would come to winter, she said; and hence we could never want for meat. The earth and atmosphere were kept warm here from the eternal springs; and grass, she said, was fresh and grew the winter through.

This is the true source of the stream which the white men call Soda; the proper Indian name of which is Numken; and here we built our cabin, reared a fortress against the approaching winter without delay, for every night his sentries were coming down bolder and bolder about the camp.

This was the famous " Lost Cabin." It stood on

a hillside, a little above the prairie, facing the sun, close to the warm springs, and on the very head of the Numken, and was not unlike an ordinary miner's cabin, except that the fireplace was in the centre of the room instead of being awkwardly placed at one end, where but few can get the benefit of the fire. This departure was not without reason.

In the first place, the two Indians, constituting nearly half of the voting population of our little colony, insisted on it with a zeal that was certainly commendable; and as they insisted on nothing else, it was only justice to listen to them in this.

" By-and-by my people will come," said Paquita, " and then you will want an Indian fire, a fire that they can sit down by and around without sending somebody back in the cold."

Again, you cannot build a cabin so strong with one end devoted to a chimney, as if it is one solid square body of logs. Then, it is no small task to build a chimney out of stone with only your hands for a trowel and black mud for mortar.

All these things considered, we placed the fire in the centre of the cabin on the earth-floor, and let the smoke curl up and out through an opening in the roof, as it always does and always will, in a graceful sort of way, if you build a fire as an Indian builds it.

The Doctor was getting strong again. As this man grew strong in a measure, it is a little remarkable that my sympathies were withdrawn proportionably.

I state this as a very remarkable fact. As the pitiful condition of the Doctor daily grew less, his crimes began to loom up and grow larger. They had sunk down almost out of sight; but now as this man began to lift up his hands to take part in the life around him, I shrank back and said to myself, There is blood on them—human blood.

No Indian had as yet, so far as we knew, discovered us. Paquita had from the first, around the fire, told her plans; how that as soon as she should be well rested from the journey, and a house was built and meat secured for the winter, she would take her pony, strike a trail that lay still deeper in the woods, and follow it up till she came to her father's winter lodges.

How enthusiastically she pictured the reception. How clearly she pourtrayed it all. She would ride into the village at sun-down, alone; the dogs would bark a great deal at her red dress and her nice new apparel. Then she would dismount and go straight up to her father's lodge and sit down by the door. The Indians would pass by and pretend not to see her, but all the time be looking slily sidewise, half-dead to know who she was. Then, after a while, some one of the women would come out and bring her some water. Maybe that would be her sister. If it was her sister, she would lift up her left arm and show her the three little marks on the wrist, and then they would know her and lead her into the lodge in delight.

One fine morning she set forth on her contemplated journey. I did not now like the place so well. For the first time, I found fault with the things around me. The forest was black, gloomy, ghostly—a thing to be dreaded. Before, it was dreamy, deep—a marvel, a something to love and delight in. The cabin, that had been a very palace, was now so small and narrow, it seemed I would suffocate in the smoke. The fires did not burn so well as they did before. Nobody could build a fire like Paquita.

Back from our cabin a little way were some grand old bluffs, topped with pine and cedar, from which the view of valley, forest, and mountain, was all that could be desired. A little way down the Numken, from the warm springs, the waters of the valley came together and went plunging all afoam down the cañon, almost impassable even for footmen. Here we found fine veins of quartz, and first-rate indications of gold both in the rock and in the placer. The Prince and the Doctor revived their theories on the origin of gold, and had many plans for putting their speculations to the test.

Klamat was never idle, yet he was never social. There was a bitterness, a sort of savage devilry, in all he did. A fierce positive nature was his, and hardly bridled at that.

Whether that disposition dated further back than a certain winter, when the dead were heaped up and the wigwams burned on the banks of the Klamat, or whether it was born there of the blood and bodies in the snow, and came to life only when a little, naked, skeleton savage sprung up in the midst of men with a club, I do not pretend to say, but I should guess the latter. I can picture him a little boy with bow and arrows, not over gentle it is true, but still a patient little savage, like the rest, talking and taking part in the sports, like those around him. Now he was prematurely old. He never laughed; never so much as smiled ; took no delight in anything and yet refused to complain. He took hold of things, did his part, but kept his secrets and his sorrows to himself, whatever they may have been.

Klamat never alluded to the massacre in any way whatever. Once, when it was mentioned, he turned his head and pretended not to hear. Yet, somehow it seemed to me that that scene was before him every moment. He saw it in the fire at night, in the forest by day. There are natures that cannot forget if they would. A scene like that settles down in the mind; it takes up its abode there and refuses to go away. His was such a nature.

In fact, Indians in the aggregate forget less than any other people. They remember the least kindness perfectly well all through life, and a deep wrong is as difficult to forget. The reason is, I should say, because the Indian does not meet with a great deal of kindness as he goes through life. His mind and memory are hardly overtaxed, I think, in remembering good deeds from the white man.

Besides, their lives are very monotonous. But few events occur of importance outside their wars. They have no commercial speculations to call off the mind in that direction; no books to forget themselves in, and cannot go beyond the sea, and hide in old cities, to escape any great sorrow that pursues them. So they have learned to remember the good and the bad better than do their enemies.

This cabin of ours in the trees on the rim of the clearing grew soon to be a sacred place to all. Here was rest absolute, unqualified repose. Eight-hour laws, late or early rising, in order to conform to the fashion of the country, did not concern us here. There were no days in which we were required to remain in to receive company, no days in which we were expected to make calls. We named the cabin the "Castle," and the Doctor cut out wooden cannon, mounted them on pine stumps before the door as on little towers, and turned them on the world below.

CHAPTER XVII

THE snow began to fall, and Paquita did not return.

Elk came down from the mountain towards spring, and we could shoot them from the cabin door. At this season of the year, as well as late in the fall, they are found in herds of hundreds together.

It seems odd to say that they should go up further into the mountains as winter approaches, instead of down into the foot-hills and plains below, as do the deer, but it is true. There are warm springs—in fact, all mountain springs are warmer in the winter than in the summer—up the mountain, where vine-maple, a kind of water-cress, and wild swamp berries grow in the warm marshes or on the edges, and here the elk subsist. When the maple and grasses of one marsh are consumed, they break through the snow in single file, led in turns by the bulls, to another.

Hundreds in this way make but one great track, much as if a great log had been drawn to and fro through the snow. The cows come up last, to protect the calves in the line of march from the wolves.

It is a mistake to suppose that elk use their splendid horns in battle. These are only used to receive the enemy upon. A sort of cluster of bayonets in rest. All offensive action is with the feet. An elk's horns are so placed on his head, that when his nose is lifted so as to enable him to move about or see his enemy, they are thrown far back on his shoulders, where they are quite useless. He strikes out with his feet, and then throws his head on the ground to receive his enemy. You have much to fear from the feet of an elk at battle, but nothing from his matchless antlers.

The black bears here also go up the mountain when the winter approaches. They find some hollow trunk, usually the trunk of a sturdy tree, and creep into it close down to the ground. Here they lie till snowed in and covered over, very fat, for months and months, in a long and delightful sleep, and never come out till the snow melts away, or they have the ill-fortune to be smelled out by the Indian dogs, and then called out by the hunters.

Whenever they find a black bear thus, they pound on the tree and call to him to come out. They challenge him in all kinds of bantering language, call him a coward and a lazy fat old fellow, that would run away from the squaws, and would sleep all summer. They tell him it is spring-time now, and he had better get up and come out and see the sun. The most remarkable thing, however, is, that so soon as the bear hears the pounding on the tree, he begins to dig and endeavour to get out; so that the Indians have but little to do, after he is discovered, but to sit down and wait till he crawls out, blinking and blinded by the light in his small black eyes, and despatch him on the spot. Bears when taken in this way are always plump and tender, and fat as possible; a perfect mass of white savoury oil.

Klamat was a splendid hunter, and even without the aid of the Indian dogs, managed to take several bears this first winter, which, after all, was not so long and dull as one would suppose. I sometimes think we partook somewhat of the nature of the bear, in our little snowy cabin among the firs that winter, for before we hardly suspected it, the birds came back, and spring was fairly upon us.

When the snow had disappeared, and our horses grew sleek and fat and strong again, Klamat and I rode far into the pines together and found a lake where the wild geese built nests in the margin among the tules.

The Prince and the Doctor went up the cañon in search of gold, for want of something better to do, and by the time the summer set in, had found a deposit in a quartz ledge, looking up towards the mountain. Gold appeared to be not over abundant nor did it seem to be much prized. No great plans, no excitement, that usually attends a discovery. These two men seemed to care more for it as a proof of their theory about the origin and growth of gold than for the gold itself.

They brought in and laid on a shelf in the corner pieces of gold and quartz with as little concern as if they had been geological specimens of slate or granite. You cannot be greatly surprised at this, however, when you remember how plentiful gold was, how little it was worth there, and that at that time it was thought to abound in every cañon in the country.

Paquita had not returned. We had come almost not to mention her now at all. Often and often, all through the spring and early summer, I saw the Prince stand out as the sun went down, and shade his brow with his hand, looking the way she had gone. I think it was this that kept him here so faithfully. He would not remain away a single night, either to hunt for gold or game, lest she might return, find him away, and need in some way his assistance.

The Doctor sometimes took long journeys down toward the valley to the south, and even fell in with white men, as well as Indians, after two or three days' ride in that direction, and thought of going down that way out of the reach of the snow, and building him a house for the winter. No one objected to this; but when he was ready to go away, the Prince compelled him to take all the gold they had taken from the mine, even against his utmost remonstrance.

"Take it," said the Prince, "every ounce of it. You may be called to use it. Here it is not worth that much lead." And he put the buckskin bag into the Doctor's catenas, and resolutely buckled them down.

Another incident worth mentioning is their agreement to never reveal the existence of the mine. Their reasons were of the noblest kind, sufficient, above every selfish consideration.

"In the first place," said they, "the gold is of doubtful utility to the world at best. But if this mine is made known, a flood of people will pour in here; the game, the forests, all this wild, splendid part of nature will disappear. The white man and the red man will antagonize, the massacre of the Klamat will be repeated; and for all this, what will be the consideration? Nothing, whatever, but gold, and we have quite enough of that,—and what do we owe the world?"

Back of all this, it was extremely doubtful whether the mine would yield anything better than this little "pocket."

For my own part, I would banish gold and silver, as a commercial medium, from the face of the earth. I would abolish the use of gold and silver altogether, have paper currency, and but one currency in all the world. I propose to take all the strong men now in the mines down from the mountains, and build ships and cities by the sea, and make a permanent commonwealth.

These thousands of men can, at best, in a year's time, only take out a few millions of gold. A ship goes to sea and sinks with all these millions, and there all that labour is lost to the world for ever. Had these millions been in paper, only a few hours' labour would have been lost. There are two hundred thousand men, the best and bravest men in the world, wasting the best years of their lives getting out this gold. They are turning over the mountains, destroying the forests, and filling up the rivers. They make the land unfit even for savages. Take them down from the mountains, throw one half their strength and energy against the wild, rich sea-border of the Pacific, and we would have, instead of these broken mountains, muddied rivers, and ruined forests, such an Eden as has not been seen by man since the days of Adam.

At last Paquita came. The Prince went forth to meet her with his arms held out, but she was too bashful and beautiful to touch.

And why had she not returned before? It is a sad story, but soon told.

When she reached the region of her father's camp, she found the grass growing in the trails. She found no sisters to receive her; no woman to bring her water; not a human being in all the lodges. The weeds grew rank, and the wolves had possession.

The white men in her absence had made another successful campaign against her people. They had become dispirited, and, never over-provident, finding the country overrun, the game made wild and scarce, and the fish failing to come up the muddied Sacramento, they had neglected to prepare for winter, and so had perished by whole villages.

These singular people perish so easily from contact with the whites, that they seem to me like the ripened fruit ready to fall at the first shaking.

She had found none of her tribe till she passed away on to the Tula lakes, and then of all her family found only two brothers. These, with some young warriors, had now come with her on her return.

They dismounted and built a fire under the trees and apart from us, and only slowly came to communicate, to smoke, and show any hospitality at all. Paquita was all kindness; but she had become a woman now; the state of things was changed. Then the eyes of her sober, savage brothers— who could ill brook the presence of the white man, much less look with favour on familiarities —were upon her, and she became the quiet, silent Indian woman, instead of the lively little maiden who had frolicked on the hill-sides and wandered through the woods the year before.

They remained camped here many days. Klamat took the young chiefs up to the mine,—only a little crevice picked out in the rotten quartz,—and they looked at it long and curiously. Then they picked up some little pieces of gold that lay there, looked at them, put them in their mouths, spit them out, and threw them down on the ground.

After that they came down to the cabin.

"You have saved our sister," the eldest said, among other things, "and we like you for that, and owe you all that we can give ; but you did not save her from a bear or a flood,—you only saved her from your own people, so that it is not so much. But even if you did save one of us in the bravest way, that is no reason why you shall help to destroy us all. If you bring men and dig gold here, we must all die. We know how that is. You may stay here, dig gold, hunt, live here all your lives ; but if you let this be known, and bring men up here, we will shoot them from behind the trees, steal their horses, and destroy them every way we can."

Paquita herself repeated this, interpreted what we did not understand, and told us emphatically that what her brothers said was true. Noble Indian woman! She was right.

The Prince answered very kindly and earnestly. He told them they were right. He told them that no one should hear of the mine ; and at the last, he lifted up his hand to Mount Shasta, and before the God of the white man and the red man, promised that no white men should come there, with his consent, while he remained.

Paquita returned soon after this with her people to her village, and it was lonely enough to be sure.

The Prince grew restless; and at last, after we had carried out some few specimens from the ledge, we mounted our horses, and set out for the settlement to procure supplies. We went by a circuitous way to avoid suspicion.

The Indian boy, our strange manner of dress, and the Prince's lavish use of money, soon excited remark and observation. New rich mines were becoming scarce, and there were hordes of men waiting eagerly in every camp for some new thing to come to the surface. We were closely watched, but did not suspect it then.

One day the Prince met a child in an immigrant camp, the first he had seen for a long long time. He stopped, took from his buckskin purse a rough nugget, half quartz and half gold, gave it to the boy, patted him on the head, and passed on. A very foolish thing.

After obtaining our supplies, we set out to return. The evening of the last day in the settlement we camped under the trees by a creek, close by some prospectors, who came into our camp after the blankets were spread, and sat about the fire cursing their hard luck; long-haired, dirty-habited, and ugly-looking men they were. One was a sickly-looking man, a singularly tall, pale man, who had but little to say. There was some gold left. It was of no possible use to us. The Prince took him to one side, gave him the purse, and told him to take it and go home. Another extremely silly thing. This man, meaning no harm of course, could not keep the secret of the few hundred dollars' worth of gold dust, and soon the whole affair, wonderfully magnified too, was blown all over the country.

When we found we were being followed, we led a sorry race indeed, and went in all directions. Klamat entered into the spirit of it, and played some strange forest tricks on the poor prospectors.

We eluded them all at last, and reached the cabin. But we had laid the foundation for many a mountain venture. What extravagant tales were told ! There was a perfect army of us—half Indians, half white men. Our horses were shod backward—an old story. Then, again, our horses' feet were bound up in gunny-bags, so as to leave no track. An impossible thing, for a horse will not take a single step with his feet in muffles.

CHAPTER XVIII

HESE Indians, and all Indians for that matter, have some strange customs, at which we laugh, or talk of in a mild, missionary, patronizing sort of a way.

Did it ever occur to an American sovereign, as he lifted up his voice in the public places, and thanked God that he is not as Indians are, that they may possibly laugh at some of his customs too? I think it never did.

When an Indian gets sick his friends have a dance. When a white man begins to lose his hair he rushes off to a barber, and has what he has left cut off to the scalp. Nature, always obliging, comes to his assistance then; and he never has to have any great portion of it cut again, but is permitted to make the rest of the journey with his head as bright and naked as a globe.

Very odd to have a dance when you get ill; but

not half so odd as it is to cut off your hair to save your hair. Indians, who never cut the hair, and women also, who until recently wore their hair nearly natural, never are bald. Yet I reckon men have gone on cutting their hair for baldness, the very thing that brings it on, for thousands of years past, and, I suppose, will still go on doing so for thousands of years to come.

We received some visits now from the chief of the Shastas. He was not a tall man, as one would suppose who had seen his warriors, but a giant in strength. You would have said, surely this man is part grizzly bear. As I have said before, he was bearded like a prophet.

I now began to spend days and even weeks in the Indian village over towards the south in a cañon, took part in the sports of the young men, listened to the teachings and tales of the old, and was not unhappy.

The Prince was losing his old cheerfulness as the summer advanced, and once or twice he half hinted of taking a long journey away to the world below.

At such times I would so wish to ask him where was his home, and why he had left it, but could not summon courage. As for myself, let it be here understood, once for all, that when a man once casts his lot in with the Indians he need return to his friends no more, unless he has grown so strong of soul that he does not need their countenance, for he is with them disgraced for ever. I had crossed the Rubicon.

It was the time of the Autumn Feasts, when the Indians meet together on a high oak plain, a sort of hem of the mountain, overlooking the far valley of the Sacramento, to celebrate in dance and song their battles of the summer and recount the virtues of their dead. On this spot, among the oaks, their fathers had met for many and many a generation. Here all were expected to come in rich and gay attire, and to give themselves up to feasting and the dance, and show no care in their faces, no matter how hard fortune had been upon them.

Indian summer, this. A mellowness and balm in the very atmosphere; a haze hanging over all things, and all things still and weary like, like a summer sunset.

The manzineta-berries were yellow as gold, the rich anther was here, the maple and the dogwood that fringed the edge of the plain were red as scarlet, and set against the wall of firs in their dark, eternal green.

The scene of the feast was a day's ride from the cabin, and the Prince and I were expected to attend. Paquita would of course be there, and who shall say we had not both looked forward to this day with eagerness and delight?

Gold, in any quantity, except in romance, is the heaviest and hardest thing to carry and keep with you in your wanderings in the mountains you can imagine.

We had saved only a trifle of dust compared to the amount report credited us with. This we put in four little buckskin bags, each taking two and placing them one in the left and one in the right pocket of his catenas. This held them to their places in hard rides; besides it was a sort of laying in of stores for some storm that might blow in upon us at any moment. Even if the lessons of the squirrels and the Indian women, all the autumn days laying up their stores for winter, had gone for nought, the lesson of the Humbug miners was not forgotten. And yet I had no idea that any grave danger could overtake us there, and I am certain I had no desire to leave the peaceful old forests and the calm delight of the mountain camp.

Of course I was very silly, as most young people are; but it seemed to me the world below was but a small affair, and all the people in it of but little consequence, so long as Paquita and the Prince were remaining in the mountains.

Had they gone down into the world, then the mountains had been rugged and cold enough, no doubt, and the world below much like home; but while they remained I had no thought of going away.

The mine did not promise much after all. We began to have a strong suspicion that we had only chanced upon a pouch in the rock—a little "chimney" that nurses a few thousand dollars' worth of dust about the flue, and nothing more—with the quartz rock back of this, as barren and hard as flint. A common thing is this, and the most disappointing of all things. Years ago, before the miners began to learn this, many a fortune was squandered in erecting mills on ledges that never offered any further reward than the one little pocket.

We went to the feast—rode through the forest in a sort of dream. How lovely! The deer were going in long bands down their worn paths to the plains below, away from the approaching winter. The black bears were fat and indolent, and fairly shone in their rich oily coats, as they crossed the trail before us.

Hundreds were at the feast, and we were more than welcome. The Chief came first, his warriors by his side, to give us the pipe of peace and welcome, and then a great circle gathered around the fire, seated on their robes and the leaves; and as the pipe went round, the brown girls danced gay and beautiful, half-nude, in their rich black hair, and flowing robes.

But Paquita was shy. She would not dance, for somehow she seemed to consider that this was a kind of savage entertainment, and out of place for her. She had seen just enough of civilized life to deprive her of the pleasures of the wild and free.

There had grown a cast of care upon her lovely face of late. She was in the secret of all the Indians' plans. At least she was a true Indian—true to the rights of her race, and fully awake to a sense of their wrongs.

She was surely lovelier now than ever before; tall,
and lithe, and graceful as a mountain lily swayed by
the breath of morning. On her face, through the
tint of brown, lay the blush and flush of maidenhood,
the indescribable sacred something that makes a
maiden holy to every man of a manly and chivalrous
nature; that makes a man utterly unselfish, and perfectly content to love and be silent, to worship at a
distance, as turning to the holy shrine of Mecca, to
be still and bide his time; caring not to possess
in the low coarse way that characterizes your
common love of to-day, but choosing rather to go
to battle for her,—bearing her in his heart through
many lands, through storms and death, with only
a word of hope, a smile, a wave of the hand from a
wall, a kiss blown far, as he mounts his steed below
and plunges into the night. That is a love to live
for. I say the knights of Spain, bloody as they
were, were a noble and a splendid type of men in
their way.

The Prince was of this manner of men. He was
by nature a knight of the chivalrous, grand old days
of Spain, a hero born out of time, and blown out of
place, in the mines and mountains of the North.

Once he had taken Paquita in his arms, had folded
a robe around her as if she had been a babe. She
was all —everything to him. He renounced all this.
Now he did not even touch her hand.

The old earnestness and perplexity had come upon
the Prince again on our coming to the feast. Once,

when the dance and song ran swift and loud and all was merriment, I saw him standing out from the circle of warriors, of young maidens and men, with folded arms, looking out on the land below. I had too much respect, nay reverence, for this man to disturb him. I leaned against a tree and looked as he looked. Once his eyes left the dance before him, and stole timidly toward the place where Paquita sat with her brother watching the dance. What a devotion in his face. I could not understand him. Now he turned to the valley again, tapped the ground with his foot in the old, restless way, but his eyes soon wandered back to Paquita. At last my gaze met his. He blushed deeply, held down his head and walked away in silence.

The next day was the time set apart for feats of horsemanship. The band was driven in, all common property, and the men selected their horses. The Prince drew out with his lasso a stout black steed, with a neck like a bull. His mane poured down on either side, or stood erect like a crest; a wiry, savage, untrained horse that struck out with his feet, like an elk at bay. He saddled him, and led him out all ready now, where the other horses stood in line, then came to me, walked a little way to one side, put out one hand and with the other drew me close to him, held down his head to my uplifted face, and said,

" Good-bye."

I sprang up and seized hold of him, but he went on calmly—

" I must go away. You are happy here; you will remain, but I must go. After many years I will return. You will meet me here on this spot, years and years from to-day. Yes, it will be many years; a long time. But it is short enough, and long enough. I will forget her—it—I will forget by that time, you see, and then there is all the world before me to wander in."

He made the sign of departure. The chief came forward, Paquita came and stood at his side. He reached his hands, took her in his arms, pressed her to his breast an instant, kissed her pure brow once, with her great black eyes lifted to his, but said no word.

The Indians were mute with wonder and sorrow. When you give the sign of going, there is no one to say nay here. No one importunes you to stay; no one says come to my place or come to mine. No such folly. You know that you are welcome to one and all, and they know that if you wish to go, you wish to go, and that is all there is of it. This is the highest type of politeness; the perfect hospitality.

The Prince turned to his steed, drew his red silk sash tighter about his waist, undid the lasso, wound the lariat on his arm, and wove his hand in the flowing mane as the black horse plunged and beat the air with his feet. Then he set him back on his haunches, sprang from the ground, and forward plunged the steed with mane like a storm, down the place of oaks, pitching towards the valley.

The trees seemed to open rank as he passed, and then to close again; a hand was lifted, a kiss thrown back across the shoulder, and he was gone—gone down in the sea below us, and I never saw my Prince again for many a year. Noble, generous, self-denying Prince! The most splendid type of the chivalric and the perfect man I had ever met.

All this was so sudden that I hardly felt the weight of it at first, and for want of something to do to fill the blank that followed, I mounted my horse and took part in the sports with the gayest of the gay.

Indians do not speak of anything that happens suddenly. They think it over, all to themselves, for days, unless it is a thing that requires some action or expression at once, and then speak of it only cautiously and casually. It is considered very vulgar indeed to give any expression to surprise, and nothing is more out of taste than to talk about a thing that you have not first had good time to think about.

During the day I noticed that my catenas were heavier than usual, and unfastening the pockets, I found that they contained all four of the bags of gold.

Why had he left himself destitute? Why had he gone down to battle with the world without a shield?—gone to fight Goliath, as it were, without so much as a little stone. I wanted to follow him and make him take the money—all of it. I despised it, it made me miserable. But I had learned to obey him, to listen to him in all things. And was he not a Prince?

"Ah!" said I to myself, at last, "he has gone down to take possession of his throne. He will cross the seas and see maidens fair indeed, nearly as lovely in some respects as Paquita;" and this was my consolation.

"Years and years," I said to myself that night as I looked in the fire, and the dance went on; "Years and years!" I counted it upon my fingers, and said—"I will be dead then."

CHAPTER XIX

NOW became almost thoroughly an Indian. The clash and struggle of the world below had ground upon my nerves, and I was glad to get away. Perhaps by nature I inclined to the dreamy and careless life of the Arabs of America; certainly my sympathies had always been with them, and now my whole heart and soul entered into the wild life in the forest. In fact from the first few months I had spent with these people—a sort of prisoner—I had a keen but inexpressed desire to be with them and them alone.

Now my desire was wholly gratified. I had seen my last, my only friend depart, and had shut the door behind him with a slam—a sort of fierce delight that I should be left alone in the wilderness.

No more plans for getting money; no more reproach from fast and clever men who managed the lower world; no more insults from the coarse and insolent; no more bumping of my head against the customs and proprieties of a half, and hence tyrannical, civilization;—nothing, it seemed to me now, but rest, freedom, absolute independence.

Did I dread and fear the primeval curse that God has put upon all men, and so seek to hide away from Him in the dark deep forests of Shasta?

I think not. I think rather that all men have more or less of the Arab in their natures; and but for the struggles for gold, the eddies and currents of commerce, and the emulation of men in art, and the like, we should soon become gipsies, Druids, and wanderers in the wild and fragrant woods that would then repossess the lands.

Maybe after a while, when the children of men are tired and weary of the golden toy they will throw it away, rise up and walk out into the woods, never more to return to cities, to toil, to strife, to thraldom.

But the Indian's life to an active mind is monotonous, and so I found it there; listless, dull, and almost melancholy. We rode, we fished, we hunted, and hunted, and fished, and rode, and that was nearly all we could do by day. If, however, we had no intense delights we had no great concern. We dreamed dreams and built castles higher than the blue columns of smoke that moved towards the heavens through the dense black boughs above. And so the seasons wore away.

Under all this, of course, there was another current, deep and exhaustless. Indians have their loves, and as they have but little else, these fill up most of their lives. That I had mine I do not deny; and how much this had to do with my remaining here I do not care to say. Nor can I bring my will to write of myself in this connection. These things must remain untold. They were sincere then, and shall be sacred now.

At night, when no wars or excitement of any kind stirred the village, they would gather in the chief's or other great bark lodges around the fires, and tell and listen to stories; a red wall of men in a great circle, the women a little back, and the children still behind, asleep in the skins and blankets. How silent! You never hear but one voice at a time in an Indian village.

The Indians say the Great Spirit made this mountain first of all. Can you not see how it is? they say. He first pushed down snow and ice from the skies through a hole which he made in the blue heavens by turning a stone round and round, till he made this great mountain, then he stepped out of the clouds on to the mountain top, and descended and planted the trees all around by putting his finger on the ground. Simple and sublime!

The sun melted the snow, and the water ran down and nurtured the trees and made the rivers. After that he made the fish for the rivers out of the small end of his staff. He made the birds by blowing some leaves which he took up from the ground among the trees. After that he made the beasts out of the remainder of his stick, but made the grizzly bear out of the big end, and made him master over all the others. He made the grizzly so strong that he feared him himself, and would have to go up on the top of the mountain out of sight of the forest to sleep at night, lest the grizzly, who, as will be seen, was much more strong and cunning then than now, should assail him in his sleep. Afterwards, the Great Spirit wishing to remain on earth, and make the sea and some more land, he converted Mount Shasta by a great deal of labour into a wigwam, and built a fire in the centre of it and made it a pleasant home. After that his family came down, and they all have lived in the mountain ever since. They say that before the white man came they could see the fire ascending from the mountain by night and the smoke by day, every time they chose to look in that direction.

This, I have no doubt, is true. Mount Shasta is even now, in one sense of the word, an active volcano. Sometimes only hot steam, bringing up with it a fine powdered sulphur, staining yellow the snow and ice, is thrown off. Then again boiling water, clear at one time and then muddy enough, boils up through the fissures and flows off into a little pool within a hundred feet of the summit. It is very unsettled and uncertain. Sometimes you hear most unearthly noises even a mile from the little crater, as you ascend, and when you approach, a tumult like a thousand engines with whistles of as many keys; then again you find the mountain on its good behaviour and sober enough.

Once it was thought a rare achievement to make the ascent of Mount Shasta; now I find that almost every summer some travellers and residents make the ascent. This must not be undertaken, however, when the arid sage brush plains of the east are drawing the winds across from the sea. You would at such a time be blown through the clouds like a feather.

Two days only are required to make the crater from the ranches in Shasta valley at the north base of the mountain. The first day you ride through the dense forest—a hard day's journey indeed—up to the snow line, where you sleep, leave your horses, and with pike and staff confront the ice and snow.

I ascended this mountain the last time more than fifteen years ago. It was soon after I first returned to the Indians. I acted as guide for some travelling, solemn, self-important-looking missionaries in black clothes, spectacles and beaver hats. They gave me some tracts, and paid me for my services in prayers and sermons. The memories of the trip were so unpleasant that I never had courage or desire to undertake it again.

There is but one incident in it all that I have ever recalled with pleasure. I had come out of the forest like a shadow, timid, shrinking, sensitive, to these men: like an Indian, eager to lead them, to do them any service for some kind words, some sympathy, some recognition from these great, good men, wise and learned, who professed to stand so near the throne eternal, who were so anxious for the heathen. I led and fed and watered and groomed their horses. I watched while they slept, spread their blankets beneath the trees on the dry soil, folded and packed them, headed the gorges, shunned the chaparral and bore on my own shoulders all the toils, and took on my own breast all the dangers of the day. I found them the most sour, selfish, and ungrateful wretches on earth. But I led them to the summit —two of them only—panting, blowing, groaning at every step. The others had sat down on blocks of ice and snow below. These two did not remain a moment. They did not even lift their eyes to the glory that lay to the right or to the left. What to them was the far faint line of the sea to the west; the long white lakes that looked like snow drifts, a hundred miles away to the east? Had they not been on the summit? Had they not said a prayer and left tracts there? Could they not have that to say, to report, to write about? Was all this not enough?

Hastily, indeed, they muttered something, hurriedly drew some tracts from their pockets, brought far away into this wilderness by these wise, good men, for the benighted heathen, then turned as if afraid to stay, and retraced their steps.

I hated these men, so manifestly unfit for anything like a Christian act—despised them, not their books or their professed work. When I had swept

my eyes around on the space below and photo-
graphed the world for myself, I turned and saw
these tract-leaves fluttering at my feet, in the wind,
in the snow, like the wings of a wounded bird. A
strange, fierce fit of inspiration possessed me then. I
drew my bowie-knife, drove it through the open,
fluttering leaves, and pinned them to the snow, then
turned to descend the mountain, with a chuckle of
delight.

These wild people of the forest about the base of
Mount Shasta, by their valour, their savage defiance
of the white man, and many commendable traits,
make good their claim to be called the first of the
land. They are much nobler, physically, than any
other tribes of Indians found between the Nez-Percés
of the north and the Apaches of the south. They
raise no grain, rarely dig roots, but subsist chiefly on
meat, acorn bread, nuts and fish.

These Indians have a great thirst for knowledge,
particularly of the location and extent of countries.
They are great travellers. The fact is, all Indians
are great travellers. In any tribe, even in the deserts
of Arizona, or the tribes of the plains, you will find
guides who can lead you directly to the sea to the
west, or the Sierras to the east. A traveller with
them is always a guest. He repays the hospitality
he receives by relating his travels and telling of the
various tribes he has visited, their extent, location,
and strength. No matter if the traveller is from a
hostile tribe, he is treated well and allowed to pass

through any part of the country, and go and come when he likes. Having no fortresses, and being constantly on the move, makes it perfectly safe for them to let their camps and locations be known to all.

A story-teller is held in great repute; but he is not permitted to lie or romance under any circumstances. All he says must bear the stamp of truth, or he is disgraced for ever. Telling stories, their history, traditions, travels, and giving and receiving lessons in geography, are their chief diversion around their camp and wigwam fires at night; except the popular and never-exhausted subject of their wars with the white man, and the wrongs of their race.

Geography is taught by making maps in the sand or ashes with a stick. For example, the sea a hundred miles away is taken as a base. A long line is drawn there, and rivers are led into the sea by little crooked marks in the sand. Then sand or ashes are heaped or thrown in ridges to show the ranges of mountains.

This tribe is defined as having possessions of such and such an extent on the sea. Another tribe reaches up this river so far to the east of that tribe, and so on, till a thousand miles of the coast are mapped out with tolerable accuracy. In these exercises each traveller, or any one who by his age, observation, or learning, is supposed to know, is expected to contribute his stock of information, and aid in drawing the chart correctly. I have seen the great Willamette valley, hundreds of miles away, which they call Pooakan Charook, very well drawn, and the location of Mount Hood pointed out with precision. They also chart out the great Sacramento valley, which they call Noorkan Charook, or South Valley. This valley, however, although a hundred miles away, is almost in sight. They trace the Sacramento River correctly, with its crooks and deviations, to the sea.

Their code of morals, which consists chiefly of a contempt of death, a certainty of life after death, temperance in all things, and sincerity, is taught by old men too old for war; and these lessons are given seldom, generally after some death or disaster, when the young men are depressed and not disposed to listen to tales or take part in any exercises around the camp. The women never attempt to teach anything, or even to correct the children. In fact, the children are rarely corrected. To tell the truth, they are not at all vicious. I recall no rudeness on their part, or disrespect for their parents or travellers. They were fortyfold more civil than are the children of the whites.

Quite likely this is because they have not so many temptations to do wrong as white children have. They have a natural outlet for all their energies; they can hunt, fish, trap, dive and swim, run in the woods, ride, shoot, throw the lance, do anything they like in like directions, and only receive praise for their achievements.

There is a story published that these Indians will not ascend Mount Shasta for fear of the Great Spirit there. This is only partly true. They will not ascend the mountain above the timber line under any circumstances; but it is not fear of either good or evil spirit that restrains them. It is their profound veneration for the Good Spirit: the Great Spirit who dwells in this mountain with his people as in a tent.

This mountain, as I said before, they hold is his wigwam, and the opening at the top whence the smoke and steam escapes is the smoke-place of his lodge, and the entrance also from the earth. Another mistake, which I wish to correct, is the statement of one writer, that they claim the grizzly bear as a fallen brother, and for this reason refuse to kill or molest him. This is far from the truth. Instead of the grizzly bear being a bad Indian undergoing a sort of purgatory for his sins, he is held to be a propagator of their race.

The Indian account of their creation is briefly this. They say that one late and severe spring-time many thousand snows ago, there was a great storm about the summit of Shasta, and that the Great Spirit sent his youngest and fairest daughter, of whom he was very fond, up to the hole in the top, bidding her speak to the storm that came up from the sea, and tell it to be more gentle or it would blow the mountain over. He bade her do this hastily, and not put her head out, lest the wind would catch her in

the hair and blow her away. He told her she should
only thrust out her long red arm and make a sign,
and then speak to the storm without.

The child hastened to the top, and did as she was
bid, and was about to return, but having never yet
seen the ocean, where the wind was born and made
his home, when it was white with the storm, she
stopped, turned, and put her head out to look that
way, when lo! the storm caught in her long red hair,
and blew her out and away down and down the
mountain side. Here she could not fix her feet in
the hard, smooth ice and snow, and so slid on and on
down to the dark belt of firs below the snow rim.

Now, the grizzly bears possessed all the wood and
all the land even down to the sea at that time, and
were very numerous and very powerful. They were
not exactly beasts then, although they were covered
with hair, lived in caves, and had sharp claws; but
they walked on two legs, and talked, and used clubs
to fight with, instead of their teeth and claws as they
do now.

At this time, there was a family of grizzlies
living close up to the snow. The mother had lately
brought forth, and the father was out in quest of
food for the young, when, as he returned with his
club on his shoulder and a young elk in his left hand,
he saw this little child, red like fire, hid under a fir
bush, with her long hair trailing in the snow, and
shivering with fright and cold. Not knowing what
to make of her, he took her to the old mother, who

was very learned in all things, and asked her what this fair and frail thing was that he had found shivering under a fir-bush in the snow. The old mother Grizzly, who had things pretty much her own way, bade him leave the child with her, but never mention it to any one, and she would share her breast with her, and bring her up with the other children, and maybe some great good would come of it.

The old mother reared her as she promised to do, and the old hairy father went out every day with his club on his shoulder to get food for his family till they were all grown up, and able to do for themselves.

"Now," said the old mother Grizzly to the old father Grizzly, as he stood his club by the door and sat down one day, "our oldest son is quite grown up, and must have a wife. Now, who shall it be but the little red creature you found in the snow under the black fir-bush." So the old grizzly father kissed her, said she was very wise, then took up his club on his shoulder, and went out and killed some meat for the marriage feast.

They married, and were very happy, and many children were born to them. But, being part of the Great Spirit and part of the grizzly bear, these children did not exactly resemble either of their parents, but partook somewhat of the nature and likeness of both. Thus was the red man created; for these children were the first Indians.

All the other grizzlies throughout the black

forests, even down to the sea, were very proud and very kind, and met together, and, with their united strength, built for the lovely little red princess a wigwam close to that of her father, the Great Spirit. This is what is now called "Little Mount Shasta."

After many years, the old mother Grizzly felt that she soon must die ; and, fearing that she had done wrong in detaining the child of the Great Spirit, she could not rest till she had seen him and restored him his long-lost treasure, and asked his forgiveness.

With this object in view, she gathered together all the grizzlies at the new and magnificent lodge built for the Princess and her children, and then sent her eldest grandson to the summit of Mount Shasta, in a cloud, to speak to the Great Spirit and tell him where he could find his long-lost daughter.

When the Great Spirit heard this he was so glad that he ran down the mountain-side on the south so fast and strong that the snow was melted off in places, and the tokens of his steps remain to this day. The grizzlies went out to meet him by thousands; and as he approached they stood apart in two great lines, with their clubs under their arms, and so opened a lane by which he passed in great state to the lodge where his daughter sat with her children.

But when he saw the children, and learned how the grizzlies that he had created had betrayed him into the creation of a new race, he was very wroth, and frowned on the old mother Grizzley till she died on the spot. At this the grizzlies all set up a dreadful howl; but he took his daughter on his shoulder, and turning to all the grizzlies, bade them hold their tongues, get down on their hands and knees, and so remain till he returned. They did as they were bid, and he closed the door of the lodge after him, drove all the children out into the world, passed out and up the mountain, and never returned to the timber any more.

So the grizzlies could not rise up any more, or use their clubs, but have ever since had to go on all-fours, much like other beasts, except when they have to fight for their lives, when the Great Spirit permits them to stand up and fight with their fists like men.

That is why the Indians about Mount Shasta will never kill or interfere in any way with a grizzly. Whenever one of their number is killed by one of these kings of the forest, he is burned on the spot, and all who pass that way for years cast a stone on the place till a great pile is thrown up. Fortunately, however, grizzlies are not plentiful about the mountain.

In proof of the truth of the story that the grizzly once walked and stood erect, and was much like a man, they show that he has scarcely any tail, and that his arms are a great deal shorter than his legs, and that they are more like a man than any other animal.

These Indians burn their dead. I have looked into

this, and, for my part, I should at the last like to be disposed of as a savage.

There is no such thing as absolute independence. You must ask for bread when you come into the world, and will ask for water when about to leave it. Freedom of body is equally a myth, and a demagogue's text; though freedom of mind is a certainty, and within the reach of all, grand duke or galley-slave, peasant or prince.

Since we are always more or less dependent, a wise and just man will seek to make the load as light as possible on his fellows. Socrates disliked to trouble even so humble and coarse a person as his jailer. Mahomet mended his own clothes, and Confucius waited on himself till too feeble to lift a hand.

If these wise men were careful not to take the time of others to themselves, when living and capable of doing or saying something for the good of their fellows in return, how much more careful we should be not to do so when dead—when we can help nothing whatever, and nothing whatever can help or harm us!

Holding this, I earnestly desire that my body shall be burned, as soon as the breath has left it, in the sheets in which I die, without any delay, ceremony, or preparation, beyond the building of a fire. There shall be no tomb or inscription of any kind. If a man does any great good, history will take note of it. If he has true friends, he will live in their hearts while they live, and that is certainly as long as he could live on marble, in a village churchyard, or elsewhere.

The waste of toil and money, which means time, taken from the poor and needy by the strong and wealthy, in conducting funerals and celebrating doubtful virtues by building monuments, is something enormous. Even good taste, to say nothing of this great sacrifice of time, should rise above a desire to ride to the grave in a hundred empty carriages, and crop up through the grass in shameless boast of all the virtues possible, chiselled there. Particularly in an age when successful soapboilers, or packers of pork, rival the most refined in the elegance of tombs and flourish of epitaphs. Another good reason why I protest against this display about the dead, is that so much is done about the worthless and worn-out body, that the mind is constantly directed down into the dismal grave, instead of being lifted to the light of heaven with the immortal spirit. One good reason is enough for anything.

Besides, there is a waste of land in the present custom that is inexcusable. Remember, all waste time, all waste labour, all waste land, is loss. That loss must be borne by some one, some portion of the country; and it is not the wealthy or refined who must bear it. True, they may directly take the money from their purses, but indirectly all such losses are borne by the poor. Sift it down and you will see.

Death to the poor man is a terrible thing, made

tenfold terrible by the present custom of interment. He sees that even in death there is a distinction between him and his master, and that he is still despised. The rich man goes to his marble vault, which is to the poor a palace, in pomp and display of carriages, attended by the dignitaries of the Church, while he, the poor and despised, is quietly carted away to a little corner set apart for the poor. Of course, a strong and philosophic mind would laugh at this, but to the poor it is a fearful contrast. "Death is in the world," and throws a shadow on the poor that may, in part, be lifted when all are interred alike—burned in one common fire.

These Indians, as I have before intimated, never question the immortality of the soul. Their fervid natures and vivid imaginations make the spirit world beautiful beyond description, but it is an Indian's picture, not a Christian's or Mahomedan's. No city set upon a hill, no palaces curtained in silk and peopled by beautiful women: woods, deep, dark, boundless, with parks of game and running rivers; and above and beyond all, not a white man there.

I have seen half-civilized Indians who are first-rate disbelievers, but never one who is left to think for himself. When an Indian tries to understand our religion he stumbles, as he does when he tries to understand us in other things.

The marriage ceremony of these people is not imposing. The father gives a great feast, to which all are invited, but the bride and bridegroom do not

partake of food. A new lodge is erected and furnished more elegant than any other of the village,
by the women, each vieing with the other to do
the best in providing their simple articles of the
Indian household.

In the evening, while the feast goes on and the
father's lodge is full of guests, the women and
children come to the lodge with a great number of
pitch torches, and two women enter and take the
bride away between them : the men all the time
taking no heed of what goes on. They take her to
the lodge, chanting as they go, and making a great
flourish with their torches. Late at night the men
rise up, and the father and mother, or those standing
in their stead, take the groom between them to the
lodge, while the same flourish of torches and chant
goes on as before. They take him into the lodge
and set him on the robes by the bride. This time
the torches are not put out, but are laid one after
another in the centre of the lodge. And this is the
first fire of the new pair, which must not be allowed
to die out for some time. In fact, as a rule, in time
of peace Indians never let their lodge-fires go out so
long as they remain in one place.

When all the torches are laid down and the fire
burns bright, they are supposed to be married. The
ceremony is over, and the company go away in the
dark. Late in the fall, the old chief made the
marriage-feast, and at that feast neither I nor his
daughter took meat, or any part. . . . . .

CHAPTER XX

HESE Indians use but few words. A coward and a liar is the same with them; they have no distinct terms of expressing the two sins. Sometimes a single eloquent gesture means a whole sentence, and expresses it, too, better than could a multitude of words.

I said to the old chief one day,

"Your language is very poor; it has so few words."

"We have enough. It does not take many words to tell the truth," he answered.

"Ah, but we have a hundred words to your one."

"Well, you need them."

There was a stateliness in his manner when he said this, and a toss of the head, that meant a whole chapter.

He seemed to say, "Yes, from the number of lies you have told us, from the long treaties that meant nothing that you have made with us; from the multitude of promises that you have made and broken, and made again, back as far as the traditions of my people go, I should say that you needed even a thousand words to our one."

"Words, umph! Tell me how my dog looks out of his eyes?"

The old Indian arose as he said this, and gathered his blanket about his shoulders. The dog lay with his nose on his two paws, and his eyes raised to his master's.

"You have not words enough in all your books to picture a single look from the eyes of my dog."

He drew his blanket closer about him, turned away, and the dog arose and followed him.

I had a pocket Bible with me once, in his camp. I was young, enthusiastic, and anxious to do a little missionary business on my own responsibility. I showed it to the chief, and undertook to tell him what it was.

"It is the promise of God to man," I said, "His written promise to us, that if we do as He has commanded us to do, we shall live and be happy for ever when we die."

He took it in his hand, upside down, and looked at the outside and inside very attentively.

"Promises! Is it a treaty?"

"Well, it is a treaty, perhaps; at least, it is a promise, and He wrote it."

"Did it take all of this to say that? I do not

like long treaties. I do not like any treaties on paper. They are so easy to break. The Indian does not want his God to sign a paper. He is not afraid to trust his God."

" But the promises?" I urged.

He pointed to the new leaves on the trees, the spears that were bursting through the ground, handed me the book gruffly, and said no more.

The Prince was gone, perhaps to return no more. I was again utterly alone with the Indians. I looked down and out upon the world below as looking upon a city from a tower, and was not unhappy.

I dwelt now altogether with the chief. His lodge was my home; his family my companions. We rode swift horses, sailed on the little mountain lakes with grass and tule sails, or sat down under the trees in summer, where the wind came through from the sea, and drank in silently the glories and the calm delights of life together. Nothing wanted, nothing attempted. We were content, silent, and satisfied. Was it not enough? Despise a love of nature, and even a love of woman, that is ranted and talked about as if it were a pain in the stomach. A dog may howl his passion, but the most of beasts are more decent in this than the mass of men.

" They will find the cabin, yet," said the chief, " if it is allowed to stand. Then they will search till they find the mine, then a crowd of people will come, like grasshoppers in the valley; my warriors will be murdered, my forests cut down, my grass will be burned; my game driven off, and my people will starve. As their father to whom they look for protection and support, I cannot allow it to stand."

" It shall be as you say. Send some men with me. What care I for the cabin, and what is a mine of gold to me here? "

We went down, we burned the cabin to the ground. We did not leave even a pine board, and after the embers had cooled and a rain had settled the ashes, we dug up the soil and scattered seeds of reeds and grass on the spot. The stumps, chips, logs, everything was burned that bore the mark of the white man's axe.

A year or two afterwards I passed there, and all was wild and overgrown with grass, the same as if no man had ever sat down and rested there below the boughs.

Some pines that stood too close to the burning cabin had yellow branches at one side, and where the bark had burned on that side they were gnarled and seared, and stood there parched up and ugly, in a circle, as if making faces at some invisible object in their midst.

That is all there is really of the lost cabin, which once created such a commotion in northern California.

Men came, less numerous of course, each season, year after year, looking for the lost cabin, for it was pleasant to come up from the hot plains of the Sacramento, and up from the cities on the sea, and camp here by the cool streams, and travel under the great trees away from even a hint of the sun; but they never found so much as a trace of the lost cabin, and at last gave it up as a myth not unlike Gold Lake, Gold Beach, and the Lost Dutchman of the earliest days of the Pacific excitements.

I did not return to the mine because, in the first place, I believed that it was only a treacherous pocket that had nothing more to give but promises. But beyond all that, I was trying to rise to the dignity of some little virtue, after the Prince had shown so much, and these Indians had set such good examples. What should I do with the gold, even if I found a mountain of it? My wants were few and simple. Except to make journeys, I did not need a dollar. I had all that I could use; what use, then, had I for more?

I could only point it out to my countrymen, and that meant toil and strife, privation and endurance for them; for the Indians it meant annihilation. With the constant sense before me that it was and is exhausted, I have been enabled to let the leaves fall there, and the moss to grow in the mine for many, many years. Sometimes we have almost to lie to ourselves to get strength to do a simple act of justice; nay, to even not do a deliberate wrong.

What, after all, if my grand, old, noble pyramid of the north, white as faith, sphinx-like looking out over the desert plains of the east, the seas of the west, the sable woods that environ it, should be built on a solid base of gold!

When the Modoc has led his last warrior to battle
up yonder in his rocky fortress, fired his last shot, and
the grass is growing in the last war-path of those
people, then, and not till then, I may go up where the
solemn trees with their dead limbs stand around,
making faces at something in the centre, pitch a tent
there, and go down in the cañon with men, and picks
and shovels, and bars of steel and iron.

At the same time, I am trying to bring myself up
to the conviction of the truth, that a great deal of
gold is rather to be avoided than sought after. Every
day I look around, and see how many thousands
there are who have gold and nothing else; I see the
sin there is in it and the getting of it. The ten
thousand temptations it brings a man, tied up in the
bags along with it, and let out when it is let out, in-
separable from it. I see that it is sinking my country, morally, every day; and yet with this steady drift
of all things toward the one goal, this sailing of every
ship in life for the one Golden Gate, barren as it is,
forgetting the green isles of palm and the warm
winds there; I say, with all this, it is hard to stand up
tall and despise it.

Save money for the children? Bosh! Are you
afraid to put them down on the track of life, to take
a fair and even start with the rest ? Do you want
to start them ahead of nine-tenths of those who have
to run the race of life ? Do you think they have not
brains or backbone enough to make their way with
the rest ? How many of all the millions can start
with a fortune?

No. Put them out on the track, well trained and strong, and let them run the race fairly and squarely with the humblest there, and then if they win they win like men. Must have money to appear well! Fiddle-sticks! To buy a new coat and furniture, so as to receive your friends. My dear sir, friends never yet came to see a man's new coat or his nice house; never! If your friends want to see new coats, they can go to the clothing stores and see a thousand every day for nothing.

No, we do not hoard up money altogether for the children, or for friends to look upon, but we heap it up because we are selfish cowards! Because we have not nerve enough to stand on our own merit, or having so little merit and so much money, we prefer to trust to the latter for a place in the eyes of the world. And then there is a low, contemptible fear that we will come to want, and so toil and toil and build a barricade of gold about us, and die at last in fear, pinched to death between twenty-dollar pieces, that the starved and hungry soul has crept between, with the last bit of young, strong manhood that we were born with crushed utterly out of us.

CHAPTER XXI

BOUT this time, tiring somewhat of the monotonous life of the Indian camp, and wishing to see the face of a white man, I descended to the settlements on the Sacramento River, and fell in with Mountain Joe, an old mountaineer who had been with Fremont. He was a German by birth and education, and remarkable as it may seem, was certainly a very learned man. I have heard him repeat, or at least pretend to repeat, Homer in the Greek and Virgil in the Latin, by the hour, though he professed to despise the translations, and would not give me a line of the English version. Possibly, his Greek was not Greek, but I think it was, for in other things in which I could not be utterly deceived I found him wonderfully well-informed.

We together located and took possession of the ranch now known as the Soda Springs, and to-day the most famous summer resort in northern California.

We employed men, built a house, ploughed, planted, and opened a trading post, all in the short period of a few weeks. Sometimes I would ride up into the mountains towards Mount Shasta, as if hunting for game, and spend a few days with my tawny friends.

Soon the rush of people subsided, and but few white men were found in the country. All up and down the streams their temporary shanties were left without a foot to press the rank grass and abundant weeds.

One day when our tame Indians, whom we had employed on the ranch, were out fishing, and Mountain Joe and I had taken our rifles and gone up the Narrow Valley to look after the horses, a band of hostile Indians living in and about the Devil's Castle, some ten miles away on the opposite side of the Sacramento, came in and plundered our camp of all the stores and portable articles they could lay hands on.

This castle is the most picturesque object in all the magnificent scenery of northern California. It sits on a high mountain, and is formed of grey granite blocks and spires, lifting singly and in groups thousands of feet from the summit of the mountain. Most of these are inaccessible. Here the Indians locate the abode of the devil. Hence its name.

I gathered up some half-tame Indians that could be relied on, while Mountain Joe went down the river ten or twenty miles to the little mining camps, and collected a company of whites. I had had no connection with these Indians, and was therefore plundered and treated as they would have treated any other settler. To have borne with the outrage would have been to fall into disgrace with the others. They would have thought I dared not resent it.

The small command moved up Castle Creek under the guide of friendly Indians. Each man carried his arms, blankets, and three days' rations. All were on foot, as the Castle cannot be approached by horsemen. We reached Castle Lake, a sweet, peaceful place, overhung by mountain cypress and sweeping cedars. This is a spot the Indians will not visit, for fear of the evil spirits which they are certain inhabit the place. They sat down in the wood overlooking the lake, while we descended, drank of the cool, deep water, and refreshed ourselves for the combat, since the spies had just returned and reported the hostile camp only an hour distant. This was on the 26th day of June, 1855. The enemy was not dreaming of our approach, and we were in position, almost surrounding the camp, before we were discovered.

Mountain Joe had distributed us behind the rocks and trees in range of and overlooking the camp. The ground was all densely timbered, and covered with a thick growth of black stiff chaparral, save one spot of a few acres, by the side of which the Indians were camped, at the foot of a little hill.

This was my first war-path. I was about to take part in my first real battle. I had been placed by Mountain Joe behind a large pine, and alone. He spoke kindly as he left me, and bade me take care of myself.

I put some bullets in my mouth, primed my pistols, and made all preparation to do my part. It seemed like an age before the fight began. I could hear my heart beat like a little drum.

The Indians certainly had not the least suspicion of danger. They were, it seemed, as much off their guard as possible. They evidently thought their camp, if not impregnable, beyond our reach and discovery. They owed the latter to their own race.

At last we were discerned, as some of the most daring and experienced were stealing closer and closer to the camp, and they sprang to their arms with whoops and yells that lifted my hat almost from my head.

The yells were answered. Rifles cracked around the camp, and arrows came back in showers.

" Close up!" shouted Mountain Joe, and we left cover and advanced. I think I must have swallowed the bullets I put in my mouth, for I loaded from my pouch as usual, and thought of them no more as we moved down upon the yelling Indians.

A little group of us gathered behind some rocks. Then a man came creeping to us through the brush to say that the other side of our company was being pressed and that we must move on. Then another came to say that Mountain Joe had been struck across the face by an arrow, and his eyes were so injured that he could not direct the fight.

" Then come on!" I cried; " let us push through
here to the camp and drive them into the open
ground." I took the lead, the men followed, and
without knowing it, I became a leader of my fellows.
We had wound our blankets about our breasts and
bodies so as to guard against arrows, but our heads
were unprotected.

Suddenly the arrows came, whiz, whistle, thud,
right in our faces.

I fell senseless. After a while I felt men pulling
by my shoulders. I could hear and understand but
could not see or rise. It seemed to me they were
trying to twist my neck from my body. Yet I
felt no great pain, only a numbness and utter helplessness.

" Help me pull it out," said one. They pulled.

" No, you must cut off the point, and then pull it
back."

Then they cut and pulled, and the blood spirted
out and rattled on the leaves.

" Poor boy, he's done for."

I could now see, but was still helpless. Half-a-
dozen men stood around leaning on their rifles,
looking at me, then around them, as if for the enemy.
By the side of me, with his head in a man's lap, lay
a young man, James Lane, with an arrow-shot near
the eye. I believe he died of his wound.

The fight was over. An arrow had struck me in
the left side of the face, struck the jaw-bone, and
then glanced around and came out at the back of the

neck. The wound certainly looked as if it must be mortal, but the jugular vein was not touched and there was hope. I was dizzy and sometimes senseless. This perhaps was because the wound was so near the brain. I constantly thought I was on the mountain slope overlooking home, and kept telling the men to go and bring my mother. We had no surgeon, and the men tied up our wounds as best they could in tobacco saturated in saliva.

That night the Indian camp was plundered and burnt. The next morning, as the provisions were out, preparations were made to descend the mountain. I here must not forget the kind but half-savage attention of these rough men. They could do but little, it is true, but they were untiring in attention and sympathy. They held my head in their laps, and talked low and tenderly of early health and my return home. I saw one man crying, the tears dropping down into his long grizzly beard; then I thought I should surely die. In the morning one kind but mistaken old fellow brought a leather bag, and held it up haughtily before my eyes in his left hand, while he tapped it gently with his bowie knife. The blood was oozing through the seams of the bag and trickling at his feet.

" Them's scalps."

I grew sick at the sight.

The wounded were carried on the backs of squaws that had been taken in the fight. A very old and wrinkled woman carried me on her back by setting me in a large buckskin, with one leg on each side of her body, and then supporting the weight by a broad leather strap passed across her brow. This was not uncomfortable, all things considered. In fact, it was by far the best thing that could be done.

The first half day the old woman was " sulky," as the men called it; possibly the wrinkled old creature could feel, and was thinking of her dead.

In the afternoon I began to rally, and spoke to her in her own tongue. Then she talked and talked, and mourned, and would not be still. " You," she moaned, " have killed all my boys, and burnt up my home."

I ventured to protest that they had first robbed us.

" No," she said, " you first robbed us. You drove us from the river. We could not fish, we could not hunt. We were hungry and took your provisions to eat. My boys did not kill you. They could have killed you a hundred times, but they only took things to eat, when they could not get fish and things on the river."

We reached the Sacramento in safety, and pitched camp on the bank of the river under some small cedars about a mile below the site of the present hotel on the Lower Soda Spring ranch. Here I lay a long long time, till able to travel. Those beautiful trees were still standing when I returned there in 1872.

It was necessary to go to San Francisco to recover my health; but I tired of the city soon, and longed for the mountains and my Indian companions.

In the spring I returned, found Mountain Joe ploughing and planting at Soda Springs, and after resting and making arrangements for the further improvement of the ranch, pushed back over the mountains to my Indians. All were there, Paquita, Klamat, the chief, and his daughter, who, although she was much to me I shall barely mention in these pages. They had learned all about my battle, and I think forgave me whatever blood was on my hands for the part I had borne in the fight, for an Indian is a hero-worshipper of the very worst kind.

CHAPTER XXII

ERE for the first time a plan which had been forming in my mind ever since I first found myself among these people began to take definite shape. It was a bold and ambitious enterprise, and was no less a project than the establishment of a sort of Indian Republic—" a wheel within a wheel," with the grand old cone Mount Shasta for the head or centre.

To the south, reaching from far up on Mount Shasta to far down in the Sacramento valley, lay the lands of the Shastas, with almost every variety of country and climate; to the south-east the Pit River Indians, with a land rich with pastures and plains teeming with game; to the north-east lay the Modocs, with lakes and pasture-lands enough to make a State. My plan was to unite these three tribes in a confederacy under the name of the United Tribes, and by making a claim and showing a bold front to the Government, secure by treaty all the lands near the mountain, even if we had to surrender all the other lands in doing so.

It might have been called a kind of Indian reservation, but it was to be a reservation in its fullest and most original sense, such as those first allotted to the Indians. Definite lines were to be drawn, and these lines were to be kept sacred. No white man was to come there without permission. The Indians were to remain on the land of their fathers. They were to receive no pay, no perquisites or assistance whatever from the Government. They were simply to be let alone in their possessions, with their rites, customs, religion, and all, unmolested. They were to adopt civilization by degrees and as they saw fit, and such parts of it as they chose to adopt. They were to send a representative to the State and the national capitals if they chose, and so on through a long catalogue of details that would have left them in possession of that liberty which is as dear to the Indian as to any being on earth.

Filled with plans for my little Republic I now went among the Modocs, whom I had always half feared since they had killed and plundered the old trader, and boldly laid the case before them. They were very enthusiastic, and some of the old councilmen named me chief ; yet I never had any authority to speak of till too late to use it to advantage.

I drew maps and wrote out my plans, and sent them to the commanding officer of the Pacific Coast, the

Governor of the State, and the President of the Republic. Full of enthusiasm and impossible theories were the letters I sent, and no doubt full of bad spelling and worse grammar; but they were honest, sincere, and well meant, and deserved something better than the contemptuous silence they received.

I thought of this thing day after day, and it came upon me at last like a great sunrise, full and complete. The Indians entered into it with all their hearts. Their great desire was to have a dividing line—a mark that would say, Thus far will we come and no farther. They did not seem to care about details or particulars where the line would be drawn, only that it should be drawn, and leave them secure in bounds which they could call their own. They would submit to almost anything for this.

Remove they would not; but they were tired of a perpetual state of half-war, half-peace, that brought only a steady loss of life and of land, without any lookout ahead for the better, and would enter into almost any terms that promised to let them and theirs permanently and securely alone. I may say here in a kind of parenthesis that the only way an Indian can get a hearing is to go to war, and thus call the attention of the Government to the fact of his existence.

How magnificent and splendid seemed my plan! Imagination had no limit. Here would be a national park, a place, one place in all the world, where men lived in a state of nature, and when all the other tribes had passed away or melted into the civilization and life of the white man, here would be a people untouched, unchanged, to instruct and interest the traveller, the moralist, all men. When the world is done gathering gold, I said, it will come to these forests to look at nature, and be thankful for the wisdom and foresight of the age that preserved this vestige of an all but extinct race. There was a grandeur in the thought, a sort of sublimity, that I shall never feel again. A fervid nature, a vivid imagination, and, above all, the matchless and magnificent scenery, the strangely silent people, the half-pathetic stillness of the forests, all conspired to lift me up into an atmosphere where the soul laughs at doubt and never dreams of failure. A ship-wrecked race, I said, shall here take rest. To the east and west, to the north and south, the busy commercial world may swell and throb and beat and battle like a sea; but on this island, around this mountain, with their backs to this bulwark, they shall look untroubled on it all. Here they shall live as their fathers lived before the newer pyramids cast their little shadows, or camels kneeled in the dried-up seas.

I went to Yreka, the nearest convenient post-office, nearly one hundred miles away, and waited for my answers in vain. I wrote again, but with the same result.

I saw that I must learn something more of the white man, mix with him, observe his manners and disposition more closely than I had done. I said to myself, I have been a dreamer. I am now awake, and I have a purpose.

That purpose became my hobby. I rode that hobby to the bitter end. Old men have hobbies sometimes as well as boys. The Civil War was born of hobbies. When a hobby becomes a success it is then baptized and given another name. I engaged in many pursuits through the summer, always leaving a place or calling so soon as it afforded me no further instruction. On Deadwood, a mining stream with a large and prosperous camp, I found some old acquaintances of The Forks, and finding also a library, a debating society, and a temperance lodge, I joined all these, took part, and on every fit and unfit occasion began to urge my hobby. Yet I never admitted that I had cast my fortune with the Indians or even had been among them. This would have been disgrace and defeat at once. I engaged as a common labourer, shovelling dirt and running a wheelbarrow with broad-backed Irishmen and tough Missourians, in order to get acquainted with the men who clustered about the library. The books—300 in number—were kept at the cabins of the men who employed me. Of course I could not stand the work long, but I accomplished my object. I got acquainted with the most intelligent men of the camp, and so enlarged my life.

I remained a month. I read Byron and Plutarch's Lives over and over again. They were the only books I cared at all to read, and they were the very books that I in that state of mind should not have read. I pictured myself the hero of all I read. Instead of being awakened, I was only dreaming a greater dream.

I returned to Soda Springs ranch, and Mountain Joe went with me to the Indian camp, but I never took him into my confidence. Not but he was a brave, true man, but that he was unfortunately sometimes given to getting drunk, and besides that, he was the last man to sympathize with the Indian or any plan that looked to his improvement. I laid in my supplies, and proposed to spend my winter with the Indians. I loved Mountain Joe fondly; and in spite of his prophecies that he would see me no more, returned to the camp on the Upper McCloud. As feed for stock was scarce on the ranch, I with my Indians took the horses on the McCloud to winter. My camp was about seventy-five miles from the Pit River settlements, and about thirty miles from Soda Springs. These were the nearest white habitations. I was partly between the two.

About mid-winter the chief led his men up towards the higher spurs of the mountain for a great hunt. After some days on the head-waters of the McCloud, at some hot springs in the heart of a deep forest and dense undergrowth, we came upon an immense herd of elk. The snow was from five to ten feet deep. We had snow shoes, and as the elk were helpless, after driving them from the thin

snow and trails about the springs into the deep
snow, the Indians shot them down as they wallowed
along, by hundreds.

Camp was now removed to this place, with the
exception of a few who preferred to remain below,
and feasting and dancing became the order of the
winter.

Soon Klamat and a few other young and spirited
Indians said they were going to visit some other
camp that lay a day or two to the east, and disappeared.

In about a month they returned. After the usual
Indian silence, they told a tale which literally froze
my blood. It made me ill.

The Indians had got into difficulty with the white
men of Pit River valley about their women, and
killed all but two of the settlers. These two they
said had escaped to the woods, and were trying to
get back through the snow to Yreka. The number
of the settlers I do not remember, but they did not
exceed twenty, and perhaps not more than ten.

There were no women or children in the valley at
the time of the massacre; only the men in charge of
great herds of stock.

This meant a great deal to me. I began to reflect
on what it would lead to. The affair, no matter who
was to blame, would be called another dreadful
massacre by the bloodthirsty savages; of this I was
certain. Possibly it was a massacre, but the Indian
account of it shows them to have been as perfectly

justified as ever one human being can be for taking the life of another.

I have been from that day to this charged with having led the Indians in this massacre. I deny nothing; I simply tell what I know and all I know of this matter as briefly as possible, and let it pass.

The massacre, as it is called, occurred in the first month of the year 1867. The whites were besieged by the Indians in a strong wooden house, a perfect fortress. The Indians asked them to surrender, offering to conduct them safely to the settlements. They felt secure, and laughed at the proposition. A long fight followed, in which many Indians fell. At last the Indians carried great heaps of hay to the walls, fired it, and the whites perished.

CHAPTER XXIII

 SPOKE to the chief about the affair; I told him it meant a bloody war; that the Indians of the valleys, wherever the Americans could reach, would be overthrown, and asked him what he would do.

He thought over the matter a day or two, then said he should keep his men together and out of the way as far as he could, and then, if attacked, would defend himself; that the Pit River Indians were not his Indians, that they had a chief of their own, and lived quite another life from his, and he could not be held responsible for their acts.

He urged, however, that they were right, that they had his sympathy, and that to assist them in the coming war would be the best and speediest way to establish the union of the three tribes, and get a recognition of rights from the Government of the United States.

I knew very well, however, that it would not do

to go to war in a bad cause; that that would ruin all concerned, and establish nothing.

From the first I had tried to get Klamat to go with me to the scene of the massacre. He refused, and the Indians put up their hands in horror at the recklessness of the proposition.

Somehow, the picture of these two men struggling through the snow, pursued, wretched, lost, half-famished, kept constantly before me. If they were making way to Yreka, I could cut across the spurs of Mount Shasta and intercept them. My camp was not thirty miles from the road leading to that city from Pit River. I resolved to go at least that far and see what could be discovered, and what I could do to assist them.

With this view I got two young strong Indians, and set out early on the hard snow, carrying snow-shoes and a little bag of ground elk meat and grass seed.

Before night, I came upon and followed the road by the high blaze on the pines for some distance, and toward the valley, but found no trace of the fugitives. I camped under a broad, low-boughed fir tree that stood almost a perfect pyramid of snow, over a dry grassy plat down about the trunk and roots of the tree.

Early in the morning we went on a few paces to the summit overlooking the valley. The sun was rising in our faces. The air was so rich and pure we seemed to feed upon it. The valley seemed to lay almost at our feet. This mountain air, in fact, all the atmosphere of the Far West, is delusive to a stranger, but this of the Sierras, and at that particular time, was peculiarly so. A tall, slanting, swaying column seemed to rise before us not five miles away. It was the smoke of an Indian camp, at least twenty-five miles distant.

We were full of fire, youth, and strength. We had been resting long in camp, and now wanted to throw off our lethargy.

" Let us go down," I said in a spirit of banter, yet really wishing to descend.

" Go !" cried the Indians in chorus. " To-ka-do; we will follow." And I slid down the mountain, laughing like a school-boy at play.

This was a turning-point in my life, taken without the least reflection or one moment's thought. Energy makes leaders, but it takes more than energy to make a successful leader.

Before night we sat down on a little hill overlooking the camp not a mile away.

I had no plan. It was while sitting here waiting for darkness before venturing further, that one of the Indians asked me what I proposed to do. I did not know myself, but told him we would take a look at the camp so soon as it got dark and then go home.

We looked at the camp, more than a thousand strong. Indians keep no guard at night. They surrender themselves to the great, sad mother—

night, with a superstitious trust, and refuse to take precaution till dawn.

I knew every foot of the ground. It was five miles to the Ferry, where had been the strongest house of the whites; I wished to go there and see first how things stood, now that I was so near. We pushed down the valley and left the Indians singing and dancing over their achievements. They did not dream that there was a white man within a hundred miles.

The houses were all burned. The ferry-boat was still chained to the bank, and in the boat lay a naked corpse with the head severed from the body.

We sat down in the boat, eat the last of our scant provisions and prepared to return. The excitement now being over, with the seventy-five miles of wilderness before us, I began to feel uneasy. We were in the " Valley of Death." Desolation was around us. Half-burnt houses were passed here and there, and now and then in the grey dawn we could see the smoke of Indian camps in the edge of the wood and along the river-banks.

We made a détour to avoid the large camp at the entrance of the valley and toiled up the mountain in silence.

Before noon we struck the route by which we entered, and on the edge of Bear Valley came suddenly upon two squaws who were on their way there to dig klara. This is the root of the mountain lily. It is a large white substance like a potato, with grains growing on the outside like Indian corn. The squaws dropped their baskets and hid their faces in their hands in sign of submission. They had not discovered us until too close to attempt escape. We greedily devoured their few roots, took them with us, and hastened on.

In the afternoon, when nearing the summit, one of the squaws dashed down the hillside through the thicket. We called to her to stop but she only ran the faster. We then told the other she could go also, and she bounded away like a deer. Our only object in keeping them with us was to prevent them giving the alarm, but since one could do this as well as two we had no occasion to keep the other.

We knew that under the excitement of fear they would soon reach camp, and, perhaps, induce pursuit, and therefore we redoubled our pace.

We travelled all night, but about dawn I broke down utterly and could stagger on not a step further.

The Indians tore off a dead cedar bark, formed it into a sort of canoe, and fastening withes to one end, placed me in it and drew me over the snow.

I ought to have recovered some strength but did not. I could not stand alone. After dark they built up a big fire in a close thicket, left me alone, and pushed on to camp.

Early in the morning other Indians came with provisions, and now being able to walk after a breakfast on elk and deer meat, we soon reached camp.

After but one day and two nights' rest I proceeded

over the mountain on snow shoes to Soda Springs, and gave the details, so far as I knew, of the destruction of the settlement in Pit River valley.

Mountain Joe advised that I should go at once to Yreka with the news. I mounted a strong nimble mule and set out.

On my way I met Sam Lockhart. This Lockhart was a leading man of the country and largely interested in Pit River valley, where he had a great deal of stock, which was in charge of his brother, who fell in the massacre. My sad news was not news to Lockhart. The two men before spoken of had made their way through the mountain to Yreka, and the whole country was already in arms.

Lockhart was on his way to Red Bluffs, two hundred miles distant, for the purpose of raising a company there, to attack the Indians from that side, while the company already started from Yreka should descend upon them from the other. There was but little military force in the country, but the miners and men generally in those days were prompt and ready to become soldiers at almost a minute's notice. But in desperate cases, as in this, men not directly interested were prepared to arm and equip a substitute such as they could pick up about the camp. Lockhart returned to Yreka with me.

We arrived in town late in the evening and I was taken at once to the law-office of Judge Roseborough. Some other lawyers were called in; I was ordered, not asked, to take a seat, and then began a series of questions and cross-questions from scowling and savage men that quite alarmed me. But I was unsuspicious, and answered naturally and promptly all that was asked.

I was very weary. I could hardly keep awake, and asked to be allowed to retire.

" You must not leave this room," said Lockhart savagely. The truth came upon me like a revelation. I was a prisoner. Lockhart, who was half drunk, now began to talk very loud, swore furiously, and wanted to murder me on the spot. I hid my face in my hands.

This, then, was the reward for my dangerous descent into the Valley of Death! This, then, was to be my compensation for all I had dared and endured!

I could not answer another question. All this is painful to remember and difficult to write.

CHAPTER XXIV

SOME of the lawyers went away. A bed was improvised for me on the floor, and I believe Lockhart, or at least some one, kept watch over me during the night.

Judge Roseborough, who is now the chief Judge of the northern district of California, with his home still at Yreka, has seen fit to give to the world an account of my singular capture, imprisonment, and this Star Chamber proceeding, and I believe claims some merit for having saved my life.

No doubt the Judge, who is really, I think, a good man at heart, did save my life. But somehow, I cannot feel any great gratitude toward him for that, under the circumstances. At the best he only prevented a foul and cowardly murder. He might have done much more. He might have said some kind words, spoken some earnest advice, and given some direction to my unsettled and uncertain life.

I was dying, morally; I was starving to death for counsel and kind words after what had just been said and done. My heart was filling full of bitterness. But perhaps he did not understand me.

Lockhart was in better temper the next morning. He told me, which no doubt was the truth, that the whole town and settlements were in a blaze of excitement about the massacre, and that I was liable to be shot by almost any one, unless I by a prudent course of conduct put down the suspicions against me.

I asked to be allowed to return to Soda Springs, but he insisted that the only safe thing for me to do was to join the expedition already on the way against the Indians. I saw that he was determined I should do this, and consented. He gave me a letter—a very friendly letter—to Joseph Rogers, a son of one of the men who had been murdered in Pit River Valley, and then with the expedition. It was an open and very complimentary letter. But other letters were sent in the hands of the two men who were sent with me.

These were men, I was told, belonging to the expedition, who had not yet left town, and would be glad to show me the way to the camp; but the truth was, I was still a prisoner, and these men were my keepers.

Very soon and very early we rode out of town against the rising sun, past the grave-yard and past the gallows toward Mount Shasta.

My heart was full of bitterness and revenge. As we crossed the crest of the little brown hill that looks above the town, I half turned in my saddle and shook a thin and nervous hand against its cold and cruel inhabitants.

I never entered that town again, save as an enemy, for more than a decade.

At dusk we came upon the camp of the expedition, noisy and boisterous, half buried in the snow.

This was the rudest set of men I ever saw gathered together for any purpose whatever. There were, perhaps, a dozen good men, as good as there were in the land; but the rank and file were made up of thieves, bar-room loafers, gutter snipes, and men of desperate character and fortunes. They growled and grumbled and fought half the time.

We travelled by night, drawing the supplies on slides, in order to get the horses over the snow when it was hard and frozen. I had told them the story of my dangerous descent into the valley, but was not believed by half the company. They could not understand what upon earth a man could mean by such a hazard. They were practical fellows. They put everything on the popular conceived basis of the age. They could not see what interest I had in going there, could not see " what I could make by it." They did not see where I could make it " pay."

One day I woke up to a strange sensation. More than once I had heard some talk about " a man living with the Indians." This man they talked of, and of whom they seemed to have but a rough idea, was to be captured, skinned alive, roasted, scalped, and, in fact, to undergo all the refined tortures known to the border.

It crossed my mind suddenly, like a flash, that I was that man.

I saw at the same time, however, that there was not the slightest suspicion that the pale, slim boy before them was "the man who lived with the Indians."

Through half-friendly savages and other means it had gone abroad among the settlers that there was a white man living with the Indians. Nothing could induce these men to believe that a man could live with the Indians for any other purpose than to take part with them in their wars, and to plunder the whites. And, as a rule, so far as I know, those who have cast their fortunes in with the Indians have been outlaws, men who could not live longer with their kind.

But these fellows expected to find the renegade a strong-limbed, bearded, desperate man. Perhaps had any one told them there and then that I was that man they would have laughed in his face.

My first impulse was to run away. Had it then been night I certainly should have fled. All day I watched my chance to escape, but no chance came. That night I had no opportunity without great hazard, and soon I began to think better of my projected flight through the snow.

Still cherishing the plan of my little Republic or independent Reservation, I saw that the Shasta Indians and their friends must show no sympathy with the Indians charged with the massacre, and determined to remain a little longer. Besides, I then liked the excitement of war, and the real men of the company were coming to be my friends.

The captain of the company was Gideon S. Whitey, a brave, resolute, and honourable man. He afterwards married a Modoc, or Pit River squaw, and now lives with her and his large family of children at Cañon City, Oregon.

At last we entered the valley. I had travelled nearly five hundred miles in the snow since leaving it ; forming a triangle in my route, with Mount Shasta in the centre.

We soon were at work. Tragic and sanguinary scenes occurred. I cannot enter into detail, it would fill a volume.

It would also fill many pages to explain how by degrees I came to enter into the spirit of the war against my allies. Nor is there any real excuse for my conduct. It was wrong, but not wholly wrong. The surroundings and all the circumstances of the time contributed to lead me to take a most active part. I could not then as now rise above the situation and survey the whole scene. From a prisoner I became a leader.

Two decisive battles, or rather massacres, took place, and perhaps five hundred Indians perished.

The men fought as well out of camp as in camp, and that is saying a vast deal for their valour.

However, I have not that high opinion of physical courage in which it is too generally held. My observation proves to me that the very worst possible man in the world may also be the very bravest man, for a day at least, that lives. I have seen too much to be mistaken in this. I have seen a row of men standing up on whisky barrels under a tree, with ropes around their necks, ready to die at the hands of the unflinching vigilantes. They sang a filthy song in chorus, howled and cursed, and then danced a breakdown till the kegs were kicked from under them. The world sets too high a mark on brute, bull-dog courage.

After a time Lockhart came up with his command from Red Bluffs, and desiring the control of the whole force, a difficulty arose and Whitey resigned. Another man was chosen as nominal leader, but the plain truth is, before we had been in the valley a month I gave direction, and had in fact charge of the expedition. Most of these men are dead now, but scattered around somewhere on earth a few may be found, and they will tell you that by my energy, recklessness, and knowledge of the country and Indian customs, I, and I only, made the bloody expedition a success. I tell this in sorrow. It is a thousand times more to my shame than honour, and I shall never cease to regret it.

Before leaving the valley, we surprised a camp by

stealing upon it at night and lying in wait till dawn.

It was a bloody affair for the Indians. More than a hundred lay heaped together about the lodges, where they fell by rifle, pistol, and knife.

The white butchers scalped the dead every one. One of the ruffians, known as Dutch Frank, cut off their ears and strung them about his horse's neck. After drawing off the force some of the men lingered behind and shot and plundered the medicine-man, or priest. This priest is a non-combatant, is never armed, and comes upon the field only after the fight to chant for the dead. This one was dressed in a costly robe of sables, with a cap made of skins of the white fox. The rear of our force, on return to camp, showed a man dressed in this singular garb still wet with blood.

I was glad when we broke camp to return. We had found the valley without a white man; we left it with scarcely an Indian.

I had had a hard time of it. I had endured insults from the roughs of the party rather than enter into their battles, which were generally fought out with the fist. It had in fact become intolerable. One morning I gently cocked my pistol, and asked the ruffian who had taken more than one occasion to insult me to step out. He declined to do this, said he was not my equal in the use of arms, but that some lucky day he would get even. He waited his time.

The snow had disappeared as we returned; spring was upon us, and the journey was very pleasant. Nearly every man carried a little captive Indian before him on his horse; most of them had Indian scalps clinging to their belts, and, dressed in furs and buckskins, cut in fantastic shapes for Indian wear, they were a strange and motley sight to look upon as they moved in single file through the deep, dark forests.

At the camp, after crossing the summit, with the McCloud and my Indian camp to the left, and Yreka in front, I determined to leave the command and seek my tawny friends at the base of Shasta.

I fancied I had made friends, and expected to have honourable mention from those who returned to the city. I do not know whether this was the case or not. Newspapers never reach an Indian camp, and I never entered Yreka again, save as an enemy, for more than a decade thereafter.

Sam Lockhart I never saw again. He was a brave man, prejudiced and reckless, but, I think, a good man at heart. He was killed in one of the hand-to-hand battles over the mines of Owyhee.

I made a little speech to the party, shook hands with about half of them, mounted my mule, and rode away alone in one direction, while they took another.

After about an hour's ride I heard some one calling after me. I turned round; they called again, and I rode back. On nearing a thicket, a double-barrelled shot gun loaded with pistol balls was fired across my breast.

The assassin nearly missed his mark. Only my right arm was shot through and disabled by a pistol ball, and the mule was hit slightly in the neck. I did not see any one. The mule wheeled and dashed through the bushes on the back track at a furious speed.

How dreadful I felt. To think that this was done by one or more of the roughs, who had followed me, after having been my companions in war!

They had sneeringly cautioned me to look out for Indians that morning as I was preparing to leave. They had taken this course to murder me, and lay it on the Indians, as is often done on the border.

My bitterness knew no bounds. I could not return and overtake the company, wounded as I was. I rode on rapidly, bleeding and faint.

I laid the matter on the whole company. I sometimes felt that a good number must have consented to this, if they had not advised it. Then I came to the conclusion that they had determined from the first who I was, and that I should die; but after finding how useful I was, deferred my attempted execution till the campaign was over. I long nursed that thought, and am even now not certain that it was incorrect.

I reached the Now-aw-wa valley, now known, I believe, by the vulgar name of "Squaw valley," and found it still as a tomb. Mountain Joe and I had

built some cabins here and sheds for the stock; but
no stock, no Indians were in sight. At last, sick
from the loss of blood, I found a camp up on a hill-
side, and there dismounted. The Indians were
silent and sullen. A woman came at last to bring
me water, and then saw my wound. That moved
their pity. I told them the white men had done it,
and that made them more than half my friends again.

CHAPTER XXV

HAT I had made a grave mistake I now saw. Indians are clannish. They may fight among each other like the other people of the earth; but let them be attacked by the common enemy, and they make common cause. I had fought against their brothers, and I was not to be at once forgiven for that. On the other hand, I had sympathized with the Indians. That also was a mortal crime, an unpardonable offence, in the eyes of the whites.

I had attempted to sit on two seats at once, and had slid between the two. It takes a big man to sit on two chairs at once. Any man who has the capacity to do such a thing, has also the good sense not to attempt it.

The Indians came slowly back into the country; but some never came. They had gone to the Pit River war. The rank grass is growing above their ashes on the hills that look upon that winding, shining river.

Klamat was never friendly after that. The defeat of the Indians on all occasions, without being able to inflict any injury in return, made him desperate, and to see me among their enemies did not add to his good nature. But dear little Paquita was the same. The same gentleness in her manner, the same deep sadness in her eyes as she tended me. I now began to think again. I now thought, I surely am awake. If I had been awake, I should have mounted my mule as soon as able to ride, and left the country for ever.

No, I said, after a long debate with myself, I will remain. I will reconsider this whole matter. I will gather these Indians together, get arms and ammunition, and around Mount Shasta make my home, and, if needs be, defend it to the end. I had done all that could be done, I thought, to convince the whites and make them do justice to the Indians and to understand me. I would try no more.

I returned the horses belonging to our ranch at Soda Springs, gave up without any consideration all my interest in the property there, bade Mountain Joe a final farewell, and returned, casting my lot wholly and entirely with the Indians.

As I crossed the little stream running through the Now-aw-wa valley, before reaching the Indian camp, I dismounted, and on a birch tree with my bowie knife I cut this word, "Rubicon."

I never saw Mountain Joe again. I never returned to the ranch, for fear of involving those there in whatever misfortune might overtake my enterprise. Dear old Mountain Joe! he had as warm a heart in him as ever beat in man, and was a kind, true friend. He wandered away up to the mines of Idaho, and there giving way to his old weakness for drink, became a common hanger-on about the saloons, and at last sunk down into a tippler's grave, after having faced death in every form in which it confronts the man of the border.

He had had his love affairs and adventures with the brown children of the Sierras, and the story was current that when he went away a little waif of humanity was left fatherless in the forest.

There were most stringent regulations and laws against selling the Indians of the border any ammunition for any purpose whatever. After the Pit River war these were enforced with a twofold vigilance.

This was particularly oppressive to the Indians. It was, in fact, saying to them, " Look here, you savages! We have superior means for taking your game. We will enter your forests when we choose. We will camp there in summer by the cool waters, and kill game at our pleasure with our superior arms, but you must only use the bow, and keep your distance from our camps. We will thin out and frighten away your game, so that it will be never so difficult for you to subsist; but you must not attempt to compete with us in the chase, even in your own forests, and in sight of your own wigwams."

The Indians felt all this bitterly. Month by month the game grew more scarce, shy, and difficult to take; the fish failed to come up from the sea, through the winding waters of the Sacramento, now made thick with mud by the miners, and starvation stared them in the face. They wanted, needed ammunition. They needed it to take game now, they wanted it to defend themselves; they were beginning to want it to go to war. Any man who attempted to furnish them with arms and ammunition was liable to the severest penalties, and likely to be shot down by any one who chose to do so, with impunity. I resolved to undertake to furnish them with arms and ammunition.

I visited the Indians in Pit River, and found that they were determined to fight rather than be taken to the Reservation, some hundreds of miles away. I knew this would involve them in war. I knew that this war would drive the Shastas into difficulties; for the whites make but little distinction between what they call tribes of wild Indians. Every Indian camp taken adds to the laurels of the officers of the campaigns; there is no one to tell to the world, or report to head-quarters, the other side, and they have it pretty much their own way in the invasion, unless checked by cold lead, which says, "Don't come this way, this is our ground, and we purpose to defend it."

I saw but two paths before me. One was to abandon the Indians, after all my plans and privations; the other was to make up such a brief and argument for our side of the case, when the threatened time came, as would convince the authorities that we were in earnest.

Early in the spring I left the mountains with a few Indians, partly warriors, partly women, and partly children, and made my way through the woods to the vicinity of Yreka, and there pitched camp in open view of town.

The women and children were taken along, in order to give to our camp the appearance of an ordinary party of vagrant, half-civilized Indians, which is always found moping about the border; and the camp was made in sight of the settlements, because it was unsafe to attempt concealment.

Any party of Indians found hidden away in the woods and hills too near the settlements, no matter how peaceful and well-disposed are its members, is at once suspected of some secret attempt to right their wrongs, and some fine morning they wake up to the tune of a volley of shot poured in from the four sides of their camp.

The plan was to buy arms and ammunition myself in small quantities, as I could, here and there, and now and then, without exciting suspicion; and also to send out the Indians to trade, and pick up as best they could the desired supplies, until we had procured as much as we could well carry in a hasty return to the mountains.

The enterprise was hazardous in the extreme. All

kind of caution was necessary. Ammunition was only to be had in small quantities, and arms only at second-hand. The stringent laws and customs compelled cunning, treachery, and deceit. We used all these. If there was any other course open, I failed, and still fail, to see it. We were preparing means to feed the half-starved children of the forest. We were preparing, if necessary, to defend homes that were older than the ancestral halls of earls or kings.

I went over to Deadwood, ten miles away, among my acquaintances, entered into many kinds of employment at different places, and procured most of the desired supplies. Indians carried them to the camp by night.

Soon we were ready to return. Horses were needed. I always kept my own horse and saddle, which was either with me or in some wood near by; but an Indian seen with a horse in the valleys then was liable to be shot down the first time he got out of sight of a house, and plundered. He would hazard about as much by the attempt to purchase a horse provided he exhibited the necessary purchase money.

The whites whenever in an Indian country helped themselves to game or anything else they needed without asking anyone. These few Indians were now in a white settlement and needed horses. It is a poor rule that will not work both ways. The test rule was to be applied.

Every year the whites were entering the Indians' forests, and destroying more game than the value of a whole herd of horses. They would only use the choicest and fattest, and carry away only the saddle of the venison. The Indians would deplore this waste. They would often, compelled by hunger, follow these sportsmen and hunters, and sullenly pick up what was left.

They had no horses now to carry them and the provisions and ammunition to the camp, nearly a hundred miles away.

They were equal to the emergency. A time was fixed for a sudden flight for the mountains with our supplies. The women and children were to come over on the hills overlooking Deadwood, and there remain with one warrior, doing what they could till our return. The purpose was to keep up this communication till the Indians were fully armed and equipped.

Whenever I felt my courage or resolution relax, I lifted my helpless arm, recalled my life of the last year, and then grew resolute and reckless, even to death.

Early one evening I rode into camp; there came an Indian on a spirited and prancing horse, looking, in his skins and long black hair, tossed about by the action of the restless and plunging horse, like a savage Gaul in the days of Cæsar. Then came another, and then another, till all were ready. They had taken their horses from different parts of the settlements, so as not to excite any suspicion of concert of action ; stolen them, if you prefer the expression, and under my direction.

Belts, saddle-bags, and catenas were loaded down with arms and ammunition. What a glorious wild ride up the Shasta valley in the moon, full against the grand old mountain. Here the strange, half-savage men about me exulted, threw back the black hair from their brows, and like giants striding in the air stretched their necks and leaned forward with eyes that were half aflame.

We met a party of miners going in a long string to the city. They stepped aside and stood so near the road as we passed that I could see their teeth as their mouths opened with wonder; but they did not lift a hand, and we were out of sight in an instant. Then we met the stage. The driver set his horses on their haunches, and heads popped out of the windows; but we were gone like a whirlwind.

We reached the wood by dawn, climbed the mountain, and made our way through rain and storm to a small camp on the head of the McCloud. The ammunition was taken into a lodge, and the delighted Indians busied themselves examining the arms. I cautioned them not to unpack the powder till dawn, but was too tired to do more, and lay down in another lodge by the fire and fell asleep.

A dull crash, a dreadful sound that has no name, and cannot be described, started me to my feet. Bark and poles and pieces of wood came raining on our roof; then there was not a sound, not even a whisper.

The poor Indians, so accustomed to arrange and

prepare their arms and such things by the camp fire, had forgotten my caution perhaps, for somehow the powder had, while the Indians were unpacking and arranging it in the lodge, ignited, and they, and all the fruits of our hard and reckless enterprise, were blown to nothing.

The Indians of the camp and the three surviving companions of my venture, were overcome. Their old superstition returned. They sat down with their backs to the dead bodies, hid their faces, and waited till the medicine-man came from the camp on the lake below.

About midnight the women began to wail for the dead from the hills. What a wail, and what a night! There is no sound so sad, so heartbroken and pitiful, as this long and sorrowful lamentation. Sometimes it is almost savage, it is loud, and fierce, and vehement, and your heart sinks, and you sympathize, and you think of your own dead, and you lament with them the common lot of man. Then your soul widens out, and you begin to go down with them to the shore of the dark water, to stand there, to be with them and of them, there in the great mysterious shadow of death, and to feel how much we are all alike, and how little difference there is in the destinies, the sorrows, and the sympathies of the children of men.

CHAPTER XXVI

 COULD not endure to remain in camp. I went down the river and rested there, and thought what I now should do. I began to recover strength and resolution. I said, if I was right at first I am still right. I resolved to return; but no Indian would venture to go back again, and I went alone. Leaving my horse on a ranch I entered Yreka, and took the stage to Deadwood. I at once went to the Indian camp, and told them of our loss. They, superstitious like the others, resolved to gather up their effects and supplies and return through the mountains to the McCloud.

After seeing my old white friends a few hours, I was told that Bill Hirst, the famous man-killer and desperado, with whom I had unfortunately previously become involved, had accused me of being with the Indians, and also taking, or having a hand in taking, his horse.

I cleaned and prepared my pistols for this man. At another time I might have been disposed to avoid this fellow. Now I wanted to meet him. It was not particularly for what he had said or done, but he had long been the terror of the camp; and with something of a spirit of chivalry and determination to revenge some wrongs of men less ready to fight, I quietly resolved to meet this man in mortal combat. Of course my own desperate condition contributed to make me reckless, and tenfold more ready to resent an insult. If I bore myself well in the scene that followed it was owing more to that, perhaps, than to manly valour.

As the men gathered into Deadwood camp, Hirst among the others, I entered the main saloon and called the boys to the bar in a long red and blue-shirted line. We took a drink, and then, after the fashion of the time, I drew a revolver, and declared myself chief of the town. This is the way a man proceeded in those days who had a wrong to avenge. If his enemy was in camp this was his signal to "heel" himself and come upon the ground. I passed from one saloon to another, making this same declaration until toward midnight. While standing with a knot of miners at the bar of Dean's billiard saloon, Hirst entered the far end of the establishment; a tall, splendid fellow, with his hat pushed far back from his brow, flashing eyes, and a pistol in his hand.

Not a sound was heard but the resolute tread of Hirst, as he advanced partly toward me and partly toward the billiard table, while the men at play quietly fell back and left the red and white balls dotting the green cloth.

Those around me sidled away right and left, and I stood alone. Hirst advanced to the table, darting his restless, keen eyes at me every second, and, standing against and leaning over the table, all the time watching me like a cat, he punched the billiard balls savagely with the muzzle of his pistol. He then drew back from the table, tossed his head, whistled something, and moved in my direction.

My hand was on my pistol. The hammer was raised and my finger touched the trigger; but Hirst, without advancing further or saying a word, quietly turned out at a side door, and I saw no more of him that night.

I had done nothing, said nothing, but answering to the rough code and etiquette of the camp, the victory was mine; for when a man enters a room where his antagonist is, it is his place to make the first demonstration. This Hirst did not openly do; still no doubt he had done enough to satisfy his ambition for that evening, and it was evident the end was not yet. It was also evident, brave and reckless as he was, that he sought rather to maintain his reputation for recklessness than to meet me as he had met so many others.

I went down the creek that night, after this event, with my white friends, the gentlemen who kept the library, and retired.

The next morning we took a walk about the mining claim, returned, sat down in the shadow of the cabin with a few friends who had gathered in, and were talking over the little event of the evening before, when Hirst and an officer came riding gaily down the road, followed by several other gentlemen on horseback, who were coming down to see the result of a second meeting.

The cabins stood on the opposite side of the stream from the road, and ditches had to be crossed by the horsemen to reach us. The officer and Hirst—both splendid horsemen as well as famous pistol-shots—leapt the ditches and came darting over; but the others, whoever they were, as they had an open view from where they stood, felt that they were quite near enough, and reined their horses.

The men I was then with, and with whom I had spent the night, were the most peaceful, noble, and gentlemanly fellows in the camp, and I had no wish to make their cabins the scene of a tragedy. I was equally unwilling to submit to Hirst in any form or manner, and hastily shaking hands with my friends as the men advanced up the hill, I made off up the mountain, perhaps fifty yards in advance of the horsemen, and on foot.

Pistols flourished in the air, the men started forward almost upon me, and it looked as if I was to be shot down and trampled under foot. The hill side was steep and rocky, and the mettlesome little Mexican horses refused to rush upon me across the steep and broken ground, but began to spin round like tops, and would not advance up the hill.

Some hard, iron-clad oaths, and then shot after shot. I turned, drew a pistol, and the battle commenced in earnest. The officer was unhorsed, and lay bleeding on the ground from a frightful wound, while Hirst, further down the hill, could only fire random shots over the head of his restless and plunging horse. It lasted but a few moments.

These men were both famous as pistol shots ; but they were not, here, equal to their reputation, and that was because they were shooting on a range they had never yet tried. They had only practised on the level ground or in a well-arranged gallery, and when it came to shooting up hill they were helpless ; and so it often happens with others. There are other men, again, who are dead pistol shots when allowed to draw deliberately and take aim slowly and fire at leisure ; but when compelled to use the pistol instantly in some imminent peril,—the only time they are ever really required to use it,— they are slow, awkward, and embarrassed.

Let us for a moment follow the fortunes of these two men before us : the one lying bleeding on the ground, and the other flying down and across the hill, firing, and trying to hold his spirited horse to the work.

CHAPTER XXVII

RADLEY the officer recovered so far, after nearly a year, as to be able to get about, and when the mines of the north were discovered, pushed out into that country.

I was there before him. I was engaged in transporting gold and letters for the miners in the mountains to and from the settlements, and doing a large and prosperous business.

I was in my express office in Wallawalla one day, when one of my friends entered with some agitation to tell me that Bradley was in town.

I reflected a moment, and then sent word that I should like to see him at my office. He soon came limping through the door and looking about for the man whom he had last met face to face in such bloody combat.

I stood behind the counter and he came forward. I gave him my hand, while with the left I held my little bulldog Derringer at full-cock in my pocket. He took my hand hastily, spoke kindly, and when I looked fairly in his face and saw the goodnature and pure manhood of the man, I let go my pistol, ashamed of my suspicion, and we went out through the town together.

He had my ugly bullet, which had been cut from his thigh, in his pocket, showed me the wound at his room, and we became sworn friends.

He opened business in Florence and flourished. Once he did me an infinite service. The country was full of robbers, and, strange to tell, many of these men were my acquaintances, and, in some cases, friends.

I always rode alone with as much gold as my horse could well carry, and that at the time was required, in the fierce opposition we were then running to Wells, Fargo and Co.'s Express, for I could not afford to employ men and horses to constitute a guard, even if I could have found men who could endure the long, hard rides I was compelled to make.

"Dave English and his party," said Bradley, "is going to rob you; one of his pigeons has told me this, and there is no doubt of its truth."

I knew English well. I wrote him a letter at once; told him I knew his plan in detail, that it was known to my friends, and that he would be held responsible. This singular man came boldly into my office, shook hands with me, and said I should not be touched.

English had five well-known followers: Scott, Peoples, Romain, and two others whose names I withhold because of their relatives, who are of most aristocratic and respectable standing in the Atlantic States.

I was not disturbed ; but shortly after this, English, Scott, and Peoples robbed some packers of a large amount of gold-dust on the highway, and were arrested.

At Lewiston the vigilantes broke into the temporary prison, improvised from a big log saloon then but partly built, overpowered the guard, and told the prisoners to prepare to die.

They were given ten minutes to invoke their Maker. At the end of that time, the only rope the vigilantes had was thrown over a beam, and they approached Scott, who was on his knees.

" No, no," cried English, " hang me first, and let him pray."

They left Scott, fastened the rope round the neck of English, and mounted him on a keg.

Then English turned to Scott, and said, " Scottie, pray for me a little, can't you ? Damned if I can pray !" Then he laughed a low, strange chuckle, and they kicked away the keg.

He hung till dead, and then the noose reached for another victim. Peoples died without a word, but when they came to Scott, he pleaded with all his might for his life, and offered large sums of gold, which he said he had buried, but finding them inexorable, he took off his necktie, strung his finger rings on it, and saying, "Send these to my wife," died as the others.

The other three of the band were arrested soon after for the murder of McGruder, and died by the civil law in the same reckless manner as their leader. All six lie together on the hill overlooking Lewiston, and the earthworks thrown up by Lewis and Clark in their expedition of 1802-3.

Bradley more than once winged his man ; made and lost several fortunes in the mountains, and is now in Arazona, one of my truest and best friends.

Hirst was a singular man. He used to say that if he got through a week without a fight it ruined his digestion.

I think his digestion did not suffer.

No one cared, so long as he fought with men who "came from the shoulder," or were on the "cut and shoot;" but he once fell upon an inoffensive man, nearly took his life, and so left camp at the suggestion of his friends (?) and drifted north.

It is but justice to this man to state that he really had lost a horse, taken by the Indians under my order for them to procure horses. Yet I had not even suspected this at the time of our encounter, or I could not have borne myself as I did.

Fate, to my dismay, threw us together at Cañon City, Oregon. I led the settlers and miners in a long and disastrous campaign against the Indians there, and Hirst was as brave and reckless there as elsewhere. Afterwards I began the practice of law, and my first client was a boy of fifteen, on trial for shooting with attempt to murder.

The court-house here was a saloon, and crowded to the utmost. A vigilance committee had been organized, and strange as it seems, Hirst was one of the leaders.

When my case had fairly opened, Hirst entered with a brace of pistols sticking loosely in his belt in front, and striding through the yielding crowd, came up and took position only a few feet from me, overlooking me, and looking straight into the face of the timid magistrate. Of course I could not remonstrate. I faltered through the case, but managed somehow to get the boy off with a nominal bail.

The energetic little rascal went into a neighbouring camp and with another boy stole some horses. They were followed by the sheriff, Maddock, and his deputy, Hart, and a desperate fight took place, in which the deputy and my client's companion were killed and Maddock left for dead.

My client was tried for life, but his youth saved his neck, and after five years in the Oregon state prison was pardoned out by the kind-hearted Governor, now Governor of Utah.

I last year saw my first client, a fine-looking young man, working gaily away at a country blacksmith's shop, on a roadside of the Willamette. May good angels keep my first client to his work!

Afterwards, Hirst appeared in the criminal court

as defendant, and I was employed as counsel. His crime was the trifling offence of snatching a curly-headed Jew from behind his counter by his curly hair, and then dragging him by his curly hair into the street.

My bold client was convicted, but the judgment was entered so awkwardly, that I had it set aside on review, and he escaped punishment.

Soon after this he married an amiable immigrant girl, and settled down as the most docile of men. But this was not to last.

One day he came to town in a perfect fury, pistol in hand, in search of the deputy sheriff Berry, who he claimed had offended his wife.

Berry was on the alert. About dusk the two men suddenly met face to face on turning a corner and the ball opened. Hirst was a very tall man, and always did things with a sort of flourish. Although quick as a trap whenever he drew his pistol, or raised it to fire, he always raised it in the air and fired as the muzzle descended.

There are two ways of firing a pistol in hand-to-hand combat, and only two. One is to fire as you raise, and the other is to raise and then fire as you fall. Every advantage, it seems to me, is with the former mode, particularly when time means everything. You can cock a pistol easier, it is true, by raising the muzzle and at the same time raising the hammer, but if strong in the thumb you should by all means cock as you draw, and fire the moment the muzzle is in range. Some men in the moment of danger go about with the pistol on cock. This is madness. At the critical instant you find yourself fumbling and feeling for the hammer which is already raised; besides, you are about as liable to shoot yourself as your enemy. There is still a worse practice than this, and that is in carrying the pistol in the belt on half-cock, where it is neither one thing nor the other. On half-cock, however, is the correct way to carry a little Derringer loose in your pocket, but never a Colt's.

Hirst raised his pistol, flourished it, let fall and fired, blowing Berry's hat to atoms, filling his face and eyes with powder, and carrying away a part of his scalp.

But he was too late. Berry cocked his revolver as he drew it, and fired the instant he got the muzzle in range.

Hirst was reaching across his breast with his left hand for his bowie knife, which hung at his right side, as Berry fired. The ball tore through the bones of the wrist that reached across his breast and entered the body squarely just below the breast bone.

Both men fell, but Berry was soon able to stand on his feet.

" Ah, boys, this is the last of old Hirst," the wounded man said, as they bore him to the surgeon's close at hand. He sent for his wife, gently and kindly bade his friends good-bye, and became insensible. I saw him just before midnight, and he scarcely breathed. They said he was dying, and preparations began to be made for the burial. I took the right hand in mine—that terrible right hand —so helpless now, so pale and thin and pulseless, kissed it gently—the kiss of forgiveness—in the dimly-lighted room, when no one observed me, and went home.

The next morning, however, Hirst was not dead. He lay as he lay through the night, and the surgeons said dissolution was only a question of time. The camp was in suspense. Was it possible that this man, who for ten years had been the terror of Oregon and northern California, could still live with a navy bullet through his body fired at two feet distance!

Another day, and the man opened his eyes and began to talk to his poor, patient little wife, who never left his side.

Hard as it may seem on the camp, I am bound to say it did not like this at all. The camp had thoroughly, and very cheerfully too, made up its mind that Hirst was a dead man, and it did not like to be disappointed.

Three days more and the surgeons announced the possibility of recovery. The camp was disgusted.

In less than forty days Hirst was walking about the claim with his arm in a sling, quietly giving directions to his labourers.

One day a man came rushing to town for the

surgeons. A little battle had been fought across the street of a little town down the creek, and half a dozen men were in need of help.

Women in the case again, and Hirst had led the fight.

His antagonists were men who claimed to be on the side of law and order. They were led by a man named Hank Rice, one of the County Commissioners, who afterwards testified that he fired at least fifty shots that day in his attempt to keep the peace.

Only able to use one arm, Hirst had, with his followers, converted the little town into a sort of miniature Paris, with barricades, fire-brands, and all the modern improvements. At last, when attempting to cross the street and drive his enemy from shelter, he received the contents of a double-barrelled shot-gun full in the breast and fell. This ended the fight.

Hirst still refused to die. He was therefore arrested on five different and very grave charges, and lodged in prison.

After he was able to be about an examination was had. I was his advocate. Bail was allowed after some delay, but it was fixed so high as to be almost beyond our reach. We tried " straw " bail, but the prosecuting attorney was too rigorous, and it was only by getting that officer out into the country to attend a case we had arranged for the occasion that we got our bail accepted.

Hirst left the country that night, his brave, faithful little wife soon followed, and I never met him

again.   After many and similar fortunes we find
him at Winemuca, on the line of the Pacific Railroad.
Here some one killed him, though only for a time,
by shooting him in the head with a Derringer.   He
recovered, but with the loss of one of his eyes and all
his ferocity, says report.

I have written of him in the past tense, because he
is said to now be a new man.   He was a year or so
ago—though the shifting fortunes of the country may
have left him by this time on other ground—a man of
wealth.

In all the experience of my life spent mostly
among the most lawless and reckless, I know of
no history so remarkable as his.   How he so con-
tinually escaped death will never cease to be a marvel
among the men of that country.   It must be remembered, however, that while he survived, perhaps a
thousand of his class perished.

Through all his stirring and bloody career, let this
be said, he was generous and open-hearted, kind to
most men, industrious, and certainly as brave as
Cæsar.

CHAPTER XXVIII

NTIRELY with my left hand had I made the fight, for my right one was still stiff and useless from the shot of the would-be assassin of the Pit River expedition. My friends and others were now running up the hill to the fallen officer, and Hirst was only now and then sending up in my direction a random shot as I turned my back on the scene, and pushed up the mountain into the forest. My Panama hat flapped and fluttered down on one side of my face like the wing of a wounded bird. A pistol ball had torn it to ribbons.

A bullet makes only a small hole in cloth, in buckskin a still smaller one; but it tears linen savagely, as well as straw. The hard, tough fibre of which Panama hats are made, particularly when rendered hard and brittle in a California sun, flies into shreds before it.

Most people imagine you can hear any bullet whistle that passes you. This is a mistake; you hear only the bullet that has first struck some object and then glanced on, catching the air, and whizzing like a bee at your ear, but almost quite as harmless. These you can hear distinctly a hundred yards away, and they sound very ugly; but a round, unmarred pistol ball can pass within six inches of your head and hardly be heard. You not only do not hear a ball strike your body, but you scarcely feel it at first, though you can hear it strike a man at your side; and the sound is dead, dull, suggestive and almost sickening.

I began to think I had escaped without a scratch; but after climbing up the hill till quite out of reach, and turning to look below, I raised my disabled right arm, and found my hand and fingers streaming with blood.

I was still strong and resolute; and, observing some men coming slowly up the hill with a show of pursuit, I hurried to the top of the hill, sat down there and examined my wound. A ball had torn across the back of the wrist and cut a vein or artery there, but done no further damage whatever.

I was wearing a linen shirt, for I always dressed as nearly like the white men as I could when amongst them, and from this I tore a strip and bound up the damaged wrist. But it still bled dreadfully, and I sat down often, as I retreated still further into the forest, and up and over the hills, and bound the wound as best I could, and tightened the bandages. The weather was intensely hot, and my blood was boiling from excitement and exertion. This made the blood stream the more profusely, and I suffered dreadfully from thirst.

I sat down at length on a log by the side of a thicket of chaparral to decide, if possible, what course to pursue, and was still tying up my wound and trying to stop the blood, with a pistol lying at my side, when I saw two men approaching on horseback.

My first impulse was to dash into the brush; but then I resolved to fight if must be, and run no farther. I took my pistol in my hand, cocked it, laid it across my lap, and sat still.

The men were strangers. They held up their hands in sign of friendship; but I was excited, weak, alone, almost helpless, and hence suspicious.

"Don't be afraid, little one," one of them called out; "we are friends, and only want to assist you."

I still said nothing, held my pistol ready, and did not move.

They talked together a moment, then one of them dismounted and came toward me, holding his pistol by the muzzle in his left hand.

"Here, take this pistol," were his first words, and he reached it out and sat down by my side. "You see we don't know much about you; you may be good or you may be bad, but we don't like to see too many on one, and we are come to help you get away."

These men proved to be miners; prominent, peaceful, and influential men.

They gave me another pistol, the best one of the two horses, and a trifle of money, and insisted that I should return to civilization.

I told them that that was impossible; that I could not abandon my Indians; besides, pursuit would run in that direction, and more blood would follow. I told them frankly that I should return to the Indians in the black forests of Mount Shasta; and they let me have my own way.

I mounted my horse, shook hands with them soon, and almost in silence. I could not speak. I was choking with a new emotion. Injury and insult, oppression, persecution, mental agony, and wrongs almost intolerable, had not roused me; but now I drew my battered hat down over my eyes and hid my face. The strong men turned their backs, as if embarrassed, looked down over the smoky camp, and I rode away in silence.

These two noble, manly-hearted men, heroes who never fought a battle, never had a quarrel, at last lie buried on the hills of Idaho. May the wild spring blossoms gather about them there; may the partridge whistle in the tall brown grass of autumn, plaintive and tenderly, and the snows of winter fall, soft and beautiful, above their peaceful breasts.

I turned a spur of the mountain, through the wood, till I came to an open space that looked down over my Indian camp, and dismounting, made a signal, such as is used by the Indians in war.

This is done by making a bunch of dry grass or

leaves into a little ball, lighting it and holding it up as it smokes and burns on the point of a stick; if you mean danger to your friends, and wish them to fly, you hold it up till it dies out, which takes some minutes. If danger to yourself, and you need assistance, you hold up the signal and let the smoke ascend, at short intervals. If you wish some one to approach you move it backwards. If you wish only to signal your own approach you move it forward, and so on through a long list of signs.

There is a great difference in the density and colour of the smoke made by different combustibles. You know, or at least all who read ought to know as much as an Indian about a thing so simple as this, that the smoke of dry straw or grass, particularly of the wild grass of California, is so much lighter than the atmosphere of even the rarest season, that it goes straight up—a long, thin, white thread, surging and veering toward heaven against the blue sky like the tail of a Chinese kite.

Another noble fellow found me here and gave me the hand of friendship; Frank Maddox, now a wealthy and influential citizen of Ummatilla, Oregon, where he has been for a succession of terms sheriff of the county.

It takes a brave man to step out from the world arrayed against you and stand by your side at such a time. Such deeds, rare as they are, make you believe in men; they make you better.

The Indian warrior at length came, stealing through

the brush and up the mountain. I told him what had happened, bade him return to his camp, and tell the women to pack up and push out through the mountains, with what arms and ammunition they had, for the McCloud. The faithful fellow went back, and before dusk returned to me with water, Indian bread and venison, and then back again to make his way with the women and children through the mountains to our home on the other side of Shasta. I never saw him again. In crossing the trail leading from the head of Shasta valley to Scott's valley they fell into the hands of some brutal rancheros who hung the Indian warrior, plundered the women and took some of the children to keep as herders, cooks, and for such other service as they might see fit to impose.

I stole down the mountain to the stage road, some miles to the east; and what a glorious ride! I was glad again, free, wild as the wind. All through that ride of fifty miles I lived a splendid song. I climbed the mountains at dawn, my horse, strong and nervous still, foaming and plunging like a flood.

That night I reached the Indian camp. Here was business,—blood. The women and children were mostly high up in the mountain, almost against the snow; but the warriors, with a few women that refused to leave them, were on the east of the McCloud, on the outskirts of their possessions. They had been assisting the Pit River Indians, and had invariably lost, until their force, weak, even at the opening of the spring, from starvation and disease and disaster, had become thinned and dispirited.

A council was held that night, and the few warriors, scared, wounded, and worn-out, talked themselves and their friends again into heart, and preparations were made to go still further, and assist the Pit Rivers against the white soldiers to their uttermost.

Little Klamat, now a man, and a man of authority, was already in the front. That fierce boy, burning with a memory that possessed him utterly, and made him silent, sullen, and desperate, cared not where he fought or for whom he fought, only so that he fought the common enemy. Paquita was also with the Pit River Indians. What was she doing? Moulding bullets? Grinding bread? Shaping arrow-heads and stringing bows? Maybe she was a sort of Puritan mother fighting the British for home and hearthstone in the Revolution. Maybe she was a Florence Nightingale nursing the British soldiers in the Crimea. No! the world will not believe it. No good deed can be done by an Indian. Why attempt to recount it?

We went down to the camp, where Klamat, Paquita, and about one hundred warriors, with a few women who were nursing their wounded, were preparing for another brush with the soldiery. Here we waited till the Modocs came down, and the three tribes joined their thinned forces, and made common cause.

In a few days we advanced, and fell in with a company of cavalry scouring the country for prisoners to take to the dreaded Reservation. Women gathering roots for their half-starved children, children whose parents had been slain, lost in the woods, and wandering they knew not whither, were about all they thus far could capture.

Shots were exchanged. The cavalry dismounted and fought on foot. The Indians shot wildly, for they were poorly armed; but the soldiers shot still more so, so that but little damage was done to either side. Now and then a soldier would be carried to the rear, and now and then they would charge up the hills or across the ravines, but that was all that marked the events of the day till almost nightfall. I was impatient of all this. We could not reach the rear of the soldiers, resting against the river, nor offend the flanks.

Toward nightfall the Indians, now almost entirely out of ammunition, withdrew, leaving the soldiers, as usual, masters of the ground.

I had taken no active part in the skirmish. I was there as an eager and curious witness. I wished to see how the Indians would bear themselves in battle. I felt that on their conduct that day depended the fate of my plans. From first to last it was not encouraging. They were brave enough, and some were even reckless; but I saw that dissension, impatience, envy, and ambition to be at the head, marked the conduct of many of the leading men. There was too much of the white man's nature here to make one confident of success in a long and bitter war. I had hoped their desperate situation had made them a unit with but one single object. I was disappointed.

For some time I had been the nominal war-chief of the Modocs, for since the Ben Wright massacre, where their great chief was killed, they had had no fit leader in battle, but policy dictated that in order to keep down jealousies, I should not at once push the Modocs too much to the front. The three tribes had never fought together before for many generations, though they had often fought against each other, and everything depended on unity and good-will. The results of the day were discouraging enough.

They retreated far up a cañon, plunging toward the river, and there in a great cave by a dim camp fire refreshed themselves on a few dried roots and venison; then after a long smoke in silence, the chief slowly rose and opened a council of war. Many speeches were made, but they mostly consisted in boasts of personal achievements. They talked themselves into sudden and high confidence, which I knew any little reverse would dispel. They were assured of success by signs, they said, and dreams, as well as by the events of the day. The spirits of their fathers had fought with them and for them.

I spoke last of all, and spoke in no encouraging spirit. I tried to tell them first how things stood, and how desperate and determined they must be before the great object—a recognition of our rights—

was reached. I told them that they had not won the fight at all; that the soldiers stood their ground, and now had possession of the field of battle.

An old Indian sitting back in a crevice of the rock called out, " Ah! what matters a few steps of ground when there is so much?"

I saw my little Republic going to pieces even before it had been fairly launched, and slept but little that night.

At midnight women were dispatched to the various camps, to give glowing accounts of the action, and also to bring provisions and whatever ammunition and arms could be had.

That night I proposed that I should cross the river with a few Indians, proceed to a temporary military camp near Hat Creek, state distinctly what the Indians desired, and try and get some recognition of their rights before they should be driven to the wall.

They would not at first consent to imperil any of their number in this way. They wanted me to go again and attempt once more to get a supply of arms and ammunition. They said that from the first I had promised this, and that now it was the only thing that would save them.

At last it was agreed that I should select four Indians, go at first to the military camp myself with the Indians a little in the background, so as to have some chance for their lives in case of treachery, and see what I could do; failing in my negotiations, I was to proceed to Shasta city at once, and endeavour to get arms and ammunition at all risks.

I chose two Modoc Indians and two Shastas—all young men, brave, resolute, and full of fire—and prepared to set out at once on my dangerous mission of peace.

The Indians had captured two stage-coaches carrying treasure and the United States mails, besides a small train with general supplies and a sum of gold and silver for the payment of soldiers, and had an abundance of money. They cared nothing for it, however. I have seen children laying little mosaic plots in the sand with silver and gold coins, which they valued only for their brightness and colour. But this now to me was of use. I took my men, with a good supply of money, crossed the river, pushed on through the woods to the stage-road, and there, after some delay, bought the best horses to be had, of several Mexican vaqueros making their way from Yreka to Red Bluffs. I also secured their sympathy and their friendship by liberal and generous dealing, and assurance of safety through the country.

These Mexicans, packers and vaqueros, ever since the war with Mexico and the conquest of California by the United States, have with reason held only ill-will toward the Americans. Speaking another tongue, adhering to another form of religion, the mass of white men have never yet come to forget the battle-fields of a quarter of a century ago.

I always found that I could approach these Mexican rovers, and obtain almost any favour I asked, most especially if it pointed to assistance of the Indians, and disadvantage to the whites.

We rode down to the military camp, and found the small force with the officers on parade. The Indians rode a few yards in the rear as I approached the officer of the day, dismounted and held my hat in one hand and lariat in the other. The officers exchanged glances, and I grew nervous.

CHAPTER XXIX

HE Indians stood behind, the two officers came towards me together, and
I told them hurriedly that the Indians
wanted peace if they could be left alone
about the base of Shasta, and that I had come from
them to say this.

My Indians, seeing me stand quietly and let the
officers approach, had dismounted, and stood watching
every movement, lariats in hand.

I began again excitedly, but the officer forgetting
himself, called out sharply to his corporal, and then
said to me,

"What! are you the ——"

I sprang into my saddle in an instant.

"*Tokadu! Kisa!*" I called to the Indians, and they
laid their hands on their Mexican horses' manes, and
sprang to their backs even as they ran, for these
horses sniff danger as quick as an Indian.

A volley of shots followed us and scattered bits of

bark across our faces from the pines as we disappeared in the forest, but did no further harm. My mission of peace was at an end. Bitterly indeed I deplored its blunt and rough conclusion. I had always hated war and despised warriors. Warriors are coarse-natured men trained to destroy what refined and gentle men build up.

Men fight for freedom of body. There is no such thing. For six thousand years men have struggled for a mistake. There is a freedom of mind, and a man can have that just as much in a monarchy as in a land even beyond the pale of law. A shoemaker or mender of nets may be as free of mind as a monarch. Give us freedom of mind, or rather let each man emancipate his mind, and all the rest will follow. It is not in the power of kings to enslave the mind, or of presidents to emancipate it. Free the mind and the body will free itself.

Poets, painters, historians, and artists generally, are responsible for the wars they deprecate, the devastation they deplore. Let the poet cease to celebrate men's achievements in battle, men, nine cases out of ten, who have not even the virtues of a bull-dog, men in debt, desperate, who have nothing to lose in the desolation they spread, and everything to gain, and wars will cease at once. Ridicule the warrior as we do the bully of the prize ring, as he deserves to be, and the pen will no longer be the servant of the sword. So long as the world goes on admiring these deeds of ruffianism, so long will wars continue. Let the historian enter into the heart, the private life of his hero; let him refuse to be dazzled by the dome of the temple, but enter in and see for himself, and let him give the world the cold, clean truth, the whole truth and nothing but the truth, as he is in duty and in honour bound, and we will find the hero of war is much the more a brute and much the less a man than the bully of the prize ring. The bully harms no one but his single antagonist; no cities are burned, no fields laid waste, no orphans made; and he risks much and makes but little, at the best. The warrior risks but little, for the chances of being hit are remote indeed. Any soldier who receives half the punishment the man of the ring must receive is sure of promotion and laudation to the skies. Say what you will, your soldier is a ruffian. The greater the ruffian the better the soldier.

Should a man not fight to defend his country? Should he not go around trained and equipped for battle, make a machine of himself in a military system, take all the time he should devote to some natural and pure pursuit, and devote it to the art of destroying cities and slaying men? No, there is not the slightest use or excuse for the soldier. Let all warriors remain at home and there will be no war. Let bullies be treated as they deserve and there will be no warriors.

If a set of men enter my fields in violation of my rights, injure my property and take away my corn, shall I not shoot them down? Shall I not arm my household, and proceed to their fields and destroy also? No, you answer, there is a law in the land to protect you, a higher authority to appeal to.

Well, I say to the nations, there is a God in the land. A higher authority. Appeal to Him.

But, you answer, there is no God: or what is much the same thing, you refuse to trust, to believe that nothing can wrong you so long as you do no wrong. Very well, even admit there is no God, and you will find there is a moral idea of right in the world to-day that will not let one nation long oppress another.

Beasts have gone back to the jungles. Theseus may sleep and Hercules put aside his club and surrender to love. Man is no more in danger from them.

Savage men have passed away. They come not down from the north nor up from the south; and even if they did, I believe they could be won to us by kindness and an appeal to their sense of right. But should that not be possible, I know their favour could be bought with a hundredth part of the time and money that is spent in a single war.

The loss of life in war is not much—it is the least of all things to be thought of. Men who fall in battle have mostly seen enough of life. Many have passed its prime, all have seen its spring, and they do not, on an average, lose more than ten or a dozen years. It is the bad moral effect. Towns grow up again; ships rebuild, and nations somehow drag through, and are going on in a little time the same as before. But only think how much time, how much talk, how much that is cruel must come out of the memory of a single war so long as any one lives to remember it. If in the great conflagration every book from Homer to the New Testament had been utterly swept away, the world had been another world. The poets, the painters, the historians, have this in their own hands. "Peace hath her victories no less renowned than war." If I were a great poet, rather than celebrate the deeds of battle, I would starve.

I now threw all my energy into the effort to keep faith with the Indians in the mountains.

I reached the Sacramento river and crossed at the ferry near Rock creek. I hid the Indians' camp in the willows near the mouth of that stream, and a few miles from Shasta city, while I took lodgings at a wayside hotel hard by, and began at once to purchase arms and ammunition, which I carried by night to the Indian camp in the willows.

I soon had a good supply, and was only waiting a fine moonlight night to push out, when it became evident one evening at my hotel that my movements were watched. I ordered my horse, left him standing at the rack, and went at the back of the house up the hill, and from a point whence I could not be seen from the hotel, signalled for one of my Indians. He came, and I hastily gave this order: "Pack up at once, three of you, swim your horses, cross the supplies in the Indian canoe, and push out for home up the Pit. One of you will come with me, for we must ride to Shasta city for pistols there, and will then overtake you before dawn."

The Indian and I rode leisurely to Shasta city, waiting for darkness. As I neared town I saw two men cross a ridge behind us, halt, and then, when they thought they were unobserved, push hard after us.

I left the Indian on the hill north of town by the graveyard, and went down to the gunsmith's, where I had some half-dozen revolvers being repaired. I hitched my horse at the rack and went in. The two men rode into town, rode past my horse, eyeing him closely sideways from under their cavalry hats, and I then knew that I had been followed from the mountains, and had something more now than the settlers to deal with. In a few minutes I saw these men watching me from the door of the shop across the narrow street.

It was now nearly dark, but I asked the gunsmith to let me take a brace of the pistols, and go out the back way and fire them into the hill. I buckled the pistols about me over my others, he opened the door, I paid him liberally, and went out, promising soon to return.

I did not discharge a shot, but hurried down a back alley to a barber's shop and had my long and luxuriant hair cut close to the scalp. I then bought a black suit of clothes and new hat at an adjoining Jew's shop, dressed in a back room, ordering the Jew to keep my cast-off clothes carefully till I returned, and then went boldly into the street. My own brother would not have known me.

I walked leisurely along, looking carefully at the hundreds of horses hitched at the racks. At length I found one that looked equal to a long and reckless ride, unhitched him, mounted and rode up past my own horse and out of town unchallenged, to my patient Indian on the hill by the graveyard.

We divided the pistols and struck out up the stage road for the bridge on the Sacramento. We reached the end of the bridge in safety, and I hastily handed the keeper his toll. He took the piece of silver, pronounced it a bad coin, returned it and demanded another; all the time talking and causing delay. I now handed him a piece of gold, and he professed to be unable to give change. Delay was what he desired. We left him and galloped across the bridge. We did not see the bar at the further end, and while the Indian's horse by some good fortune cleared it, mine struck it with all his force and fell over it, throwing me over his head, and bruising me fearfully. I got on his back again, but was bleeding from my mouth from internal injuries, and could scarcely keep my seat. I had lost one of my pistols in the fall. There was now a sound of horses' feet in the rear, men calling in the dark, and horsemen thundering across the bridge. At this point some men came riding down the narrow road, with its precipitous bluff on one side and perpendicular wall on the other, and called out to us to stop.

We set spurs to our horses, and dashed up the hill right into their faces. They did not fire a shot as we approached, but halted, let us pass, and then, as if recovering their senses, sent several random shots after us. An innocent good-night.

I had my pistol in my hand; and as I could hear but imperfectly, and was otherwise suffering fearfully, I hardly knew what I was doing. I fancied I heard our pursuers upon us, and attempting to wheel and fire, I accidentally discharged my pistol into the shoulder of my own horse as we turned the top of the hill.

The poor beast could only spin around on three legs now, and as we could not get him to follow the road farther, the Indian led him off to a thicket of chaparral, left him, and we hastened on.

I now rode the remaining horse, and the Indian ran along the dusty walk at my side. We reached a little mining camp called Churn Town,—a camp which I had visited often before,—and there finding a number of horses tied to a rack, we determined to procure another, since it would be impossible to overtake our companions half mounted as we were.

The Indian took some money, and went through the town, in hope of meeting some Mexican with whom he could deal, and I went down to the saloon to see what I could do in the same direction. I found a large number of miners and settlers engaged in a political meeting. A popular lawyer was making a great speech on Popular Sovereignty.

I stood in the doorway a little while, noting the strange proceedings of the strange men in the strange land, till I saw my Indian leading a horse triumphantly out of town, then turned, mounted the other horse, and followed at a good pace. I continued to suffer and grow weak. It was evident I could not keep my saddle for the long hard ride, now necessary from our delay, to overtake our friends.

It was finally decided that when we struck the stage road I should attempt to make the Indian camp at the foot of the high backbone mountains of the McCloud, about twenty-five miles distant, and there remain till recovered, while the Indian pushed on. When we came to separate, the kind-hearted Indian gave me the fresher and stronger horse, mounted his own tired and bruised mustang, and rode away in the dark and dust at a gallop.

What a night I had of it! It grew chill towards morning, and I could not straighten myself in my saddle. Night birds screamed wickedly in my ears, and it seemed to me that I had almost finished my last desperate ride in the mountains.

At dawn, after slowly threading a narrow bushy trail, around mountains and over gorges, I came down to the deep and dark blue river.

An Indian set me across in a wretched old boat, and I took my course across the mountains for the McCloud. There were some few miners here, and sometimes I would meet half-tame Indians, and then half-wild white men.

At dusk I dismounted at the Indian camp, more dead than alive, and turned the horse out on the luxuriant grass of the narrow valley ; for here the trail ended, and I could use him no further.

I did not like the look of things here altogether. The Indians mixed too much with the whites. They were neither one thing nor the other. I was compelled to spend the night here, however, but determined to go on over the high mountain the following day, on foot, to *Hubet Klabul*, or " Place of Yellow Jackets," where I knew more noble Indians than these would receive me.

I rose in great pain next morning, and went down to the brook to bathe my head. While leaning over the water, my pistol slid from the scabbard into the stream, and was made useless till it could be taken to pieces and cleaned. I went back, laid down, and was waiting for an Indian woman to prepare me some breakfast, when I saw two suspicious-looking, half-tame Indians coming down the hill ; then three suspicious-looking white men, with the muzzles of their rifles levelled at my head, and I was a prisoner.

My faithful Indian companion of the night before had almost cost me my life by his kindness. We had taken the saddle-horse of an honest settler, then a judge of the Court of Sessions. Some strange hand had led me by his very door the day before, and I had been followed in my slow and painful flight.

They took my arms, tied me, and talked very

savagely. I said in a low tone to one of the men who stood close at my side, "Please don't hang me, but shoot me. That will be better for us all." Maybe it was my boyish face, maybe it was some secret chord in his heart that only my helplessness could touch; I do not know what it was, but he looked at me with a gentleness that I could not mistake, and I knew at once that I had at least one friend among my captors.

I soon found that they had no connection with the soldiers, and that they had no suspicion as to who I was. This was a great relief, and by the time we began to return I began to see a possibility of escape. Soon we came to a little mountain stream. I was feverish and thirsty, and asked for a drink of water. One of the men filled a cup and raised it to my lips. I could not take hold of it, for I was bound like a felon on his way to the gallows. I did not touch the water, but turned away my head, and in spite of all my efforts I broke down utterly and burst into tears.

The men looked the other way for awhile, and then after some consultation they told me if I would promise not to attempt to escape they would unloose my arms. I had never been bound before. To have the spirit of an eagle, and then be fettered like a felon! That is crucifixion. After two days we reached Shasta city. I could have escaped on the way. I could have dashed down one of the hundred steep and bushy mountain-sides from the trail and laughed at the shots that would have followed ; could have escaped in spite of my wounds and wasted strength, but I had made a solemn promise to men who were humane and honourable, and I was bound to keep it. I kept my promise, and I kept it at a fearful cost, and I knew the cost at the time. At every rugged and bushy pass on the way to prison I fought a battle with myself against a reckless and impulsive spirit that almost lifted me out of the trail, and almost forced me to dash down the mountain through the chaparral in spite of my resolution and promise.

CHAPTER XXX

ET us pass hurriedly over those dreadful events; but remember I kept my promise like a man. There are a thousand things you will condemn and denounce, but if you endure what I endured to keep faith with your captors, I for one will pronounce you not wholly bad, whatever you may do.

I was surrendered to the sheriff and taken before a judge. I feared an investigation, lest something might be revealed which would connect the pale-faced boy in black with the long-haired renegade living with the Indians, and thus throw me into the hands of the military, which I had just escaped.

The Prince was in Nicaragua battling for the establishment of an order of things even more impossible than my Indian Republic, and I had not a friend with whom I dared communicate. I pleaded not guilty, declined an examination, and was taken to prison. And what a prison! A box, ten feet by ten; a little window with iron grates looking to the east over the top of another structure that clung to the steep hill-side on which the rude and horrible prison was built. A mattress on the floor; filth and vermin everywhere; not a chair, not a drop of water half the time ; not a breath of air. The food was cold refuse of some low chop-house. You could sometimes see teeth-marks in the soggy biscuits. Some sovereign, no doubt, had a contract for feeding the prisoners, and was doing well.

Low-bred and half-read lawyers beset me. They would tell the jailer I had sent for them, and thus gain admittance. Somehow they thought I had or could obtain money. They were coarse, insolent, and persistent in their efforts to get into the secrets of my life. At last, when they got what jewelry and few available gold pieces I had, and could not get my secrets, I saw them no more. If the treatment I received at the hands of these wretches is a fair example, then here is a wrong that should be corrected, for a prisoner, let him be never so guilty, has more to fear from these fellows than from his judges.

Many people visited me, but they could not remain long in the wretched pen; and as I would never speak to them, I had but little sympathy. Sometimes for a while I was out of my mind. At such times I would write strange, wild songs, in the Indian tongue, all over the walls.

At length the kind young man mentioned at my capture came with a young lawyer named Holbrook. This young lawyer was a gentleman, kind-hearted and intelligent. After a few visits I told him my story with perfect confidence. I do not think he believed it altogether, for he now insisted on putting in a plea of insanity. I scorned to do this, and grew indignant as he persisted. He never betrayed a word of my history, however, and went on, honestly, no doubt, making up his case to prove his client insane.

Brave, noble Holbrook! he was doing, or thought he was doing, all in his power to serve his client. This man became a brilliant lawyer, a leading spirit in Idaho, and twice represented the Territory in Congress with distinction. He was killed in the prime of manhood in a hand-to-hand encounter—a sort of duel.

One night, as I lay half-awake in the steaming little den, I heard the call of the *cakea*, or night bird, on the steep hill-side above the prison. It stopped, came nearer, called again, called three times, retreated, called thrice, came again nearer, and called as at first. I sprang to the window and answered through the bars, till I heard the jailer turn in his bed, where he lay in a large room into which my cell opened, and then I was silent. But ah, how glad! All night I paced eagerly around the room, trying to strengthen my legs, and throwing out my arms to harden them for action. I knew my friends the red men had followed and found me. Here was something to be done. I forgot about my lawyers, refused my food no longer, and filled my head with plans.

The next day I waited for night, and it seemed the sun would never go down. Then I waited for midnight; and at last when it came, and no call from the hill, I began to despair. I could hardly repress my anxiety; my heart beat and beat at every breath, as if it would burst. After all, I said to myself, I am really insane.

I lay down with my face to the low window, looking out to the dim, grey dawn breaking and flushing like a great surf over the white wall of the sierras to the east.

Maybe I slept an instant, for there, when I looked intently, sat Paquita on the roof of the lower building, peering through the rusty bars right into my face.

I had learned the virtue, if not the dignity, of silence, and arose instantly and stole up to the bars.

The poor girl tried, the first thing, to pass me a pistol through the bars, as if that could have been of any use to me there; but it could not be passed between. Then she passed through a thin sheath knife, but never said a word.

She made signs for me to cut away the bars with the knife, that she would come and help me, motioned to the grey surf breaking against the sky in the east, and disappeared.

I hugged that knife to my heart as if it had been a bride come home. I danced mercilessly and Indian-like about my cell, and flourished the knife above my

head. I was now not so helpless. I was not alone.
This knife was more to me than all the lawyers.

I will kill that dreadful jailer with this knife some
night when he comes in with my supper, I said, pass
out, slip into town, mount a horse and escape to the
mountains. I lay down at last, hid the knife in my
bosom, and hugged it till I fell asleep.

Paquita came early the next night. Indians are
too cunning to come twice at the same hour.

I had done nothing all day. This time she spoke
and told me that the bars must be filed and cut
away, that this was now the only hope, since all
other attempts of hers had failed. An Indian warrior was waiting, she said, with horses out of town;
only get the bars away and we could almost step
from the house-top to the steep hill-side, and then all
would be well.

She had hacked two thin knives together, making
a kind of saw, and we set to work. The bars were
an inch in diameter, but made of soft iron, and the
knife-blades laid hold like vipers.

At dawn she filled up the little gashes we had cut
across the bars with a substance she had prepared
just the colour of the rusty bars, and again disappeared.

For more than a week we kept at this work. No
one passed on the brushy hill-side or dwelt there, and
we were never disturbed. At last three bars were
loosened, and on Saturday night, when, as was then
the custom, the men of the city, officers and all,

would be more or less in their glasses, our time was set for the escape.

She came about midnight, the true and faithful little savage, the heroine, the red star of my dreadful life, crouching on the roof, and laid hold of the bars one by one, and bent them till I could pass my head and shoulders. Then she drew me through, almost carried me in her arms, and in another moment we touched the steep but solid earth.

She hurried me up the hill-side to the edge of a thicket of chaparral. I could go no further. I fell upon my knees and clasped my hands. I bent down my face and kissed and kissed the earth as you would kiss a sister you had not seen for years. I arose and clasped the bushes in my arms, and stripped the fragrant myrtle-leaves by handfuls. I kissed my hands to the moon, the stars, and began to shout and leap like a child. She laid her hand on my mouth, and almost angrily seized me by the arm. I turned and I kissed her, or rather only the presence and touch of her. I lifted her fingers to my lips, her robe, her hair, as she led me over the hill, around and down to a trail. There, in answer to the night-bird call, an Indian, a brave, reckless fellow, who had been with me in many a bold adventure, led three horses from a thicket.

The tide was coming in again. The great grey surf was breaking over the wall of the Sierras in the east. They lifted me to my saddle, for I was as weak as a child. We turned our steeds' heads, we plunged away in the swift, sweet morning air, and as we climbed a hill and left the town behind, I looked across my shoulder, and threw a bitter curse and threat . . . .

But the prison only was burned. The town, Shasta city, stands almost a ruin. The great men who made it great in early days have gone away. Chinamen and negroes possess the once crowded streets, bats flit in and out through broken panes, and birds build nests in houses that are falling to decay. The city of twenty years ago looks as though it had felt the touch of centuries.

How grandly the eternal old snow peak lifted his front before us! How gloriously the sunlight rolled and flashed about his brow before its rays got down into the pines that lay along our road.

We plunged into the Sacramento river at full speed, and swam to the other side.

When you swim a river with a horse, you must not touch the rein; that may draw his nose into the water, and drown you both. You drop the rein, clutch the mane, and float free of his back, even using your own limbs, if strong enough, to aid your horse in the passage. You wind a sash tightly about your head or hat, and thrust your pistols in the folds. Keep your head above water, and you are ready to fight the moment you touch land on the other side.

As the first rays of the sun shot across the mighty ramparts to the east, we climbed the rocky bluff and set our course through the open oaks for a crossing on Pit River, not far from the military camp spoken of before. We hoped to reach it and cross at dark, and rode like furies. Where did the Indian get these horses?

The escape so far was a success. At first I had had no hope. The idea of cutting away iron bars with knives seemed a delusive dream. But Indian patience can achieve incredible things. At first the knives would pinch and bite in the little grooves, for the back was of course thicker than the edge. But Paquita was equal to all that. By day she would grind the knives on the rocks, while hiding away in the bushes, till they were thin as wafers. A watch-spring is a common instrument used to cut away bars or rivets. The fine steel lays hold of the iron like teeth. Mexican revolutionists, liable at any time to imprisonment, sometimes have their watch-springs prepared especially for such an emergency; and I have known common cut-throats on the border to have a watch-spring around the arm under the folds of a garment. Prison-breaking in the Old World, owing to the massive and substantial structures, is almost a lost art. "But few escapes are made now," said a Newgate prisoner to me, "and those are mostly by strategy, like that of the illustrious prisoner of Ham."

It was nearly dusk when we touched the bank of the river, up which we must ride a mile or so before we came to the crossing.

Our horses fairly staggered under us, but we kept on, full of hope, and certain of security.

We descended the hill that sloped to the crossing, winding our scarfs about our heads, and preparing for the passage, which, once accomplished, would make our rest secure.

Suddenly, from a clump of low fir-trees, an officer with a platoon of soldiers stepped out, with rifles to their faces, and called to us to surrender.

The soldiers were there concealed, waiting for Indians that might attempt to cross at this favourite pass, and we were upon them before we suspected an enemy within miles of us.

They were almost between us and the deep cut leading to the river that had been made by animals and Indians from time immemorial, and we could not reach it. To attempt to ascend the hill, up the trail, on our tired horses, had been certain death.

The officer called again. The Indian drew his pistol, called to us to leap our horses down the bank into the river, and as we did so, fired in the face of the officer. Then, with a yell of defiance, he followed us over the precipice into the boiling, surging river, cold and swollen from the melting snows of Mount Shasta.

It was a fearful leap; not far, but sudden and ugly, with everything on earth against us. My horse and myself went far down in the blue, cold river, but he rose bravely, and struck out fairly for the other side.

But poor Paquita and her brave companion were not so fortunate. The river ran in an eddy, and their weak and bewildered horses were spun around like burrs in a whirlpool. The soldiers had discharged a volley as we disappeared, but I think none of us were touched from this first fire. My horse swam very slow, and dropped far down the current. The soldiers came up, stood on the bank, deliberately loaded, aimed their pieces, and fired every shot of the platoon at me, but only touched my horse. They had not yet discovered Paquita and her companion struggling in the eddy, almost under their feet, else neither of them had ever left it. Now, they got their horses turned and struck out, diving and holding on to the mane.

They were not forty feet from the soldiers when discovered. The guns were dropped, pistols were drawn, and a hundred shots, and still another hundred, rained down upon and around those two brave children, but they gave no answer.

I was down the stream out of reach, and nearing the shore. I witnessed the dreadful struggle for life, looking back, clinging to my almost helpless horse's mane.

They would dive, then the black heads and shiny shoulders would reappear, a volley of shot, down again till almost stifled; up, again a volley, and shouts and laughter from the shore.

It seemed they would never get away from out the rain of lead. Slowly, oh! how slowly, their weary, wounded horses struggled on against the cold, blue flood that boiled and swept about them.

At last my spent horse touched a reach of sand far below, that made a shoal from shore, and I again looked back. I saw but one figure now. The brave and fearless warrior had gone down pierced by a dozen balls.

My horse refused to go further, but stood bleeding and trembling in the water up to his breast, and I managed to make land alone. I crept up the bank, clutching the long wiry grass and water-plants. I drew myself up and sat down on the rocks still warm from the vanished sunshine.

When I had strength to rise, I went up the warm grassy river-bank, peering through the tules in an almost hopeless search for my companions. Nothing was to be seen. The troops on the other bank had gone away, not knowing, perhaps not caring, what they had done. The deep, blue river gave no sign of the tragedy now. All was as still as the tomb. I stole close and slowly along the bank. I felt a desolation that was new and dreadful in its awful solemnity. The bluff of the river hung in basaltic columns a thousand feet above my head; only a narrow little strip of grass, and tules, and reeds and willows, nodding, dipping, dripping, in the swift, strong river. Not a bird flew over, not a cricket called from out the long grass. " Ah, what an ending is this!" I said, and sat down in despair. My eyes were riveted on the river. Up and down on the other side, everywhere I scanned with Indian eyes for even a sign of life, for friend or foe. Nothing but the bubble and gurgle of the waters, the nodding, dipping, dripping of the reeds, the willows, and the tules.

If earth has any place more solemn, more solitary, more awful than the banks of a strong, deep river rushing, at nightfall, through a mountain forest, where even the birds have forgotten to sing, or the katydid to call from the grass, I know not where it is.

I stole further up the bank; and there, almost at my feet, a little face was lifted as if rising from the water into mine.

Blood was flowing from her mouth, and she could not speak. Her naked arms were reached out and holding on to the grassy bank, but she could not draw her body from the water. I put my arms about her, and, with a sudden and singular strength, lifted her up and back to some warm, dry rocks, and there sat down with the dying girl in my arms.

She was bleeding from many wounds. Her whole body seemed to be covered with blood as I drew her from the water. Blood spreads with water over a warm body in streams and seams; and at such a time a body seems to be covered with a sheet of crimson.

Paquita?

I entreated her to speak. I called to her, but she could not answer. The desolation and solitude was now only the more dreadful. My voice came back in strange echoes from the basalt bluffs, and that was all the answer I ever had.

The Indian girl lay dead in my arms. Blood on my hands, blood on my clothes, and blood on the grass and stones.

The lonely July night was soft and sultry. The great white moon rose up and rolled along the heavens, and sifted through the boughs that lifted above and reached from the hanging cliff, and fell in lines and spangles across the face and form of my dead.

Paquita!

Once so alone in the awful presence of death, I became terrified. My heart and soul were strung to such a tension, it became intolerable. I would have started up and fled. But where could I have fled, even had I had the strength to fly? I bent my head, and tried to hide my face.

Paquita dead!

Our lives had first run together in currents of blood on the snow, in persecution, ruin, and destruction; in the shadows and in the desolation of death; and so now they separated for ever.

Paquita dead!

We had starved together; stood by the sounding cataracts, threaded the forests, roamed by the river-banks together; grown from childhood, as it were, together. But now she had gone away, crossed the dark and mystic river alone, and left me to make the rest of the journey with strangers and without a friend.

Paquita!

Why, we had watched the great sun land, like some mighty navigator sailing the blue seas of heaven, on the flashing summit of Shasta; had seen him come with lifted sword and shield, and take possession of the continent of darkness; had watched him in the twilight marshal his forces there for the last great struggle with the shadows, creeping like evil spirits through the woods, and, like the red man, make a last grand battle there for his old dominions. We had seen him fall and die at last with all the snow-peak crimsoned in his blood.

No more now. Paquita, the child of nature, the sunbeam of the forest, the star that had seen so little of light, lay wrapped in darkness. Paquita lay cold and lifeless in my arms.

That night my life widened and widened away till it touched and took in the shores of death.

CHAPTER XXXI

ENDERLY at last I laid her down, and moved about. Glad of something to do, I gathered fallen branches, decayed wood, and dry, dead reeds, and built a ready pyre.

I struck flints together, made a fire, and when the surf of light again broke in across the eastern wall, I lifted her up, laid her tenderly on the pile, composed her face and laid her little hands across her breast. I lighted the grass and tules. So the fire took hold and leaped and laughed, and crackled, and reached, as if to salute the solemn boughs that bent and waved from the cliffs above, as bending and looking into a grave. I gathered white stones and laid a circle around the embers. How rank and tall the grass is growing above her ashes now! The stones have settled and settled till almost sunk in the earth, but this girl is not forgotten. This is the monument I raise above her ashes and her faithful life.

I have written this that she shall be remembered, and properly this narrative should here have an end.

The " Tale of the Tall Alcalde," which men assert on their own authority to be a true story of my life here and her death, was written for her. I could not then make it literally true, because the events were too new in my mind. It had been like opening wounds not yet half healed. I was then a judge in the northern part of Oregon. I had, with one law book and two six-shooters, administered justice successfully for four years, and was then an aspirant for a seat on the Supreme Bench of the State. Men who had some vague knowledge of my life with the Indians were seeking to get at the secrets of it and accomplish my destruction. I wrote that poem, and took upon myself all the contumely, real or fancied, that could follow such an admission.

At sunrise I began to make my way slowly up the river, towards the Indian camp, which I knew was not more than a day's journey away. I ate berries and roots as I could find them in my way, and at night I entered the village and sat down by the door of a lodge.

An old woman brought me water, but she could not restrain her eagerness to know of my companions, and at once broke the accustomed silence.

" Uti Paquita? Uti Olale?"

I pointed my thumbs to the earth.

She threw up her arms and turned away. The camp was a camp of mourning, for nothing but defeat and disaster had followed them all the summer. Still they would mourn for Paquita and the brave young warrior, and they went up to the hill-top among the pines and filled the woods with lamentations.

Let us hasten to the conclusion of these unhappy days. I rested a little while, then took part in a skirmish, captured a few cavalry horses, and two prisoners, whose lives I managed to save at the risk of my own, for the Indians were now made desperate. The Indians were now doing what little fighting was done, entirely with arrows.

The Modoc Indians had exhausted all their arrows and were returning home. A general despondency was upon the Indians. No supplies whatever for the approaching winter had been secured. The Indians had been kept back from the fisheries on the rivers and the hunting grounds in the valleys. The Indian men had been losing time in war and the Indian women in making arrows and nursing the wounded. Even in the plentiful season of early autumn a famine was looking them in the face.

No gentleness marked our actions now; I did not restrain my Indians in any ruthless thing they undertook.

I made a hurried ride through the Modoc plains around Tula lake and saw there but little hope of continuing a successful struggle as it was then being conducted. Lieutenant Crook, now the General Crook famous in American history, had established a military post on the head-lakes of Pit river. This was in the heart of the Indian country, and almost on the spot where the three corners of the lands of the three tribes met, and he could from this point reach the principal valleys and the great eastern plains of the Indians with but little trouble.

A new and most desperate undertaking now entered my mind. It was impossible to dislodge the military from the Indian country as things then stood. I resolved to " carry the war into Africa."

I laid my plan before the Modocs, and they, poor devils, made desperate with the long and wasting struggle, were mad with delight.

It was resolved to gather the Indian forces together, send the women and children into the caves to hide and subsist as best they could, leave our own homes, and then boldly descend upon the white settlements. This we were certain would draw the enemy, for a time at least, from our country.

I never witnessed such enthusiasm. These battle-scarred, worn-out, ragged, half-starved Indians arose under the thought of the enterprise as if touched by inspiration.

I was to go down to Yreka, note the approaches to town, the probable strength of the place, the proper time to attack, while they gathered their forces together for the campaign and disposed of the women and children.

The attack was to be made on the city itself.

There we were to strike the first blow. The plan was to move the whole available Indian force to the edge of the settlement and there leave the main body. Then I was to take the flower of the force, mounted on the swiftest horses, and, descending upon the town suddenly, attack, sack, and burn it to the ground.

We had had many a lesson in this mode of warfare from the whites and knew perfectly well how the work was to be done.

I mounted a strong, fleet horse and set out. On reaching the mountain's rim overlooking the valley I was struck by the peaceful scene below me. All the fertile plain was dotted yellow, and brown, and green from fields of grain. It looked like some great map. Peace and plenty all the way across the valley to the city lying on the other side, and thirty miles ahead.

At dusk I came to a quiet farm-house and asked for hospitality.

The old settler came bustling out bare-headed and in his shirt-sleeves, as if he was coming to welcome a son.

He took care of my horse, hurried me into the house, hurried his good wife about the kitchen, and I soon was seated at the table of a Christian eating a Christian meal.

It was the first for a long, long time; I fell to thinking as of old, and held down my head.

After supper the old man sat and talked of his

cattle and his crops and the two children climbed about my knees.

No sign of war here. Not a hundred miles away a people all summer had been battling for their firesides, for existence, and yet it had been hardly felt in the settlements. Such is the effect of the quiet, steady, eternal warfare on the border. It is never felt, never hardly heard of, till the Indians become the aggressors.

The old lady came at last and sat down with her knitting and a ball of yarn in her lap. She talked of the price of butter and eggs, and said they should soon be well-to-do and prosperous in their new home.

I retired early, and rising with the dawn, left a gold coin on the table, and rode rapidly toward the city.

I was not satisfied with my desperate and bloody undertaking. As I passed little farm-houses with vines and blossoms and children about the doors, I began to wonder how many kind and honest people were to be ruined in my descent upon the settlements.

The city I found assailable from every side. There was not a soldier within ten miles. Fifty men could ride into the place, hold it long enough to fire it in a hundred places, and then ride out unhindered.

It seems a little strange that I met kindness and civility now when I did not want it. Of course I was utterly unknown, and having taken care from the first to dress in the plainest and commonest dress of the time, there was not the least suspicion of my name or mission.

As I rode back, the farmers were gathering in their grain. On the low marshy plains of Shasta river they were mowing and making hay. I heard the mowers whetting their scythes and the clear ringing melody came to me full of memories and stories of my childhood. I passed close to some of these broad-shouldered merry men, as they sat on the grass at lunch, and they called to me kindly to stop and rest and share their meal. It was like merry hay-making of the Old World. All peace, merriment and prosperity here; out yonder, burning camps, starving children, and mourning mothers; and only a hundred miles away.

I did not again enter a house or partake of hospitality. I slept on the wild grass that night, and in another day rode into the camp where the Indians had gathered in such force as they could to await my action.

A council was called, and I told them all. I told them it was possible to take the city, that my plan was feasible, and yet I could not lead them where women and children and old men and honest labourers would be ruined, and perish alike with the arrogant and cruel destroyers. An old man answered me; his women, his children, his old father, his lodges, his horses had all been swept away; it was now time to die.

Never have I been placed in so critical a position, never have I been so crucified between two plans of life. But I had said when I climbed the mountain and looked back on the green and yellow crops below, that I would not lead my allies there, come what might, and I doggedly kept my promise through all the stormy council of that long and unhappy night.

Time has shown that I was wrong; I should have taken that city and held on, and kept up an aggressive warfare till the Government came to terms, and recognized the rights of this people.

I rode south with my warriors, and we gathered in diminished force on a plateau not far from Pit River, and prepared to make another fight.

If there is a race of men that has the gift of prophecy or prescience I think it is the Indian. It may be a keen instinct sharpened by meditation that makes them foretell many things with such precision; but I have seen some things that looked much like the fulfilment of prophecies. They believe in the gift of prophecy thoroughly and are never without their seers. Besides the warriors are constantly foretelling their own fate. A distinguished warrior rarely goes into battle without telling what he will do, whom he will encounter, who will be killed, and how the battle will be determined. They often foretell their own deaths with a singular accuracy. They believe in signs of all kinds: signs in the heavens, signs in the woods, on the waters, anywhere; and a chief will sometimes suddenly, in the midst of battle, call off his warriors even when about to reap a victory, should a sign inauspicious appear.

Klamat, shadowy, mysterious, dark-browed little Klamat, now a tall and sinewy warrior, was strangely thoughtful all this time. He went about his duties as in a dream, but he left no duty unperformed. He prepared his arms and all things for the approaching battle with the utmost care. He bared his limbs and breast and painted them red, and bound up his hair in a flowing tuft with eagle feathers pointing up from the defiant scalp-lock.

At last he painted his face in mourning. That means a great deal. When a warrior paints his face black it means victory or death. When a warrior paints his face black before going into battle he does not survive a defeat. It is rarely done, but an Indian is greatly honoured who goes to this extreme, and when he goes out to battle the women sit on the hills above the war-path and sing a battle song with his name in a kind of chorus, calling their deity to witness his valour to defend him in battle, and bring him back victorious. I was standing down by the river alone, waiting and looking in the water, when he came and laid his hand upon my shoulder. He had his rifle in his other hand and his knife, tomahawk, and pistol in his belt. He looked wild and fierce. He scarcely spoke above a whisper.

" I will not come back," he began, " I have seen the signs, and I shall not come back. It is all right, I am going to die like a chief. To-morrow I will be with my people on the other side of darkness. They will meet me on my way, for I have had their revenge."

He looked at me sharp and sudden, and his black eyes shot fire. He lifted his hand high above his head and twirled it around as if shaping a beaver hat. His eyes danced with a fierce delight as he hissed between his teeth,

" The Judge ! Spades ! "

He struck out savagely, as if striking with a knife; as if these men stood before him, and then laid his hand upon his own breast.

Great Heavens ! I said to myself, as he shouldered his rifle and joined his comrades, and it was this boy that killed them ! The Doctor and the Prince had understood this all the time and could not trust me with the secret. They had borne the peril and reproach that they might save these two and bring them back beyond the reach of the white man. I never till that moment knew how great and noble were the two men whose lives mine had touched, spoken to, and parted from as ships that meet and part upon the seas.

We had to fight a mixed body of soldiers and settlers, and a short, but for the Indians bloody, battle took place.

The chief of the Pit River Indians fell, and many of his best warriors around him. Early in the fight I received an ugly cut on the forehead, which bled profusely and so blinded me that I could do nothing further for my unhappy allies. It was a hopeless case. While the fight waxed hot I stole off up a cañon with a number of the Shasta Indians and escaped. I came upon an old wounded warrior leaning on his bow by the trail. The old man said "Klamat!" bowed his head and pointed to the ground.

The prophecy had been fulfilled.

Do not imagine these were great battles. Other events had the ears of the world then, and they were probably hardly heard of beyond the lines of the State. Half armed, and wholly untrained, the Indians could not or did not make a single respectable stand. The losses were almost always wholly on their side.

Had they been able to make one or two bold advances against the whites, then negotiations would have been opened, terms offered, opinions exchanged, rights and wrongs discussed, and the Indians would at least have had a hearing. But so long as the troops had it their own way, the only terms were the Reservation, or annihilation.

The few remaining Modoc warriors now returned to their sage-brush plains and tule lakes to the east; the Shastas withdrew to the head-waters of the McCloud, thus abandoning lands that it would take you days of journey to encompass ; and the Pit River Indians, now almost starving, with an approaching winter to confront, sent in their remaining women and children in sign of submission. They were sadly reduced in numbers, and perhaps less than a thousand were taken to the Reservation. To-day the tribe is nearly extinct.

And why did the Government insist to the bitter end that the Indians should leave this the richest and finest valley of northern California? Because the white settlers wanted it. Voters wanted it, and no aspirant for office dared say a word for the Indian. So it goes.

The last fight was a sort of Waterloo. There was now no hope. My plans for the little Republic were utterly overthrown. I could now only bring ruin upon the Indians and destruction upon myself by remaining. I resolved to go.

At last a thought like this began to take shape. I will descend into the active world. I will go down from my snowy island into the strong sea of people, and try my fortunes for only a few short years. With this mountain at my back, this forest to retreat to if I am worsted, I can feel strong and brave; and if by chance I win the fight, I will here return and rest.

My presence there, instead of being a protection, was only a peril now to the Indians. I told Warrottetot, the old warrior, frankly that I wished to go, that it was best I should, for the white men could not understand why I was there, except it was to incite them to battle or plunder.

I sat down with him by the river, and with a stick

marked out the world in the sand, showed him how narrow were his possessions, and told him where all his wars must end. He gave me permission to go, and said nothing more. He seemed bewildered.

The old chief, the day before my departure, rode down with me from the high mountains to the beautiful Now-aw-wa valley, where I had built a cabin years before. We stopped on a hill overlooking the valley and dismounted; he took fragments of lava and built a little monument. He pointed out high landmarks away below the valley embracing almost as much land as you could journey around in a day's travel.

"This is yours. All this valley is yours; I give it to you with my own hand." He went down the hill a little way, and taking up some of the earth brought it to me and sprinkled it upon and before my feet.

" It is all yours," he said, " you have done all you could do, and deserve it; besides, I have no one to leave it to now but you."

" You will go on your way, will win a place in life, and when you return you will have lands, a home and hunting-grounds. These you will find here when you return, but you will not find me, nor one of my children, nor one of my tribe."

The poor old Indian, battle-worn, wounded and broken in spirit, he was all heart, all tenderness and truth and devotion. He could not understand why that land should not be wholly mine. He had not the shadow of a doubt that this gift of his made the little valley as surely and wholly mine as if a thousand deeds had testified to the inheritance. He could not understand why he was not the lord and owner of the land which had been handed down to him through a thousand generations, that had been fought for and defended from a time as old, perhaps, as the history of the invader.

Under the madroños my horse stood saddled for a long, hard ride. Good-byes were said, I led my steed a little way, and an Indian woman walked at my side.

Some things shall be sacred. Recital is sometimes rofanity.

It was a sudden impulse that made me set my horse back on his haunches as he bounded away, unwind my red silk sash, wave a farewell with it, toss it to her, and bid her keep it till my return. In less than forty days, I rested beneath the palms of Central America.

CHAPTER XXXII

ORE than a dozen years had passed away. And what years! I had gone through almost every stage and experience of human life. I had gone far out and away from my life in the mountains among the Indians. I had come to look upon it as upon the life of another. It seemed to be no longer a part of my nature or myself, much as I loved it and fondly as I cherished the memory of the dead days and their dead. Irresistibly I was drawn to return at the first possible opportunity, and now in the yellow autumn I was nearing my old home. The narrow trails were no longer in use. A broad stage road was hewn from out the mountain-sides, and we dashed through the forests as if on the highway of an old civilization.

I was an utter stranger to all. I saw no familiar faces among the few worthless Indians about the stations, and no white man suspected that I had once held dominion in all that wild and splendid region.

I sat with the driver as the six horses spun us at a gallop around the spurs of the mountain crags overhanging the Sacramento river. Our road, cut from the rocks, had looked like a spider web swinging in the air when we saw it first from the waters of the Sacramento, that boiled and foamed in a bed-rock flume now thousands of feet below us.

The passengers, who had been very loud and hilarious, were now very quiet, and an old gentleman, who was engaged in some quartz speculation, and had been extremely anxious to get ahead, here stuck his head out of the window as he gasped for breath, and protested to the driver that he had changed his mind about reaching camp so soon, that, in fact, he was in no hurry at all, and that, if he was a mind to, he might go a little slow.

The driver then gently threaded the ribbons through his fingers as if to get a firmer hold, threw his right arm out, and snapped the silk under the heels of his leaders.

This was the nervous man's only answer.

It was perfectly splendid. We were playing spider and fly in the heavens. Down at the mountain's base and pressed to the foamy rim of the river, stood the madroño and manzanita, light, but trim-limbed, like sycamore; and up a little way were oak, and ash, and poplar trees, yellow as the autumn frosts could paint them; and as the eye ascended the steep and stupendous mountain that stood over across the river against us, yet so close at hand, the fir and tamarack grew dense and dark, with only now and then a clump of yellow trees, like islands set in a sea of green.

Here and there a scarlet maple blazed like the burning bush, and, to a mind careless of appropriate figures, might have suggested Jacob's kine, or coat of many colours. How we flew and dashed around the rocky spurs! Some chipmunks dusted down the road and across the track, and now and then perched on a limb in easy pistol-shot; a splendid grey squirrel looked at us under his bushy tail, and barked and chattered undisturbed; but we saw no other game. In a country famous for its bear, we saw not so much as a track.

Down under us on the river-bank the smoke of a solitary wigwam curled lazily up through the trees, and the Indian that stood on the rocks spearing the autumn run of salmon looked no taller than a span.

Again we dashed around a rocky point, and the driver set his leaders back on their haunches with a jerk that made six full groans issue from inside the stage, and as many heads hurry through the windows. The driver pushed back his hat, the hat that stage drivers persist in wearing down on their noses, pointed with his whip into the air, and said,

" How 's that for high?"

Then again he snapped his silk, settled the insiders in their seats, and we were dashing on as before.

Mount Shasta! Shasta the magnificent was before us, above us! And so sudden! And at last, and after so many many years!

As if a great iceberg of the north had broken loose, and, seamed and scarred by the sun, drifted through the air upon us.

The driver felt and silently acknowledged the power of this majestic presence, for he held the silk in his hands very quietly, and let the tired horses have it their own way till he drew the reins and called out at the end of the next half hour, "Fifteen minutes for supper!" Even the foaming horses, weary as they were, lifted their ears a little and stepped more alert and lively when the sun flashed back upon us from the snowy breastplate of kingly Shasta.

Here I determined to cross the Sacramento, climb the mountains of the other side, pierce the splendid forests, and reach the valleys of McCloud at the base of Shasta.

In my mind, the wigwams still sent up their smoke through the dense firs of the McCloud, and pretty maidens still bore water on their heads in willow baskets from the river to the village. I almost heard the ancient, wrinkled squaws, grinding acorn bread, and the shouts of the naked children at their sports.

I could get no ponies, and so had to take little lean Mexican mules, old and lazy as possible, the remnant of some of the great pack trains that strung across these mountains in the days when they were only marked by narrow trails, and everything was transported on the backs of these patient little animals.

My guide, sent along by the ranchero to take care of the mules and return them, was a singular Indian. His name was "Limber Jim." I should have known his name was Limber Jim before I heard it. Out here things take their names just as they impress you. Once a six-foot desperado said to a man with a freckled face, who had wedged himself into a party as they were lifting glasses, "What is your name?"

" P. Archibald Brown."

" P. Archibald Hell!—your name is Ginger."

A Californian desperado is not a fool; he is oftener a genius. "P. Archibald Brown" was never heard of after that. Down in Arizona is now a board at the head of a little sandy hillock marked "Ginger."

When Limber Jim moved, every limb and muscle was in motion. When he opened his mouth he also opened his hands, and when he opened his hands he would helplessly open his mouth. After we had forded the Sacramento and climbed the long and rugged trail on the other side, we rested in the shade and I asked the creature his history. His short and simple annals were to the effect that he was an Indian lad in good standing with the whites while they were at war with his fathers, and was a great pet among them. But one morning after a pack train had disappeared a rancheria was surrounded and all the men and boys taken to the camp for execution, in case the mules were not returned in a given time.

The animals, of course, did not come back, and the Indians, a dozen or more, were punctually suspended to the nearest tree, and Jim was hung among the rest. He said he was hung by mistake; and was very confident there was no intention of hanging him, but that he got mixed up with the rest, and that men who did not know his face suspended him, where he hung all day by the neck till it got very dark, when they took him down and told him they were very sorry. He added mournfully, that his nerves had never been reliable since.

We pushed our little Spanish mules along the worn trail that stretched across the mountain. At noon we came down to the McCloud, which we found too deep to ford, and therefore bore up the stream a little way till we could find a lodge and log canoe. It looked so very lonely. Here stood lodges, but they were empty. There, on a point where I had left a thriving, prosperous village, the rye grass grew rank and tall as our shoulders as we rode along. The lodges stood still as of old. An Indian never tears down his house. It will serve to shelter some one who is lost or homeless; besides, there is a superstition which forbids it. From one of these lodges a small black wolf started out and stole swiftly across the hill. When a white man leaves a habitation he changes the face of things; an Indian leaves them unimpaired. His deserted house is the perfect body with only the soul withdrawn. An empty Indian village is the gloomiest place in the world.

We crossed the McCloud, and our course lay through a saddle in the mountains to Pit river; so called from the blind pits dug out like a jug by the Indians in places where their enemies or game are likely to pass. These pits are dangerous traps; they are ten or fifteen feet deep, small at the mouth, but made to diverge in descent, so that it is impossible for anything to escape that once falls into their capacious maws. To add to their horror, at the bottom, elk and deer antlers that have been ground sharp at the points are set up so as to pierce any unfortunate man or beast they may chance to swallow up. They are dug by the squaws, and the earth taken from them is carried in baskets and thrown into the river. They are covered in the most cunning manner; even footprints in an old beaten trail are made above the treacherous pits, and no depression, no broken earth, nothing at all indicates their presence except the talismanic stones or the broken twigs and other signs of a sort of rude freemasonry which only the members of a tribe can understand.

Here we passed groves of most magnificent oak. Their trunks are five and six feet in diameter, and the boughs were then covered with acorns and fairly matted with the mistletoe.

Coming down on to the banks of Pit river, we heard the songs and shouts of Indian girls gathering acorns. They were up in the oaks, and half covered in the mistletoe. They would beat off the acorns with sticks, or cut off the little branches with tomahawks, and the older squaws gathered them from the ground, and threw them over their shoulders in baskets borne by a strap around the forehead. I must here expose a popular delusion.

I have heard parents insist that their girls should wear shoes, and tight ones at that, in childhood, so that their feet should be small and neat when grown. Now, I am bound to say that these Indian women, who never wear anything closer than a moccasin or Mexican sandal, and not half of the time either of the two, have the smallest and prettiest feet, and hands also, I have ever seen.

These few Indian girls were pretty. Some of them were painted red; and their splendid flow of intense black hair showed well in the yellow leaves and the rich green mistletoe. Some warriors watched a little way off on a hill, lest some savage border ruffians, under a modern Romulus, should swoop down upon them and carry them off.

We rode under the oaks and they laughed playfully and crept closer into the leaves. One little sun-browned savage pelted Limber Jim with acorns. Then he opened his mouth and laughed, and opened his hands and let go his reins, and rolled and shook in his saddle as if possessed by an earthquake.

Toward evening, in the bend of Pit river, we came upon an old Indian herding ponies, and it occurred to us to leave our mules to rest and get fresh horses. Accordingly, we approached the old fellow, sunning himself on the sand before his lodge, and said, in the old words by which a favour was asked when first I knew this people, and had for the asking,

" Brother, the sun goes on. Your brothers are weary and have far to go. Bring us better horses."

The old tender of herds turned his head half way, and informed me in broken English and butchered Mexican, badly put together, that he had some horses to sell, but none to give away. Consternation ! These Indians are getting civilized, I said to myself. Here has been a missionary in my absence; and we rode on.

Every foot of ground here, even up to the rugged base of Shasta, was familiar to me. Sometimes, to the terror of Limber Jim, I took the lead in the trail. I knew as well as he the stones or the broken twigs that pointed out the pit. All the afternoon we rode along the rim of the bright blue river, except when forced to climb a spur of mountain that ran its nose fairly into the water and cut us off.

All along the shores stood deserted lodges, and the grass grew rank and tall around them. They had been depopulated for years. I had not as yet met a single old acquaintance.

It was fairly dark before we dismounted at an empty lodge and pitched camp for the night.

Early we set out next morning on our solitary

ride for the camp, where the little remnant of the Shastas were said to be gathered high up on the mountain. More empty lodges, right and left only solitude and desertion.

We left the river and turned up a gorge. Sometimes, in the great cañon running to the sun, the air was warm and fresh of falling leaves; and then again as we turned a point it came pitching down upon us, keen and sharp from the snows of Shasta. But few birds sing here. There are some robins and larks, and also some turtle-doves, which the Indians will not harm. Partridges in splendid crests ran in hundreds across the trails, and these whistle all the year; but there was an unaccountable scarcity of birds for a country so densely timbered.

At last, when the shadows were very long, we climbed a rugged, rocky hill, nearly impassable for man or mule, and saw on a point in a clump of pines, that could only be reached by crossing an open space of rocks and lava, the camp we sought.

Indians have no terms of salutation. If the dogs do not celebrate your arrival, all things go on the same as if you had never been. You dismount, unsaddle your mule, turn it to grass, take a drink of water, and then light your pipe, when the men will gather about you by degrees and the women bring refreshments. But our arrival here was an uncommon occasion. No white man had as yet set foot on this rocky ridge and natural fortress; and then when it was known that one had returned to their mountains whom they had known of old, and whose exploits and manners they had magnified by repeated narration, no Indian stolidity could keep up their traditional dignity. Children peeped from the lodges, and squaws came out from among the trees, with babies in willow baskets. There was a little consultation, and we were taken to a lodge of great dimensions, made of cedar bark fastened by withes and weights to a framework of fir and cedar poles. The walls were about eight feet high; the roof sloping like that of an ordinary cabin, with an opening in the comb for the smoke.

We had refreshments; meats roasted by the fire, and manzanita berries ground to powder, and acorn bread.

Runners were sent to the Modoc camp, a half-day distant, and the few warriors came. But I did not know a single face. The old warriors had all perished. New men had grown in their places. It seemed as if I had outlived my generation even in my youth. Then a long smoke in silence, a little time for thought, and preparations were made for a great talk.

And what a talk it was! Indians, like white men, talk best about themselves. They spoke by turns, each rising in his place, speaking but once, and few or many minutes, according to his age and inclination. They gesticulated greatly, and spoke rapidly; sometimes striking with imaginary knives, twanging bows, and hurling tomahawks; and all the time boast-

ing of their own deeds or those of their fathers.
One young man who had not yet been in battle told
of killing a bear; this made another young man
laugh, and then all the Indians frowned terribly. To
think that a young man should so far forget himself
as to laugh in council!

Nearly all the speeches were mournful, sad, and
pathetic, but some very fine things were said. As of
old, all their invectives were hurled at their hereditary
enemy. One old man said, "The whites were as the
ocean, strong and aggressive; while the red men
were as the sand, silent, helpless, tossed about, run
upon, and swallowed up." He was the only one
that stood up tall and talked like a reasonable man.
He wore a robe of panther skins thrown back from
his shoulders.

I saw that even these few surviving people would
not die in silence. They were as a wounded serpent
that could yet strike if a foot was set in reach.

To me all this was sad beyond recital. What had
these people seen, endured, felt, suffered in all the
years of my absence! And the end was not yet.

The struggles of many years were recounted many
times, by each man telling the part he had borne in
the battles, and from an Indian's standpoint it looked
sad enough. The old savage spoken of had not much
to say of himself, but now and then his long fingers
would point to scars on his naked breast, when
alluding to some battle.

"Once," said he, in conclusion, "we were so many

we could not all stand upon this hill; now we are all in one little cawel;" and here he made a solemn sweep with his arm, which was very grand. Then after a pause he said: " Once I had seven wives, now I have only two."

At midnight, with solemn good-nights, the men arose one by one and retired. Over all things there hung a gloom. I went out into the village of a dozen houses that crouched down under the dense black pines. What a glorious moon! Only such a moon as California can afford. A long white cloud of swans stretched overhead, croaking dolefully enough; the sea of evergreen pines that rolled about the bluff and belted the base of Shasta was sable as a pall, but the snowy summit in the splendours of the moon, flashed like a pyramid of silver! All these mountains, all these mighty forests, were to me as a schoolboy's play-ground, the playmates gone, the master dead!

CHAPTER XXXIII

LEANED from the black stone wall that sheltered the lodges from the south, and watched the white McCloud riding like a stream of light through the forest under me, and thought of many things.

Yonder lay my beautiful Now-aw-wa valley; that was wholly mine, that I should never possess, to which I should never dare assert my right, and there, not far away, were the ashes of the great Chief of the Shastas. Strangely enough he had fought his last fight there, not far from the spot where he had stood and given me possession of the cherished part of his old inheritance.

How still, how silent were all things! Not a camp-fire shining through all the solemn forest. It was a tomb, dark and typical;—the cyprus and the cedar trees drooped their sable plumes above the dead of a departed race.

Why had I returned here? The reasons were

many and all-sufficient. Among others I had heard that another had come upon the scene. A rumour had reached me that a little brown girl was flitting through these forests; wild, frightened at the sight of man, timid, sensitive, and strangely beautiful. Who was she? Was she the last of the family of Mountain Joe? Was she one of the Doctor's children, half prophetess, half spirit, gliding through the pines, shunning the face of the Saxon, or was she even something more? Well, here is a little secret which shall remain hers. She is a dreamer, and delights in mystery. Who she was or who she is I have hardly a right to say. Her name is Calle Shasta.

What was I to do? Leave her to perish there in the gathering storm that was to fall upon the Modocs and their few allies, or tear her away from her mother and the mountains?

But where was the little maiden now, as I looked from the battlement on the world below? They told me she was with my Modocs away to the east among the lakes. I waited, enquired, delayed many days, but neither she nor her mother would appear. Her mother, poor broken-hearted Indian woman, once a princess, was afraid I would carry away her little girl. At last I bade farewell, and turned down the winding hill. I heard a cry and looked up.

There on the wall she stood, waving a red scarf.

Was it the same? Surely it was the same I had thrown her years and years before, when I left the land a fugitive.

There was a little girl beside her, too, not so brown as she, waving one pretty hand as she held to the woman's robe with the other. I stopped and raised my hat, and called a kind farewell, and undertook to say some pretty things, but just that moment my mule, as mules always will, opened his mouth and brayed and brayed as if he would die. I jerked and kicked him into silence, and then began again; and again the mule began, this time joined by Limber Jim's. Limber Jim swore in wretched English, but it was no use—the scarlet banner from the wall was to them the signal of war, and they refused to be silenced until we mounted and descended to the glorious pines, where I rode and roved the sweetest years of my life.

Yet still the two hands were lifted from the wall, and the red scarf waved till the tops of the pines came down, and we could see no more.

Then I lifted my hat and said, " Adieu! I reckon I shall never see you any more. Never, unless it may come to pass that the world turns utterly against me. And then, what if I were to return and find not a single living savage?"

I think I was as a man whose senses were in another world. Once I stopped, dismounted, leaned on my little mule, looking earnestly back to the rocky point as if about to return; as if almost determined to return at once and there to remain. There was a battle in my heart. At length awakened, I mounted my mule mechanically, and went on.

The Doctor still lived. I would see him once more before I left the land for ever. It was a hard and a long day's journey, and was nearly sundown when we reached the little path planted with cherry trees, and overhung in places with vines of grape, leading from the river up the hill to his house. I heard the shouts of children in the hills, and saw the old man sitting in his cabin porch that overlooks the river. He had some books and papers near him. His face and demeanour were majesty itself.

He arose as he saw us through the trees and vines, and shaded his brow with his hand as he peered down the path. Men in the mountains do not forget faces. Mountaineers never forget each other, though they may separate for twenty years. In a city you may meet a thousand new faces a year; there a new face is a rare thing.

He came down the steps in moccasins and a rich dress of skins and fur. His thin hair fell in long silver tresses on his shoulders. He was stouter than before, and seemed quite strong. He took my hands, led me up to a seat, sat down by my side, and we two together looked up the river and up to the north. The same old golden glory rested like a mantle on the shoulders and about the brows of Shasta; the same sunset splendour as of old; the purple tint, the streaming bars, the banner of red and blue and gold was stretching away from the summit across the sky.

He had learned the Indians' custom of silent

salutation, which means so much; but I knew his thoughts. He was saying in his heart so loud that I heard him: "You and I are changed, the world has changed, men and women have grown old and ugly, and a new generation now controls and possesses the world below. Here there is no change."

I looked often at my old companion there, as he looked away across the scarlet and yellow woods in the dying sunlight or lifted his face to the mountain. The old, old face, but nobler now, a sort of strength in its very weakness, an earnestness very finely marked, a sincerity not stamped in broad furrows or laid in brick and mortar, but set in threads of silver and of gold. He had settled here in a stormy time. For the good he could do he came down here on the line between the white man and the red, where the worst of both men are always found, and you have nothing to expect from either but suspicion, treachery, and abuse, and here gathered a few Indians about him, and took up his abode.

He had planted trees, tilled the soil a little, grew some stock, and now had a pleasant home, and horses and cattle in herds up and down the river.

As the sun went down, the children,—brown, beautiful, and healthy children, strong and supple,— came in from the hills with the herds, and dismounted, while some Indians came up from the river and led their ponies down to water.

A little girl came up the steps; the eldest, a shy child of not more than a dozen years, yet almost a woman, for this Californian sun is passionate, and matures us early. A great black pet bear was by her side, and she seemed to shrink as she saw me, a stranger, there, and half hid behind his shaggy coat. She took an apple from the ground that had fallen in the path, and then the huge bear reared himself on his hind legs before her as she turned, showing the white of his breast to us, and opened his red mouth, and held his head coaxingly to one side to receive the apple. The bear was as tall as the little woman.

The next morning, when I persisted that I could not remain, fresh horses were saddled for us, and an Indian given to return the tired mules to the station.

"Why did you not tell me," said I, as we walked down the path to the canoe, "that you bore nothing of the blood of those men?"

The old nervousness swept across his face, but he was composed and pleasant.

"Would men have believed me? And if they had believed me, was I not as able to bear the blame as the poor, desperate and outraged little Indian? As a true Indian, he could not have done otherwise than he did. If ever men deserved death those did. Yet, had it even been believed that they fell by an Indian's hand, not only those two children, but every Indian that set his foot in camp had been butchered."

I could not answer. I could only think how this man must have suffered to save those two waifs of the forest, how he had thought it all out in the old mining camp, balanced the chances, counted the cost, and deliberately at last decided to be known as a murderer, and to become an outcast from the civilized world.

He stood with his moccasins down to the river's rim, and took my hand, as the Indian seated himself in the canoe and lifted his paddle.

"Come back," he said, "to the mountains. The world is fooling you. It will laugh and be amused to-day, as you dance before it in your youth, and sing wild songs, but to-morrow it will tire of the forest fragrance and the breath of the California lily; your green leaves will wither in the hot atmosphere of fashion, and in a year or two you will be more wretched than you can think; you will be neither mountaineer nor man of the world, but vibrate hopelessly between, and be at home in neither capacity. Come, be brave! It is no merit to leave the world when it has left you, and requires no courage; but now—"

"Say no more," I cried, "I will come! Yonder, across the hills, where the morning sun is resting on the broad plateau, there among the oaks and pines, I will pitch a tent, and there take up my everlasting rest."

A pressure of the hand for the promise; the canoe swung free, the Indian's paddle made eddies in the bright blue water, the horses blew the bubbles from their nostrils, and their long manes floated in the sweeping tide.

*   *   *   *   *   *

I am now in my new home where I have rested and written this history of my life among the Indians of Mount Shasta. I have seen enough of cities and civilization—too much. I can endure storms, floods, earthquakes, but not this rush and crush and crowding of men, this sort of moral cannibalism, where souls eat souls, where men kill each other to get their places. I have returned to my mountains. I have room here. No man wants my place, there is no rivalry, no jealousy; no monster will eat me up while I sleep, no man will stab me in the back when I stoop to drink from the spring.

And yet how many noble and generous men have I met away out in the sea of human life, far from my snowy island in the clouds! Possibly, after all, I am here, not that I love society less, but the solitude more.

The heart takes root like a tree when it is young and strong, and fresh and growing. It shoots tendrils like a vine. You cannot tear it from its place at will. You may be very strong ; you may even uproot and transplant, but it will never flourish in the new place or be satisfied.

We have a cabin here among the oaks and the pines, on a bench of the mountain, looking down on the Sacramento valley, a day's ride distant.

A stream, white as cotton, is foaming among the mossy rocks in a cañon below the house, with balm and madroño on its banks, and I have some horses on the plain below. I have cattle on the manzanita hills above me, towards the snow, where the grass is fresh the season through. You can hear the old white bull, the leader of the herd, lift up his voice in the morning, and challenge the whole world below to battle, but no David comes to meet him. When we want a fresh horse here, we mount one of those staked out yonder by lariat and hackamore, ride down to the band in the plain, take, with the lasso, the strongest and fastest of them all, saddle him, mount, and turn the other loose to run till strong and fresh again.

I have a field too, down yonder, where we lead the water through the corn, and the rich, rank growth of many kinds of vines. We have planted an orchard, and grape vines are climbing up the banks, and across the boulders that time has tumbled down from the manzanita hills. We will remain here by our vine and our fig tree till we can take shelter under their boughs.

We will yet eat fruit from the trees we have planted.

We? Why, yes! That means little "Calle Shasta," the little shy, brown girl that tried to hide, and refused to see me when I first returned to the mountains. She is with me now, and wears a red sash, and a scarf gracefully folded about her shoulders under her rich flow of hair. I call her Shasta because she was born here, under the shadows of Mount Shasta, many stormy years ago. How she can ride, shoot, hunt, and track the deer, and take the salmon!

Beautiful? I think so. And then she is so fresh, innocent, and affectionate. Last night I was telling her about the people in the world below, how crowded they were in cities, and how they had to struggle.

" Poor things!" she said, "poor things! how I pity them all that they have to stay down there. Why cannot they come up here from their troubles and be happy with us ?"

She is learning to read, and believes everything she has yet found in the school books—George Washington with his hatchet and all. The sweet, sweet child! I am waiting to see what she will say when she comes to the story of Jonah and the whale.

The Prince is here, and happy too, back from his wanderings. Up from the world, up to this sort of half-way house to the better land.

To-day, when the sun was low, we sat down in the shadow of the pines on a mossy trunk, a little way out from the door. The sun threw lances against the shining mail of Shasta, and they glanced aside and fell, quivering, at our feet, on the quills and dropping acorns. A dreamy sound of waters came up through the tops of the alder and madroño trees below us.

The world, no doubt, went on in its strong, old way, afar off, but we did not hear it. The sailing of ships, the conventions of men, the praise of men, and the abuse of men; the gathering together of the fair in silks, and laces, and diamonds under the lights; the success or defeat of this measure or of that man; profit and loss; the rise and fall of stocks: what were they all to us?

Peace! After many a year of battle with the world, we had retreated, thankful for a place of retreat, and found rest—peace. Now and then an acorn dropped; now and then an early leaf fell down; and once I heard the whistle of an antlered deer getting his herd together to lead them down the mountain; but that was all that broke the perfect stillness. A chipmunk dusted across the burrs, mounted the further end of the mossy trunk, lifted on his hind legs, and looked all around; then, finding no hand against him, let himself down, ran past my elbow on to the ground again, and gathered in his paws, then into his mouth, an acorn at our feet. Peace! Peace! Who, my little brown neighbour in the striped jacket, who would have allowed you to take that, even that acorn, in peace, down in the busy, battling world? But we are above it. The storms of the social sea may blow, the surf may break against the rocky base of this retreat, may even sweep a little way into the sable fringe of firs, but it shall never reach us here.

I looked at the Prince as the sun went down. I had so longed to know the secret of his life. Yet I had never doubted that he was all he looked and seemed: a genuine, splendid Prince.

Strange, nay, more than strange, that men should live together in the mountains, year after year, and not even know each other's names, not even the place of their birth. Yet such is the case here, and all up and down the Sierras. A sort of tacit agreement it seems to have been from the first, that they should not ask of the past, that they began a new life here. The plains and the great seas they had crossed were as gulfs of oblivion. Was it an agreement that we should all begin life even here, and equal? or was it because these men were above any low curiosity, because they had something to do beside prying into the past lives of their neighbours? I should say that this fine peculiarity grew largely out of the latter.

But here it seemed the Prince and I had at last pitched our tent for good, together. I had told him of my ten years' battle just past, and he had recounted his. He had crossed and recrossed the Cordilleras and the Andes, sailed up and down the Amazon, fought in Nicaragua, and at last raised an old Spanish galleon from Fonseca filled with doubloons and Mexican dollars that had gone down in the sea half a century before.

But the past! Was he really a Prince, and if he was really a Prince why follow the mountains so far? Why seek for gold, and why at last return to Shasta, instead of to his people and his possessions? My faith was surely shaken. So many years of practical life had taken something of the hero-worship out of my nature. There was no longer the haze of sovereignty about the head of this man, and yet I believe I loved him as truly as ever.

Little Shasta came dashing up with the hounds at

her horse's heels. A chill breath came pitching down from the mountain tops, keen and crisp, and we arose to enter the cabin.

I put my hand on his arm, reached up and touched the long, black curls that lay on his shoulder, for I am now as tall as he.

"Nevertheless," said I, "you are really a Prince, are you not?"

"A Prince!" said he with surprise. "Why, what in the world put that into your head?" and he put my hand playfully aside and looked in my face. He patted the ground in the old, old way, smiled so gently, so graciously and kind, that I almost regretted I had spoken. "A Prince! indeed!"

"Then pray, once for all, tell me who you are, and what is your real Christian proper name."

He laughed a little, tossed his black hair back from his face, stooped, picked up an acorn and tossed it lightly after a chipmunk that ran along the mossy trunk, and said:—

"Why, a man, of course, like yourself. An American, born of poor parents, so that I had to make the best of it; drifted into Mexico after awhile, and have been drifting ever since; aimless, idle, till I met you and undertook to pull you through the winter. As for my name, it is Thomas, James Thomas." Here he stooped, picked another acorn from the ground, and cast it at the hounds that stood listening to the whistle of the deer.

"Ah, Prince! Prince! You should at least have

had a romantic and prince-like name," I said to myself, as I filled a pipe with killikinick and reclined on the panther skins in the cabin when we had entered.

" But see," I said with paternal air, to Calle, as I blew the smoke towards the thatch, and she came bounding in, filling the house, like sunshine, with cheerfulness and content, to prepare the evening meal; " see what silence, coupled with gentlemanly bearing, may do in the world. Even plain Mr. Thomas may be named a Prince."

He is indeed a Prince, none the less a Prince than before. Here we shall dwell together. Here we shall be and abide in the dark days of winter and the strong full days of the summer. Here we have pitched our tents, and here we shall rest and remain unto the end.

I have seen enough, too much to be in love with life as I find it where men are gathered together. As for civilization, it has been my fate to see it in every stage and grade, from the bottom to the top. And I am bound to say that I have found it much like my great snow peaks of the Sierras. The higher up you go the colder it becomes.

Yet a good and true man will not withhold himself utterly from society, no matter how much he may dislike it. He will go among the people there much as a missionary goes among the heathen, for the good he can do in their midst.

How it amuses me to see my friends, the men I have

met in civilization, denying and attempting to dispute the story that I am the man who lived with the Indians and led them in war. Ah, my friends, you do not know me at all.

There is much, no doubt, in my life to regret, but there is nothing at all to conceal.

And let it be understood once for all that the things I have to regret are not of my life with the Indians or my attempt to ameliorate their condition. I only regret that I failed.

Nay, I snap my fingers at the world and say, I am proud of that period of my life. It is the only white spot in my character, the only effort of my life to look back to with exultation, the only thing I have ever done or endeavoured to do that entitles me to rank among the men of a great country.

And what has been my reward? . . . . . No matter, I appeal to time. It may be that a Phillips will rise up yet to speak for these people, or a John Brown to fire a gun, and then I will be remembered.

*　　　*　　　*　　　*　　　*　　　*

Ah, thus I wrote, felt and believed in the few days that I sat again in the shadows of Shasta, where I wrote all but the opening and concluding lines of this narrative. But I had mixed too much with the restless and bustling life below me. I had bound myself in ties not to be broken at pleasure.

Besides, it was now so lonely. The grass grew tall and entangled in the trails. It was rank and green from the dust and ashes of the dead. It flourished with all that rich and intense verdure that marks the grasses growing above your friends. Here it was like living in one great graveyard.

We went down to the busy world below, the Prince and I, and ships have borne us into other and different lands; wanderers again upon the earth; drifting with the world, borne up and down, and on, like the shifting levels of the sea.

The origin of the late Modoc war, which was really of less importance than the earlier ones, and in which the last brave remnant of the tribe perished, may be briefly chronicled.

Among the Indians, as well as Christian nations, there is often more than one man who aspires to or claims to be at the head of the people. It is a favourite practice of the Indian agents to take up some coward or imbecile who may be easily managed, and make him the head of a tribe, and so treat with him, and hold the whole tribe to answer for his contracts. In this way vast tracts of land and the rights of a tribe are often surrendered for a mere song. If anyone dissents, then the army is called to enforce the treaty.

The old treaty with the Modocs was not much unlike this. Every foot of their great possessions had been ceded away by one who had not authority to cede, or influence to control the Indians.

They were mostly taken from their old possessions to a reservation to the north, and on the lands of the Klamat Indians, their old and most bitter enemies. It was a bleak and barren land, and the Indians well-nigh starved to death

Captain Jack, who was now the real and recognized chief among the Indians, still held on to the home of his fathers, an honest and upright Indian, and gathered about him the best and bravest of his tribe. Here they remained, raising horses and cattle, hunting, fishing, and generally following their old pursuits, till the white settlers began to want the little land they occupied.

Then the authorities came to Captain Jack, and told him he must go to the Reservation, abandon his lands, and live with his enemies. The Indians refused to go.

"Then you must die."

"Very well," answered Captain Jack; "it is die if we go, and die if we stay. We will die where our fathers died."

At night—that time which the Indians surrender to the wild beasts, and when they give themselves up in trust to the Great Spirit—the troops poured in upon them. They met their enemies like Spartans.

After long holding their ground, then came the Peace Commissioners to talk of peace. The Indians, remembering the tragedy of twenty years before, desperate and burning for revenge, believing that the only alternative was to kill or be killed, killed the Commissioners, as their own Peace Commissioners had been killed. They were surrounded, yet did this deed right in the face of the desperate consequences which they knew must follow.

If we may be permitted to exult in any deeds of war, how can we but glory in the valour of these few

men, battling there in the shadows of Shasta for all
that is sacred to the Christian or the savage, holding
the forces of the United States at bay for half a
year, looking death firmly in the face and fighting
on without a word day by day, every day counting
a diminished number, shrinking to a diminished
circle ; bleeding, starving, dying; knowing that annihilation was only a question of time. Knowing the
awful cost and yet counting down the price bravely
and without a murmur. There is nothing nobler in
all the histories of the hemispheres. But they shall
not be forgotten. Passion will pass away, and even
their enemies of to-day will yet speak of them with
respect.

I know that men will answer that it is impossible
to deal peaceably with the Indians. I ask, who has
tried it ? Penn tried it, and found them the most
peaceable, upright, and gentle of beings. The
Mormons, certainly not the most noble type of men
at first, tried it, and they were treated like brothers.
A destitute and half-desperate band of wanderers, they
sat down in the midst of the wildest and the worst of
Indians, and the red men gave them meat to eat,
lands to plough, and protection and food till they
could protect and feed themselves. These are the
only two examples of an honest and continued
attempt to deal peaceably and fairly with the Indians
that you can point to since the savage first lifted his
hands in welcome to Columbus.

When I die I shall take this book in my hand
and hold it up in the Day of Judgment, as a sworn

indictment against the rulers of my country for the destruction of these people.

Here lies a letter giving a long account of the last struggle of the Indians of Mount Shasta. Strange how this one little struggle of the Modoc Indians has got to the ears of the world, while a thousand not much unlike it have gone by in the last century unwritten and unremembered; perhaps it is because it came in a time of such universal peace.

Brave little handful of heroes! if ever I return to Mount Shasta I will seek out the spot where the last man fell; I will rear a monument of stones, and name the place Thermopylæ.

And little Calle Shasta, the last of her race?

At school in San Francisco. Her great black eyes, deep and sad and pathetic, that seem to lay hold of you, that seem to look you through and understand you, turn dreamily upon the strange, strong sea of people about her, but she gazes unconcerned upon it all. She is looking there, but she is living elsewhere. She is sitting there in silence, yet her heart, her soul, her spirit, is threading the dark and fragrant wood. She is listening to the sounding waterfall, watching the shining fish that dart below the grassy border. Seeing all things here, she understands nothing at all. What will become of her? The world would say that she should become a prodigy, that she should at once become civilized, lay hold of the life around her, look up and climb to eminence; crush out all her nature, forget her childhood; compete with those educated from the cradle up, and win distinction above all these. The world is an ass !

" And whose child is she?" I hear you ask. Well now, here is a little secret.

On her mother's side you must know that the last and best blood of a once great tribe is in her veins. And her father? Ah, that is the little secret. We only know. We laugh at the many guesses and speculations of the world, but we keep the little maiden's secret.

If I fail in my uncertain ventures with an un-schooled pen, as I have failed in all other things, then she is not mine; but if I win a name worth having, then that name shall be hers.

Getting along in her new life?

Well, here is a paragraph clipped from an article of many columns in a San Francisco journal:—

" She is now fifteen years old, and is living in San Francisco, supported from the poet's purse. She is described as strikingly beautiful. She has her mother's deep, dark eyes, and wealth of raven hair, and her father's clear Caucasian skin. Her neighbours call her the beautiful Spanish girl, for they know not her romantic history ; but to her own immediate friends she is known as the poet's gifted child. It is but justice to this rough, half-savage man, to say that he is exceedingly fond of her, and does everything in his power to make her comfortable and happy."

What a joke it would be on this modern Gorgon,— this monster daily press of America that eats up men and women, soul and body,—this monster that must be fed night and morning on live men who dare to come to the surface, if it should in this case be utterly mistaken !

What if this busy, searching, man-devouring press, which has compelled me to add to this narrative, or live and die misunderstood, should discover after all that this little lady is only the old Doctor's daughter sent down to the city in my care to be educated ?

What will become of her ? The poor little waif, when I look into her great wondering eyes, I fancy she is a little rabbit, startled and frightened from the forest into the clearing, where she knows not whether to return or bound forward, and so sits still and looks in wonderment around her. A little waif is she, blown like some strange bird from out the forest into a strange and uncertain land.

Will she succeed in the new scene ? Poor child, the chances are against her. Only fancy yourself the last one of your race, compelled to seek out and live with another and not an over-friendly people. And then you would be always thinking in spite of yourself; the heart would be full of memories; the soul would not take root in the new soil.

How lost and how out of place she must feel! Poor little lady, she will never hear the voices of her childhood any more. There is no one living now to speak her language.

Touch her gently, O Fate, for she is so alone ! she is the last of the children of Shasta.

THE END

AFTERWORD

The History Behind *Unwritten History*

When America was still free to dream her utopian dreams, a boy of seventeen left his father's Oregon farm and journeyed to the Siskiyou Mountains of California. The writings he produced eventually caused him to be called the creator of the "Western Archetype"[1]—and in his own lifetime he was recognized as the first authentic spokesman to whom Western America had given birth.[2] This was Joaquin Miller, better know to the world as "The Poet of the Sierra." As soon as *Life Amongst the Modocs: Unwritten History* was published in 1873, the English claimed it was superior to his poetry and "a contribution to the knowledge of human nature in some of its most peculiar conditions."[3] It was the first significant attempt in a reform novel to change the attitude of the whites toward the Indians. Twenty years before the massacre at Wounded Knee, Miller predicted what would happen to the Native Americans, and revealed the methods then being used by the Indian Bureau, settlers, and military in denying the Indians their rights. The fate of the Indians, the novel warned, constituted a danger to the settlers as well. Though the Europeans' dream of a New World had been fulfilled, it was quickly being betrayed.

The story behind Miller's novel and the way it was received by the press is a poorly understood chapter in the history of Americans writing. Bret Harte, who was jealous of Miller's spectacular fame, had been telling American editors that nothing Miller wrote was true.[4] Harte did not know how much of the book was or was not based on fact, but the American editors were more interested in Miller's flamboyant style of dress in London and his relations with his estranged wife than in his predictions about a fragile California Eden.

Mark Twain—attending social and literary gatherings with Miller in London—liked him[5] and recommended *Life Amongst the Modocs* to his American publisher, who brought it out a year later under the title *Unwritten History: Life Amongst the Modocs*. Hastily, however,

Twain noted in his jottings that Miller was supposed to be marrying Iza Hardy, "the only daughter of Sir Thomas Hardy, Baronet," and that he had "made love to Clara Spaulding!" and "sat with his hat on."[6] Twain was under the censorious eye of his new wife, Livy, and, like everyone else in America, believed Miller to be a married man. This was how the press was representing him, and Miller (who three years earlier had been granted a divorce in an Oregon court) was given front-page abuse for having left a woman who was still calling herself his wife. "Is he a villain?"[7] one of Twain's correspondents wrote to ask.

This divorce accompanied by lurid scandal had a profound effect on Miller's career. When the record of the Oregon trial was finally dug out of the archives and some of the testimony printed for the first time in 1967,[8] it was discovered that the court held in question the paternity of at least one of the children, and Theresa Dyer Miller's taste for extramarital relations was described in the records. Like her husband she nurtured dreams of becoming a celebrated poet, and she was no better suited to traditional marriage roles than her spouse. The press in the 1870s stuck very close to a melodramatic formula, depicting him as the domestic villain who had deserted his wife and children, while she was given the role of tragic defender of the home. However, both representations were inaccurate. The details of the divorce trial were so painful to him that he didn't discuss them—with anyone. If he did speak to the newspapers, it was only to defend his wife from criticism. He took upon himself the shame of the divorce for which he would not have been so bitterly attacked had he spelled out the details of the court's decision.

Though the English in 1873 immediately recognized the great beauty of *Life Amongst the Modocs* and declared, "It is well that the red men have at last found a witness to speak for them,"[9] the death knell for Miller's book as a novel and cultural document was rung on the other side of the Atlantic, for the American press refused to review it. The book went through several editions, nevertheless, and from 1873 until the time of his death, Miller, besides writing widely celebrated poems and several more novels, also wrote successfully for the stage. He became an acclaimed public figure. He established

Arbor Day in California, and admirers of his work included Walt Whitman, Tennyson, Browning, Charles Warren Stoddard, James Whitcomb Riley, John Muir, and the redoubtable Bierce. Before the discrepancy between 19th century critical opinion and the authentic value of his most significant book can be assessed in detail, the novel's factual background must first be understood.

The year Miller left his father's farm in Oregon and made his way to California's Siskiyou Mountains, he was not "Joaquin" yet, but Cincinnatus Hiner Miller, aged seventeen. This was in October of 1854. News from the east traveled slowly on boats around the Horn, and there were practically no roads.[10] His stopping place was a region to which he would return many times during the next five years. From the McAdams, Humbug, and Cherry Creek areas, millions of dollars in gold[11] was being carried away by the miners who were rolling northward to the "sea of sombre firs." Miller calls this place "a savage Eden" in *Life Amongst the Modocs.* Already the miners had clashed with the Klamath and Rogue River Indians.[12]

While living through his first winter in a deep, sunless canyon, he met a man named Harry Lockhart, who owned a hotel on Humbug Creek.[13] In just two years, Harry would be killed by Pit River Indians. Harry's twin brother Sam would then capture Miller and accuse him of cooperating with the Pit River Indians in the killing of his brother Harry and other white settlers along the Pit River.[14] This imprisonment and false accusation would become the psychological center of *Life Amongst the Modocs.*

But long before those events, and before Miller was captured by Sam Lockhart, the youngster was predisposed to like Indians. His father as justice of the peace in Indiana had settled disputes among them—frequently providing a place at his dinner table for them.[15] Nevertheless, Miller, like his fellow miners, was in essence a hungry intruder on Indian lands, an unskilled worker. In June of 1855 he became involved in an action against the Modoc and Trinity Indians. It took place in the crags which still look down on Lower Soda Springs south of the present-day town of Dunsmuir. Miller, "unhappy everywhere"[16] (as Walt Whitman later described him) had left the Humbug Creek region and had joined his mentor from

Oregon days, Mountain Joe, who was tending a rest station that supplied the miners who were on their way north to the rich diggings near Yreka.[17] Joe was a packer who had lured Miller to the Siskiyou Mountains with tales of the rich gold strikes to be found there. Known to Indians and whites alike as an engaging talker, Joe had a brain that had been fertilized with a smattering of the classics (some of which he could recite in Latin). Towering above Joe's rest station loomed enormous granite pinnacles, many of them narrow and needle-like, the famous Castle Crags. Joe created much confusion by passing along the rumor that the fabulous Lost Cabin Mine had been rediscovered near Soda Springs.[18] Joe's story about this legendary strike brought hundreds of men out of the neighboring mining areas, and what little fishing or hunting could have been done was spoiled for the Indians. The frantic whites churned up the area of Soda Creek and the Upper Sacramento. The most complete history of these events relates that "the miners became enraged because they found almost nothing. Mountain Joe disappeared and there was talk of lynching Mountain Joe's boy...."[19]

At this point, the main threat to Miller and Joe came from angry miners, not Indians. Joe and his young disciple made themselves scarce, and while they were away from the station, a band of Modoc, Trinity, and Shasta Indians came down from the heights, attacked the encampment, looted the supplies, and burned the buildings. When Miller and Joe joined the party of settlers and miners who hastened up the Crags to punish the Indians and recover stolen property, leaking bundles of foodstuffs showed the path the Indians had taken. An account of the battle is given on pages 259-63 of *Life Amongst the Modocs*. The fictionalized version, though in general outlines true, is not very detailed, and it portrays Mountain Joe as the leader of the pursuing whites. In the actual engagement a man named Squire Gibson, justice of the peace from nearby Portuguese flat, let the expedition.[20] He convinced his Indian father-in-law, Chief Wielputus of the Shastas, to bring twenty-nine of his men. To this group was added Ross McCloud, Sheriff Drebelbis of Shasta City, and about thirty whites, including Miller and Mountain Joe. They circled the crags and coming upon the Modoc and Trinity Indians from an unexpected direction, were able to surprise them and drive them off the heights. That Miller was wounded in this battle was reported by Squire Gibson in his account of the battle and by the Shasta newspaper a couple of months later. "Mr. Miller was wounded in the right corner of the mouth by an arrow entering there and coming out below the left ear."[21] Miller's arch-detractor, M. M. Marberry, claimed that a "secret diary" proved that Miller had been elsewhere during the battle. In fact, the diary does not include the period during which the battle was fought. More than a few of Marberry's suggestions fail to square with the historical record. Marcelle Masson, a descendent by marriage of Ross and Mary McCloud, said that the trail from their inn near Portuguese Flat "led down the hill to the river where there was an Indian encampment, where Mrs. McCloud would go to get the Indian girls to help her; and this is where she saw this white boy, Joaquin Miller, the future poet, lying down in one of the huts."[22] A second account indicated that Miller's wound had not been dressed properly. Mary McCloud questioned him, "learning of his part in the Castle Crag fight, and then told him she would care for his wound if he would help her with the work at the inn."[23] Whether or not Miller's future wife, the McCloud Indian, Sutatot, was in this particular Indian encampment cannot be known for sure. The Indians of this region were Wintu-speaking, and Miller added some of their words to his vocabulary. Later on, an extensive list of these words was found in the manuscript of his *California Diary.*[24]

By August, Miller was well enough to move around, but the following year brought him little in the way of enjoyment or riches.[25] Since he later became famous in the region for the easygoing way he collected other people's horses, the purchase of his first saddle horse should be mentioned.[26] After scrimping and saving a dollar at a time, he was able to buy a roan mare, but the ninety-dollar animal was stolen within a few weeks. Hoping to recover her, he traveled to Red Bluff, went to bed tired and supperless, (spending a night there that was "bad enough") but he finally succeeded in leading her home. Within six weeks other miners had found the mare appealing. It cost him a "quarrel such as I hope to never see again" (with two employees at the American Ranch) to recover her.[27] With his mare trotting handsomely beneath him, he followed the trail up the Sacramento River, heading north to rejoin Mountain Joe at Lower Soda Springs. Early in the winter of 1856, he set up housekeeping with a McCloud Indian woman named Sutatot in Squaw Valley between the Upper Sacramento and McCloud Rivers.[28] Sutatot would one day serve as a model for Paquita, the Indian heroine of *Life Amongst the Modocs*.[29]

We know that Miller and Sutatot had a daughter named Cali-Shasta,[30] and years later, while he was away (probably in Oregon), the mother and daughter were captured by Modocs and lived in slavery until rescued by a scout named Jim Brock. Sutatot married Brock, had children by him, and was thereafter known to Californians as Amanda Brock. In 1872, Miller escorted Cali-Shasta from northern California to San Francisco to complete her education, placing her in the care of Ina Coolbrith. Almost forty years later, Cali-Shasta's mother, Amanda Brock, was still enough of a celebrity to have her death reported in the San Francisco newspapers.[31] Her age at the time was said to be seventy-five years. This meant Amanda was about three years older than Miller when they began living together on the McCloud.

Much of her life with Miller was occupied with cooking and storing foods. She also helped him prospect for gold between snow-falls.[32] When food was scarce, he crossed across the mountains to the white communities on the Upper Sacramento to obtain supplies. (Hardly a model husband for very long, by August of this same year, during a trip north to Eugene, Miller was attracted to a Miss Mary J. Tompkins of Willamette Forks and wrote her a love letter.)[33]

In February of 1856, with the band of Indians under the old chief Blackbeard, he went on an elk hunt and came upon a small herd in the snow.[34] From then on meat was plentiful. He wrote of this period, "If I were to look back over the chart of my life for happiness, I should locate it here if anywhere." And he might have observed— regarding the miners and settlers of the Shasta region—"All around them was the beauty of the first day, but they could not see it."[35] He was in sympathy with the Indians' belief that in the woods at the base of Shasta they were living in the presence of a deity. For hours he studied the McCloud, the "brightest stream"[36] he had ever seen, and in the morning he could look at the south face of the mountain and see the dawn like a "grey surf breaking over the wall of the Sierras." For Miller, the purity of the white streams and untouched forests, as actualities and taken as symbols, led back to an inexhaustible cleansing source. This turn of mind was to link him with John Muir. Decades later, when Muir put together an anthology of the best writing done in California up until that time (entitled *Picturesque California*), he relied on Miller's prose sketches for many of the articles in his book. The two devotees of nature were almost the same age, but were as different from each other as a walnut tree from a pine. While Muir was happy as a loner, he often denounced "all things morally or religiously amiss in old or young." In his early twenties, Muir had little ambition to "be someone" and practiced a chaste rectitude. Both men had a contemplative side, but Miller believed in indulgence. Comparatively easygoing, Miller kidded friends and foes alike, and when someone took his originality as an affront, he welcomed the challenge. "Hurrah for little me," he wrote several times in his diary. In a more reflective mood he set down some lines of poetry:

> Can gold calm passion or make reason shine?
> Can we dig peace or wisdom from the mine?
> Gold banished honor from the mind
> And only left the name behind.[37]

The gold Miller found was never enough to live on. Though in his lifetime he would explore some of the richest gold fields in the world (and in 1861 was in the vanguard of those who discovered the fabulous Idaho strikes), he was like Mark Twain in being "close to a millionaire" several times, but always had to support himself by other means—as cook, express rider and surveyor.

While he was camped with Chief Blackbeard's tribe on Squaw Creek, he "heard that John Hale was coming with a co[mpany] of men to kill the Indians." For a time the tribe remained on the alert. Though the rumor proved false, there were more threats of this kind—many of them real enough—during the months Miller lived with the McClouds. The Indians had already been handed some of their worst defeats, not only on the battlefield, but in the California State Legislature. Laws had been passed defining their status as little more than indentured servants, a people who were not permitted to give evidence against white men in court. Not until 1863 (the same year as the Emancipation Proclamation) were laws of this kind erased from California's books.[38]

Miller began to wonder what vital stake, if any, he had in the civilization of white towns. He could see for himself that Native Americans were not the godless demons Christian civilization often made them out to be. But their way of life could hardly be called perfect. The neighboring tribes of Achomawi and Modocs took slaves in war. Class played an important part in the McCloud tribe's social life, and when Miller attended Indian dances, he noticed that no one "was allowed to dance but those of high family." On the other hand, the Indians' reliance on intuition, their lack of hypocrisy, and their rapport with nature made him admire and sympathize with them. Certainly, if they continued to be provoked, they might have good reason to become the cruel demons they had been labeled.

One night he surprised himself by dancing with them:

> Yes I the high-minded proud souled Hiner Miller join in a digger Indian dance for a change in weather. well really I must laugh and wonder at myself.... I who have been raised in a Christian country who have been taught to go weekly to the house of God and there offer up my prayers and to kneel at the family altar when the shades of evening gather round I say that in their prayers offered up to the God of their being there is more true faith more pure religion and less hypocrisy than there is in the best branch of worshipers that the Christian religion ever gave birth to.[39]

Early in March of 1857, Miller learned of a massacre of white settlers in the Pit River Valley. The scene of the massacre lay to the southeast of his location in Squaw Valley.[40] With two Indians as companions, he left the campground to find out what he could about the tragedy.... and from about a hundred miles south, near the American Ranch, Sam Lockhart set out by a different route to learn about the destruction of his ferryboat operation on the Pit River.[41] Both Miller and Sam had good reason to be distraught. Sam's twin brother

Harry, along with several other whites in the valley, had been killed by the Achomawi (Pit River) Indians. Miller later said that the whites had been abusing Achomawi women and this had caused much of the trouble. But Sam never needed justification for hating Indians. It seemed to be a part of his nature. A Sacramento newspaper for March of 1857 reported that Sam had been lacing flour with strychnine and leaving it where hungry Indians would find it.[42] He "boasted of his poisoning achievement... last summer while living with his brother. According to his own story, a number of the Indians of that section of the country were poisoned by him." A man whose rage needed no motive or justification, Sam Lockhart had become a source of danger to anyone who favored reason in dealing with the tribes of the area. While on his way to gather an army with which to attack the Pits, he encountered Miller, and learning that the nineteen year old had an Indian "pokona," Lockhart suspected him of helping the Indians in the murder of the settlers.[43] Fortunately, he did not kill him on the spot but took him to the office of Judge A. M. Rosborough in Yreka. In *Life Amongst the Modocs,* Miller's *persona* states that he would have appreciated helpful counsel from the judge that he did not receive. "Rosborough only prevented a foul and cowardly murder.... He might have said some kind words, given some direction to my unsettled and uncertain life."

The first historian to describe the incident, Harry Wells, reported that Sam Lockhart "became satisfied that Miller was not connected with the affair and let him depart; but had it been otherwise, the poet's days in the land of the living would have been few."[44]

An account by Judge Rosborough's son, Alex J. Rosborough, adds a few details to the picture. Alex was a tax collector for Alameda County and wrote down what he remembered hearing from his father.

> One day Sam Lockhart came to my father's office in Yreka bringing with him a boy. "Judge," said he, "I found this young fellow out here in a Modoc Indian Camp.[45] I have questioned him about the Pit River killings and I'm not certain he has told me the truth as to where he was at the time. I don't know yet whether he had anything to do with the murder of my brother, but I am going out to verify what he has told me and if he has been lying to me, I'm going to kill him. I would like to leave him in your care until I return." [Later on Lockhart returned and

is quoted as saying:] "Well, Judge, I have verified his statement to me
and with what you have said about him, I'm going to let him go."[46]

Judge Rosborough was, by nature, both idealistic and practical.[47]
His attempts to control, or at least moderate, the tempers of violent
men in the area had caused him to be appointed special Indian agent
for northern California in 1854. Leaders of the Modoc, Shasta,
Rogue, and Klamath tribes trusted him—and he was one of the few
officials in the region who had never betrayed them. In 1856, as county
judge, he began a judicial career that lasted more than twenty years.

Miller was released—perhaps on the condition that he join up
with the volunteer expedition that was being organized to punish
the Pits.[48] The two men who had escaped from the scene of the December massacre and made their report of the tragedy to Yreka were
both former employees of Lockhart's.[49] (See pages 272 and 275 of
Life Amongst the Modocs.) Their names were Whitney and Fowler.
Miller believed that Fowler had helped start the trouble by mistreat-
ing Achomawi women (See page 34), and supposedly Fowler was
an Indian hater like Lockhart. It was Whitney, however, who was
placed in command of the volunteer company,[50] and Miller expressed
admiration for him rather than dislike. By mid-March the men were
ready for service with Miller mounted and expected to take part in
the action. Whitney's name is found in Miller's *California Diary,*
and it seems fair to assume that Lockhart placed the nineteen-year-
old Miller under Whitney's surveillance.

After the volunteers from Yreka went into action, Miller came to
be trusted by Whitney to the extent that he was given a portion of
the force, and with this detachment he succeeded in setting up an
ambush for the Achomawi.[51] For some reason, maybe because of a
dispute with Lockhart, Whitney was later replaced by Captain
Langly.[52] Miller's figures and accounts of the battles in his *California Diary* are accurate when measured against those of the best historian of the battle, May Southern.[53] That he helped to punish the
Pits is clear: an affidavit in the Bancroft Library from the Adjutant
General's office testifies to Miller's part in the March campaign.
But Miller regretted it. As he later said in his short story "The Pitt
River Massacre," the attack on the whites by the Indians had been

justified by past wrongs. "After a quarter of a century, looking at the matter with mature sense, and from all sides and in all lights, I do not see how the Indians could have done anything else and retain a bit of self-respect.... The Rape of the Sabines was as nothing compared to the ruthless way in which these men had seized upon the handsomest Indian women of the valley and murdered their fathers, brothers, husbands, who dared protest or even ventured to beg about their doors as the winter went past...."[54] The tribe Miller had lived with, the McCloud band of Wintu, were primarily peaceful, and as far as he was concerned, led admirable lives. But he later decided that he had no business fighting against any tribe—even the warlike Pits. On pages 285-86 of *Life Amongst the Modocs,* he deliberately exaggerates the magnitude of his guilt. This distortion has to do with the central expiatory purpose of the book.

For three long weeks following the war, he went into seclusion, returning to Sutatot and their retreat on the McCloud River.[55] In the *California Diary* he notes with a certain pleasure that no one in the mountain camp could speak English. With nothing but roots, cold water, and venison to eat, he is nevertheless happy. Even in this portion of the diary, however, there is a degree of ambivalence. Before long, he misses the society of his friends from the settlements and the sound of his own "sweet" language.

For the time being Miller's mind seems to have been washed clean of the conflict, but this could not be said of Sam Lockhart. For the rest of his life he held all Indians in the country responsible for his brother's death.[56] Near the end of his days, he claimed that he had killed every Indian who had had anything to do with the massacre. His standing in the community did not seem to suffer—though his morals degenerated even below what they had been previously. Reports of his murdering Indians and leaving poisoned food for them continued to circulate. After he rebuilt the ferry, his business practices were said to include fraud and murder.[57] One report had to do with a competitor named McElroy, who built a toll bridge across the Pit River a short distance from Lockhart's establishment. He was shot. When his brother took over the business, he too was shot. A friend of McElroy's held Lockhart responsible. Judge Rosborough's brother Joseph saw Lockhart during the last year of his life and described him as a man "bitter to the end." Sam liked to brag about killing two Indians around a campfire with one bullet, emphasizing the fact that he waited until they got lined up so he wouldn't need a second shot. When Lockhart was dying of a gangrenous wound, Joseph Rosborough went to say good-bye to him and expressed the hope that he would see him again. Lockhart's reply was, "don't care if you never come back."[58] Such was the nature of the man who might have ended Miller's career before it began.

During the two years that followed the Pit River War, Miller was emotionally vulnerable and did not always know where his sympathies would lead him. In this sense he was still a victim rather than a master of his contradictions. His understanding of the positions of top dog and underdog gave him a fundamental uncertainty about the categories some of the settlers were so adamant about, such as white and red, civilized and uncivilized. He knew that whites who lived with Indians were held in contempt, and that the "very worst offense a white man can commit is to cast in his lot with the Indians."[59]

He seemed to be habitually on the wrong side of the law in 1859—perhaps the most troublesome year in his long career. His main antagonist was Bill Hurst, who owned a mining operation on McAdams Creek.[60] A certain kind of attraction-repulsion seemed to exist between the two men, and as a result of their long quarrel Miller had to leave northern California.

It was Miller's custom—long before he became renowned for his leather boots and long hair in England—to dress as he pleased, sometimes in ordinary clothes, other times extravagantly. On Sundays he would stroll into the town of Deadwood dressed in a buckskin suit and gloves and sit all day in the barroom reading the papers. The historian Harry Wells tells us that on one occasion "Bill Hurst, arrayed in a capacious pair of gloves, seated himself before Miller and began to imitate the poet's manner of reading."[61] This was probably not the first time the two men had seen each other. Hurst's little parody irked Miller, and someone heard the youngster make the vague but not altogether empty threat that he might have to kill someone in the town. Not long after that, Hurst hired Miller to do some work for him in his camp. When it came time for the poet to receive his wages, Hurst declined to pay. Miller left the job and as compensation took one or two of Hurst's horses. He sold the animals in Shasta county, and finding himself much wanted by people in pursuit, he looked around for a handy means of conveyance. He spotted a gelding that belonged to Thomas Bass, mounted up, and went back to his life with the Indians on the McCloud River. Before many weeks had passed, Miller was captured and locked up in the Shasta City jailhouse, six miles west of present-day Redding. The formal deposition, dated July 19, 1859, charged him with a felony as follows:

> That the said Hiner Miller at the county of Shasta on the 10th day of July A.D. 1859 [took] one gelding horse of the value of eighty dollars, one Saddle of the value of Fifteen dollars, and one bridle of the value of Five of the property, goods and chattels of one Thomas Bass then willfully did steal, drive and take away, contrary to the Statute in such case made and provided and against the peace and dignity of the People of the State. James D. Mix District Attorney.[62]

Miller succeeded in breaking out of his cell, and the newspaper that reported his achievement mentioned a note he had left behind.

> BROKE JAIL—On Saturday night last, during the performance of Lee's Circus in this place, two prisoners, Miller and Walton—the former charged with horse-stealing—made their escape from the jail, by sawing the iron bars in the windows. We understand they left rather a saucy letter to the Sheriff, which contained sundry quotations from the scriptures in justification of their action.[63]

In *Life Amongst the Modocs* (See pages 340-44) Miller gives a fictionalized account of the jailbreak. He has the heroine Paquita hand the young narrator the saw blades that do the work. It's possible that Sutatot or some of Miller's other Indian friends helped with the actual escape, but not likely. Wells says that a third man, Jack Marshall, was with Miller at the time and that Miller and Marshall headed north. This acquaintanceship continued for a while, and the historian adds that Miller "lived on the island in Scott Valley with a band of notorious characters among whom were Jack Marshall, Nels Scott, Dave English, and Frank Tompkins.[64] The coincidental meeting with

Nels Scott and Dave English may have helped Miller survive his career as a gold carrier in Idaho, because by the time he became an Idaho express rider, his two former friends had joined the Plummer gang—an organization that specialized in robbing gold carriers. More will be said about this connection in a moment.

But there were further developments in Miller's conflict with Bill Hurst. After hiding out for a time in Scott Valley, Miller decided to challenge Hurst, and perhaps he was just angry enough to settle matters with more bravado than was wise. He reentered Deadwood one day, walked up to the bar in one of the saloons, bought everyone a drink and was recognized. Historian Harry Wells tells it this way:

> The fugitive poet, divested of his buckskin suit and his waving yellow locks, had returned. When he heard his name spoken, the stranger raised his filled glass high in the air and brought it down upon the counter with a blow that shivered it to atoms and made the glasses on the counter dance like manikins. "Yes," said he, "I'm Hiner Miller. Is there any one here wants anything of Hiner Miller?" Laying his hand on his pistol, he slowly backed out of the room and was gone.[65]

This was not the 1920s, but the 1850s. The picturesque showdown, the fearless hero who summons his enemies to a public gun battle, had yet to be immortalized in popular novels and films. Miller was bodying forth a prototype as yet unsung.

Learning Miller had come out of hiding, Hurst obtained a warrant for his arrest. The charge was the theft of the livestock Miller had taken from Hurst in the mountain camp. While Hurst was trying to find the young fugitive, it was learned that Miller "had gone to collect some money due him from his old employer, Will Thompkins."[66] Hurst and Constable Bradley finally caught up with Miller when he was in a cabin by a streambed, talking with friends. Historian Wells account of what happened next is fairly close to the picture given in *Life Amongst the Modocs*.[67] Wells says:

> This was daylight. Miller saw them coming and ran up a hill back of the cabin, followed by Bradley and Hurst on horseback. He fired several times at Hurst who was in the rear, and then, being closely pressed by Bradley, fired upon and wounded him, then making his escape up the hill. Several persons trailed him for some distance and lost his track.

That night, C. H. Pyle, John Hendricks, Wesley Morse, Philip Pencil,
and Bill Hurst went to an Indian Rancheria a number of miles distant,
surrounded it and made a search, without finding the fugitive, who had
gone to the Warren place in the valley, where Thompkins paid him two
hundred dollars, as they had agreed that day.[68]

An ironic situation developed: Judge Rosborough, who less than
two years before had protected Miller from Sam Lockhart, now issued a bench warrant for the young fugitive's arrest, ordering "Hiner
Miller be admitted to bail in the sum of two thousand dollars" for
"assault with an intent to commit murder."[69] Perhaps this was better
for him than "earnest advice" from Rosborough, for it helped Miller
escape from a situation in northern California that would only have
grown worse.

During the next two years, Miller earned his living as a surveyor
and express rider. While carrying gold in Idaho, he had the opportunity to reminisce about old California days with Dave English and
Nels Scott. His former trailmates had signed on with the notorious
Plummer gang, an organization which, according to Governor W.T.
McConnell of Idaho, literally outnumbered the peaceful citizens of
the Lewiston area and tyrannized over them.[70] By the time Miller
arrived in Idaho, he had reached the conclusion that the day-to-day
workings of respectable, law-abiding society sometimes constituted
a series of interlinked frauds. Wild was often better than tame, and an
honest thief might do a great deal less harm than a politician of good
family. Some of his most famous lines of poetry express it this way:

> In men whom men condemn as ill
> I find so much of goodness still,
> In men whom men pronounce divine
> I find so much of sin and blot,
> I do not dare to draw a line
> Between the two, where God has not.
> ("Byron")

His experiences in Idaho confirmed these beliefs. It would not be
amiss to glance for a moment at the careers of Nels Scott and Dave
English. Miller not only bothered to keep track of the outlaws, he
sometimes dramatized their deeds in his stories. He described En-

glish in the story "Rough Times in Idaho" as a man who was irresistibly forceful, but "unusually good-natured." Scott seemed to enjoy being flattered and had a face "fine and delicate as a woman's." (See *Life Against the Modocs,* pages 306-8.) The Plummer gang specialized in roadhouse ploys. Unknown to hotel guests, false bills of sale would be written up for livestock while the owners slept inside. Later, at another Plummer-operated roadhouse or perhaps just a few miles down the road, the travelers would be stopped by members of the organization, who would then produce documents for the livestock and "claim" their goods. According to Governor McConnell, an important step in ridding Idaho of this gang was the arrest of Nels Scott and Dave English. Their capture came about after they, along with a third outlaw, held up a packer named Joseph Berry. The bandits did not kill Berry, who later identified them. Miller's erstwhile friends were then hanged in Lewiston by a citizens' committee.[71]

Miller's generous view of the outlaws had something to do with the necessities that sometimes arose on the frontier. A surprising irony is illustrated in the story "Rough Times in Idaho" in which Miller portrays Dave English as the benefactor of the travelers he is planning to rob. During a fearful snowstorm, English draws all the travelers' horses into a circle and shoots the animals, then forces everyone to lie down inside the protective warmth of the dead horses, thus saving the travelers' lives. Such blurring of the lines of morality occurred under extreme conditions, and a higher order, above good and evil, seemed to evolve of itself.

The "mysterious leveling"[72] of the frontier brought Miller to the conclusion that a brave robber "may be better than many legal thieves who infested the land." By the time English, Scott, and Peoples were executed in Lewiston, Miller had already left the region and was editing an Oregon newspaper. But the minute he heard about their execution, he informed his readers of the event, using details he had received from a correspondent in Idaho. It's no exaggeration to say that had Miller traveled into northern California, a little more than two hundred miles south from Eugene, Oregon, he would have been in danger of long-term confinement himself.

The social issue that gave him the final impetus to complete *Life Amongst the Modocs: Unwritten History* and publish it when he did was the hysteria being worked up against the California Indians during the Modoc War of 1872-73. The settlers had forced the Modocs onto a reservation with their enemies, the Klamaths. The physically handsome and intelligent Modoc chief Kientpoos (Captain Jack) decided to lead his band back to their ancestral lands on the northeast side of Mount Shasta. By the time Miller returned to northern California in late 1872,[73] internationally famous for his volume of poems *Songs of the Sierras,* on his way to bring his daughter Cali-Shasta from Oregon to San Francisco, some of the Modocs had gone to work on the ranches of white settlers and could be seen on their days off in Yreka, dressed in levis and store-bought cowboy shirts.[74] As far as some of the whites were concerned, the Modocs were a model tribe. They even helped the townspeople put out a fire that began during some festivities on Independence Day. In the opinion of Judge Rosborough and other leaders of the area, the Modocs deserved a portion of land where they would not be disturbed. But the most fearful and acquisitive of the settlers wanted possession of all the Modoc lands, and even the Indians' request for a home in the Lava Beds was denied. Finally, when the Modocs were attacked by the U.S. Army on Lost River, a war resulted which is still famous in military history. In defending themselves against more than one thousand U.S soldiers, the Modocs with only fifty-two warriors, lost six men in battle and created a casualty list of one hundred sixty-five dead and wounded.[75] Miller wanted to alert the English and American public to the fact that the Indians' demands were quite reasonable, that a policy very much like genocide was being practiced in the Mount Shasta region, and that to a certain extent the situation was irreversible. When *Life Amongst the Modocs* first appeared, the English press had no trouble understanding Miller's intentions:

> Is it possible that, after all, our just indignation with the savage Modocs, and our satisfaction that the Americans are likely to extirpate them, there is a second side to the story, and that what the Modocs have done was brought about by both provocation and necessity?
>
> (*Illustrated London News,* August 23, 1873, p. 178)

Joaquin Miller... is able to lift up his voice and tell us what the red
man thinks of it... the government of the United States seems to have
been guilty of at least culpable negligence by the manner in which it
condoned or even assisted... [the settlers'] courses of unsparing cru-
elty and shameless treachery.

(*Spectator,* August 9, 1873, p. 1016)

Praising *Life Amongst the Modocs* for its aesthetic beauty, the London *Examiner* added, "besides being as interesting as a novel and as
picturesque as a poem, it is an eloquent and most timely apology for
the unfortunate people whom the progress of American 'civilization' is rapidly exterminating."[76]

But when the American edition of the book came out a year later,
the U.S. press was still angry with Miller for capturing female hearts
in London; according to them he was callous about his many love
affairs in England, and the rumors circulating about him implied
that any day he might become a bigamist by marrying one of his
admirers. (That he was officially divorced was not reported.) American newspapers continued to publish articles by his ex-wife, and
her charitable tone only created more dislike for him.[77]

William Dean Howells, who had been reviewing Miller's poetry
in the *Atlantic,* said of him "It is rather a ruinous thing to be a phenomenon," and he turned his back on Miller's most significant book.[78]

The few notices that did appear were both cold and obtuse. The
Alta California remarked, "How much is true we do not know, and
do not much care...."[79]

The leaders and educated men for whom the volume was intended
had no desire to take a second look at America's Indian policy, or to
admire Miller's beautifully synchronized novel.[80] The book sold well
anyway, despite being ignored by the press.

From a modest Oregon homestead in the sparsely settled Willamette
Valley, the seventeen-year-old Miller had walked into a scene of
cultural friction and had been transformed by it. The day-to-day existence of the McCloud Indians in northern California seemed to
coincide perfectly with the Anglo-Europeans' projection of what
life was supposed to be like in a free New World. In this sense,

Miller had encountered the dream born of Old World longing. It had magnetized millions of wayfaring Europeans, and Miller's poetic sense quickly responded to it. But it was unsettling to watch the myth shatter upon contact with the worst elements of Anglo-American society. The historical unfolding of the process of European request and New World answer did not change certain laws having to do with human downfall. In *Life Amongst the Modocs* Miller predicted that the Indians' paradise would be destroyed as the biblical garden had been. However, he was enough of a cultural relativist to know that even if these unhappy predictions came to pass, it would not mean the destruction of all potential for good. In essence, he was an anti-perfectionist who thought man actually needed his defects in order to discover truth. As he said on one occasion, "Error is a phase of truth."[81] Though human progress might be a matter of stumbling, human love would ultimately transcend failure. It was his hope that this tragic passage in California's history would lead to an enlightened future.

The narrator of *Life Amongst the Modocs* says he is "dying morally." While Miller was writing the first draft of the book (probably as early as 1867), he was performing his duties as first judge of Grant County, Oregon and was married to his second wife, Theresa Dyer, who later brought him so much negative publicity. He had not only fought against the Pits and lost touch with his Indian wife Sutatot and his daughter Cali-Shasta, who were still living in the Shasta region, but he was living with a woman for whom, as time went on, he cared less and less. The tide of guilt and his sense of failure were rapidly increasing.

In organizing his thoughts about what had happened to him in the Shasta region, he created one of the West's angriest protest novels, narrated by a *persona* who is almost too cringing and helpless to be a violent spokesman for justice. For what is the boy searching? Something that by the industrial world's standards is almost laughable: pure manhood; more specifically, an ideal man to serve as a guide for his own development. But the young idealist becomes the victim of his propensity for disaster. In depicting the boy's fate, Miller came close to outlining what the psychologist Carl Jung has defined as "the shadow personality." The shadow side of a man's nature consists of those impulses that make him want to cheat, destroy, and obtain power unfairly rather than through efforts that involve self-discipline or moral struggle. Jung said, "Today it is no longer a question of 'How can I get rid of my shadow?'—for we have seen enough of the curse of one-sidedness. Rather we must ask ourselves, 'How can man live with his shadow without its precipitating a series of disasters?'"[82]

Life Amongst the Modocs poses the same question. Though the narrator is idealistic and in the early portions of the novel innocent, his "shadow" qualities upset most of his heroic efforts. Not even aware of them, he becomes their victim. An interesting representation of this "shadow" is figured dramatically on page 53 of the novel when the youth stands before an ugly stable hand, a Nicaraguan. The narrator finds himself hypnotized by the one-eyed man. "This black man to me was a nightmare. I stood before him like a convict before his keeper. I felt that he was my master. Had he told me to do this or that I would have gone and done it, glad to get from under his one and dreadful eye, that seemed to be burning a hole in my head." In keeping with the strong contrasts in the book, the differences between the two individuals are made to be shocking. The blonde, feminine boy faces a squat, black, older man. Opposing the youth's love and innocence is the unexplained, irrational malevolence of the stable keeper. The boy is glad to get away from this individual, who drains away his strength. But Miller's *persona* must eventually understand and face up to what his own negativity means.

In the second half of the book, though his love does not deteriorate (an all-pervading tenderness characterizes his descriptions of the men and the woods), the boy's "shadow" begins to undermine the efforts of his conscious will. He presents the case of the just against the unjust, makes efforts to unite the tribes into a republic, risks his life for them, and fights for them. But even after most of the tragedies that can befall a man have taken place and almost all of his friends are murdered, he does not know how to acknowledge the self-destructiveness that makes him ineffective in carrying out his plans. Then, in the Pit River War, the narrator blackens himself with guilt, turns from hero to demon within a few pages:

> It would... fill many pages to explain how by degrees I came to enter into the spirit of the war against my allies. Nor is there any real excuse for my conduct.... From a prisoner I became a leader. Two decisive battles, or rather massacres, took place, and perhaps five hundred Indians perished.... Another man was chosen nominal leader, but the plain truth is, before we had been in the valley a month I gave direction, and had in fact charge of the expedition. Most of these men are dead now, but scattered around somewhere on earth, a few may be found, and they will tell you that by my energy, recklessness and knowledge of the country and Indians' customs, I, and I only, made the bloody expedition a success. I tell this in sorrow. (Pages 285-86)

This admission of treachery is the central expiatory rite of the novel. The narrator tells us that he was trying to rise to the dignity of some little virtue... after... these Indians had set such good examples." Then after the massacres, with the benefit of hindsight, he observes, "I now thought, surely I am awake. If I had been awake, I should have mounted my mule as soon as able to ride, and left the country forever." For the reader, the situation is best summed up in the complaint, "I was drying morally." Loving both the Indian and the white man, without conscious awareness of his shadow, he oscillates, first creating then destroying, now idealizing, now undermining. Obviously, Miller was not attempting to enhance the boy's popular image by introducing this important element, because the reader never quite recovers from the shock of the boy's confession. In blackening his *persona* with guilt, Miller offers himself up for humiliation and censure. Vicariously, he subjects himself to the disgust the reader feels for the youth (a disgust Miller, as judge in Canyon City, no doubt felt for himself.) Yet, despite repeated failures, the boy continues to dream and to act. Ultimately he learns,[83] and much of the book's power comes from the acknowledgment that love in a mysterious way survives disaster. In later life Miller continued to write about the inevitability of human failure,[84] but he also insisted that the forgiveness of others and of oneself is the key to overcoming despair. The advice he gave to others is revealing:

> Sit down a little time as you stumble headlong in the dust up and down the steeps of life,—steeps of your own making or imagining, as a rule.... You will then see that all the world is beautiful.... And meantime get a

little acquainted with your own soul. You will find that you are better, a great deal better, than you believed.... You will also find that those about you are... vastly better than you believed.[85]

I fill myself with asceticism, get drunk on abnegation, recite my own poems, and dance a two-step inspired by self-sacrifice. I am touched with madness, but sane enough to know it. I have a good time on nothing....[86]

There are spots even in the sun. There is also an infinity of light. God made the spots, and He will look to the spots. Let us concern ourselves with the light.[87]

Life Amongst the Modocs is a successful attempt at self-revelation—one which few writers in 1873 would have attempted and, as such, it is a more honest and insightful rendering of the workings of Miller's inner self than a purely factual narrative would have provided. He goes beyond the facts to an inner truth, and the language and structure lift the book to an aesthetic truth as well.

His novel was also a poignant warning that at the edge of the frontier—a place in his lifetime considered to be the focal point of democratic hope—the possibility of self-betrayal was present, a predilection for overturning one's own most cherished cultural dreams. The policy toward the Native Americans was only one proof of this. His book—so rich in experiences unique to American life—contained this archetypal American presentiment.

Alan Rosenus

Notes

1. Everson, *Archetype West,* p. 27.
2. George Francis Armstrong, "Mr. Miller's 'Songs of the Sierras,'" *The Dark Blue* (London), September 1871, p. 120.
3. *Spectator*, August 9, 1873, p. 1016.
4. See Martin S. Peterson, *Joaquin Miller, Literary Frontiersman* (Stanford, Calif.: Stanford University Press, 1937), p. 117; Richard O'Connor, *Bret Harte, A Biography* (Boston: Little Brown, 1966), p. 204.
5. See *Mark Twain to Mrs. Fairbanks,* p. 174. Twain's letter reads, "We see Miller every day or two, and like him better and better all the time. He is just getting out his Modoc book here ane I have made him go to my publishers in America with it (by letter) and they will make some money for him."
6. Ibid., pp. 174-77.
7. Ibid., p. 165. Mary Fairbanks was secretly hoping Miller would reform. On his return to America she saw him and reported to Twain, "he has grown so delicate and gentle and unaffected. He has dropped the barbaric element and is ambitious to seem a refined gentleman. He has shorn his Absalom locks, he wears kid gloves and black neck-tie." Both in Europe and America, Miller was often seen in ordinary dress, but as time was to prove he was not eager to satisfy Mrs. Fairbanks' genteel expectations.
8. See Frost, *Joaquin Miller*, pp. 44-46. If any critic prior to Frost read the divorce proceedings, no report was ever made of it.
9. *Spectator,* August 9, 1873, p. 1017.
10. See J. Roy Jones, *Saddle Bags in Siskiyou* (Yreka, Calif.: News Journal, 1953); Wells, *A History of Siskiyou County.*
11. This region was so profitable for gold mining that by the 1940s it had been worked over more than five times. Ecological damage, especially from dredges, is still visible.
12. See Stephen Dow Beckham, *Requiem for A People* (Norman, Okla.: University of Oklahoma Press, 1971).
13. See Wells, *A History of Siskiyou County*, p. 209.
14. Ibid., p. 119, and references in discussion below.

15. See *Selected Writings of Joaquin Miller,* pp. 212-17.

16. See *The Correspondence of Walt Whitman*, 2 Vols. (New York: The New York University Press, 1961), Vol. 1, Pt. 2, pp. 182-83. Whitman's letter to Charles Eldridge of July 19, 1872, reads: "Charley, who do you think I have been spending some three hours with to-day, from 12 to 3—(it is now 4 1/2)—*Joaquin Miller*—He saw me yesterday toward dusk at 5th av. on a stage, and rushed out of the house, and mounting the stage gave me his address, and made an appointment—he lives here 34th st. in furnished rooms—I am much pleased, (upon the whole) with him—*really pleased and satisfied—his presence, conversation, atmosphere*, are infinitely more satisfying than his poetry—he is, however, mopish, ennuyeed, a *California Hamlet*, unhappy every where—but a natural prince...." [Emphasis Whitman's]

17. See Rosena A. Giles, "The Battle of Castle Rocks," *The Covered Wagon*, (Shasta Historical Society), 1956, pp. 19-20. This article gives the correct spelling of Mountain Joe's name as known to local informants (Joe De Blondy). For confirmation of this see "Clarification on Joaquin Miller News Article," which presents information given by Marcelle Masson, a descendent by marriage of Ross and Mary McCloud: "Mrs. Masson further notes that the old [Wintun] Indian, Grant Towendolly, an uncle of our Ted Towendolly, local city employee, told him that the Lockhart brothers were the ones who built the log cabin, known as the Joaquin Miller cabin, which was on the site of the James Consentino home.... The real name of "Mountain Joe" was Joe De Blondy. Grant Towendolly relates that he knew of Mountain Joe as did most of the old time Indians." (Undated news clipping, Siskiyou County Historical Museum, Scrap Book File, Book 26, p. 22.)

18. See May Hazel Southern, "The Legend of the Lost Cabin Mine," *The Covered Wagon*, 1967, pp. 1-2; also, Rosena A. Giles, "The Battle of Castle Rocks," *The Covered Wagon*, 1956, pp. 19-20; "Castle Crags Park Hard to Beat," *Oakland Tribune*, June 12, 1959.

19. May Hazel Southern, "The Legend of the Lost Cabin Mine," *The Covered Wagon*, 1967, pp. 1-2.

20. For additional accounts of the Battle of Castle Crags see Southern, *Our Stories Landmarks*, pp. 65-68; Miller's "The Battle of Castle Crags," in *Selected Writings of Joaquin Miller*, pp. 28-37; Giles, *Shasta County, California: A History*, pp. 37-38; Ruth T. Jones, "Upper Soda Springs," *Siskiyou Pioneer and Year Book*, Vol. 4, No. 1 (1968), pp. 41-44.

21. *Shasta Courier*, August 11, 1855, p. 2. On the other hand, we have M.M. Marberry's assertion in *Splendor Poseur* (New York: Thomas Y. Crowell, 1953), p. 21, that "All residents of the area and all those who fought in battle scoffed at the idea that Joaquin had been there." Marberry does not document his statement or cite local historians. In support of Miller's participation we have the above contemporary newspaper report, a statement by Reuben P. Gibson, the leader in the battle, quoted in the Bear Edition of *Joaquin Miller's Poems*, Vol. 4, p. 98; and the confirming statement regarding Gibson and Miller by Southern in *Our Stories Landmarks*, p. 68; also the account of Marcelle Masson, a descendent by marriage of Ross McCloud, who fought in the battle ("Clarification on Joaquin Miller News Article," undated news clipping, Siskiyou county Historical Museum, Scrap Book File, Book 26, p. 22), and her confirming article in the *Dunsmuir News* for October 3, 1963. Marberry's book is not always the well-researched biography it pretends to be, and in this case he deliberately misrepresents local opinion. He also refers to a "secret diary" to suggest Miller was elsewhere during the battle, but the secret diary does not exist. Marberry's book is inaccurate on peripheral matters as well, such as the whereabouts of Bret Harte and the character of Mrs. Frank Leslie, and though it is at best a witty piece of journalistic libel, it has continued to influence opinion about Miller to this day.

22. See "Clarification on Joaquin Miller News Article," undated news clipping, Siskiyou Historical Museum, Scrap book File, Book 26, p. 22.

23. *Dunsmuir News*, October 3, 1963.

24. *Selected Writings of Joaquin Miller*, pp. 181-87. On the rela-

tionship between the whites and the Wintuns in the Dunsmuir area see Ruth T. Jones, "Upper Soda Springs," *Siskiyou Pioneer and Year Book*, Vol. 4, No. 1 (1968), pp. 41-44.

25. *Selected Writings of Joaquin Miller*, pp. 148-68.

26. Ibid., p. 156.

27. Ibid., pp. 158, 163, 165.

28. Since Miller is "crossing" over to Lower Soda Springs, he is living in Squaw Valley. See entries in the *California Diary* in *Selected Writings of Joaquin Miller*, pp. 168-69.

29. Paquita, evocative, perhaps, but so little realized as an individual character, probably does not resemble the real Sutatot in many respects. James Thomas, though a prototype of the heroic gambler, is far better fleshed out, and Miller said the model for the character was a man named Thomas from Leon, Nicaragua. Miller dedicated the poem "King of Tigre" to him, and in a note on the poem indicated that Thomas had been with him in London. When asked by some members of London's Savage club how Thomas had managed to supply himself with such an abundance of ready cash, Joaquin Miller's answer was playfully evasive. "I am not certain whether it was as a pirate of the South Seas or merely as a brigand of Mexico." (*Joaquin Miller's Poems*, Bear Edition, Vol. IV, p. 170.) Charles Warren Stoddard's article, "The King of Tigre," is helpful. (*National Magazine*, 25, October, 1906, pp. 17-21). Finally, in a manuscript of Ina Coolbrith's in the Bancroft Library entitled "Joaquin Miller," there is an unnumbered page on which Iza Hardy identifies the Prince of *Life Amongst the Modocs* as "Col. Thomas of Leon, Nicaragua." That such a person as Thomas of Leon existed is all we know. We can't say how much he resembled or differed from James Thomas of *Life Amongst the Modocs*.

30. See Wagner, *Joaquin Miller and His Other Self*, pp. 238-39. For Cali-Shasta's relationship with Ina Coolbrith, see Rhodahamel and Wood, *Ina Coolbrith*, p. 178.

31. In *Joaquin Miller and His Other Self*, Harr Wagner cites the *San Francisco Call* for June 8, 1908. See Minnie Lee's article on Miller in the *Portland Oregonian*, January 9, 1938.

32. *Selected Writings of Joaquin Miller*, p. 170.

33. Ibid., p. 188.

34. Ibid., pp. 170-71. In *Life Amongst the Modocs*, Miller fuses Blackbeard and his son Worotitot into one character. But in his *California Diary* (see *Selected Writings*, p. 180) Miller makes a clear distinction between father and son. In real life, Blackbeard was a war chief who after some successful campaigns eventually lost almost one-half his territory. According to anthropologist Jeremiah Curtin, Blackbeard's son Worotitot was half-Wintu, half-Pit River Indian—a savvy warrior who could speak three languages. In her article "Joaquin Miller: Fact and Fiction," Margaret Guilford-Kardell speculates that Sutatot was indeed Worotitot's daughter as Miller tells us in *Life Amongst the Modocs*, and that after Sutatot married a scout named Jim Brock, she named her son after her father-chief. See *The Californians*, Nov./Dec. 1991, 7-13.

35. These are Matisse's sentiments regarding his French compatriots in Tahiti. His exact words were, "Above them, and all around them, was that wonderful light of the first day, that magnificence, but they no longer noticed it." Escholier, *Matisse from the Life*, p. 112.

36. *Selected Writings of Joaquin Miller*, p. 171.

37. Ibid., p. 198.

38. Ibid., p. 171. See the so-called "Act for the government and Protection of the Indians." California Legislature, *Statutes of California*, 1st sess., Chap. 133 (1850).

39. *Selected Writings of Joaquin Miller,* p. 172.

40. Ibid., p. 174.

41. See Neasham, *Fall River Valley: A History*, p. 67; also Heizer's *They Were Only Diggers*, p. 31; Southern, *Our Stories Landmarks*, pp. 75-76.

42. The *Sacramento Union* for March 18, 1857, cited in Boggs, *My Playhouse Was a Concord Coach*, p. 265; also see Heizer, *They Were Only Diggers*, p. 31.

43. See Wells, *A History of Siskiyou County*, p. 119; Neasham, *Fall River Valley: A History*, pp. 67-68.

44. Wells, *A History of Siskiyou County*, p. 119.

45. Lockhart was using the word *Modoc* in much the same way the word *Digger* was used. Miller was camped with Wintu-speaking McCloud Indians in Squaw Valley.

46. Siskiyou County Historical Museum, Scrap Book Files, Book 4.

47. See Alex J. Rosborough, "A.M. Rosborough, Special Indian Agent," *California Historical Quarterly*, Vol. 5, No. 3 (September 1947), p. 201. More details are given in an article published in April of 1895 in the *Columbia* (Tenn.) *Maury Democrat*, which states in part that Judge Alexander Madison Rosborough (born in 1814) was a graduate of Tennessee University and fought against the Seminoles in Florida. In 1841 he began to devote his time to journalism and worked for the *Columbia Observer* and the *Nashville Whig*. In San Francisco, he worked for the *San Francisco Evening Picayune*—having come to the state in 1850. Beginning in 1856, he was elected county judge and won that post four times, serving for fourteen years, after which he resigned and became judge of the district court, serving in that capacity ten years. The newspaper clipping titled "A Judicial Veteran" is in the files of the Siskiyou County Historical Museum. For more on the activities of Judge Rosborough see Beckham, *Requiem for a People*; Riddle, *The Indian History of the Modoc War*; and Dillon, *Burnt-Out Fires*.

48. Neasham in *Fall River Valley: A History*, p. 68, comes to this conclusion and it seems justified.

49. See Southern, *Our Stories Landmarks*, pp. 75-76.

50. See *Selected Writings of Joaquin Miller*, p. 176; Neasham, *Fall River Valley: A History*, pp. 68-70.

51. *Selected Writings of Joaquin Miller*, p., 177.

52. See Neasham, *Fall River Valley: A History*, p. 71.

53. In the California Diary (*Selected Writings of Joaquin Miller*, p. 177) Miller notes fifty-six dead, with many others wounded, and says sixteen children were taken into the settlement. In Southern's *Our Stories Landmarks* (p. 77) fifty-nine are reported killed, with thirteen children being brought to Yreka. May Hazel Southern (1867-1943) was born May 1, 1867, at Southern's

Stage Stop in the Sacramento Canyon north of Redding and enjoyed lifelong contact with the pioneers of the region. Compared with most of the histories produced in the area, her *Our Stories Landmarks* is unusually accurate.

54. *Selected Writings of Joaquin Miller*, p. 46.
55. Ibid., p. 178.
56. See Neasham, *Fall River Valley: A History*, p. 74.
57. Ibid., p. 75.
58. Lockhart's being a "man bitter to the end," his words, "don't care if you never come back," and the cause of his death are from a statement by Alex J. Rosborough made on July 23, 1954, to Ernest R. Neasham, who interviewed Rosborough (quoted with permission of Ernest R. Neasham).
59. One overzealous militia leader had such contempt for the feelings that existed between whites and Indians that he forced his volunteers to give up their native women as part of a campaign against the Pits. See Albert L. Hurtado, *Indian Survival on the California Frontier* (New Haven and London: Yale University Press, 1988), p. 176.
60. See Wells, *A History of Siskiyou county*, p. 119.
61. Ibid., p. 119
62. Quoted in full in Boggs, *My Playhouse Was a Concord Coach,* p. 342.
63. *Shasta Courier*, July 9, 1859, p. 2.
64. Wells, *A History of Siskiyou County*, p. 119.
65. Ibid., p. 120.
66. Ibid.
67. Ibid. Ina Coolbrith gives a slightly different version of the story but it undoubtedly refers to the same events. She got her information from James Barrett, "Pretty Jim," who was in Hurst's camp when Miller wounded the sheriff. Barrett said that Miller had taken one of Hurst's horses, had sold the animal, then returned to give his employer the proceeds, after first deducting the unpaid wages. Hurst sent for the law. Meantime, according to Barrett, Miller had "gathered his belongings, mounted his horse, taken his gun across his saddle, and started down the

trail, to meet the Sheriff coming up. All the camp followed 'to see the fun'—their sympathy entirely with the cook (Miller). To the Sheriff's repeated summons to stop, Joaquin's only answer was the quiet, 'I'm not stopping today'; until, following the Sheriff's threat to shoot, and the click of his pistol, Joaquin, like a flash, raised his gun and fired." The bullet hit the Sheriff in the shoulder, which put him out of commission. As Miller 'was not stopping that day' he quietly rode on. These events took place in June of 1859. Within less than two weeks, Miller took a horse belonging to Thomas Bass and was jailed for the offense in Shasta City. According to the local newspaper, he escaped from jail on July 9. This leaves us with the question of why Judge Rosborough waited such a long time before issuing the bench warrant for Miller's arrest on the charge of "assault with an intent to commit murder." The warrant was issued in early 1860, six or seven months after the shooting of Bradley took place. It is also interesting that when Miller was jailed in Shasta County for theft, no mention was made of the fact that he was wanted in Siskiyou County, not far north, for the more serious offense of assault with intent to commit murder. Ina Coolbrith's account can be found in an unpublished article, "Joaquin Miller," which is among her papers in the Bancroft Library. Her informant, "Pretty Jim" Barrett, is undoubtedly the same J.M. Basset who published an essentially identical account of the Miller-Hurst feud in the August 23 and 30 issues of the Fort Jones *Farmer and Miner* (1911). In the printed version, however, Basset states that Miller took not one horse, but a team of horses Hurst used for hauling.

68. Wells, *A History of Siskiyou County*, p. 120.
69. Court of Sessions, Siskiyou County, II, 85.
70. See McConnell, *Early History of Idaho* (Caldwell, Idaho: Caxton, 1913), pp. 71-72.
71. See John Hailey, *The History of Idaho* (Boise, Idaho: Syms-York Co., 1910), p. 34.
72. The phase is Chuang Tzu's. See *The Complete Writings of Chuang Tzu*, Trans. Burton Watson (New York: Columbia University Press,

1968), p. lll. Chuang Tzu's sentiments go: "Cudgel and cane the sages and let the thieves and bandits go their way; then the world will at last be well ordered!… wipe out and reject benevolence and righteousness, and for the first time the Virtue of the world will reach the state of Mysterious Leveling."

73. Boggs, in *My Playhouse Was a Concord Coach* (p. 564), records Miller as being in Lower Soda Springs in November of 1871.

74. For other information on the Modocs see Riddle, *The Indian History of the Modoc War*, and Dillon, *Burnt-Out Fires.*

75. See Dillon, *Burnt-Out fires*, p. viii.

76. *Examiner*, (London) August 2, 1873, p. 785.

77. See the *San Francisco Call* for Sunday, November 22, 1874, p. 6, and the change in the *San Francisco Chronicle's* attitude toward Miller between October and November of 1874. Look in particular at the front page of the *Chronicle*, November 15, 1874.

78. *Atlantic Monthly*, Vol. 28 (December 1871), p. 770.

79. *Alta California*, November 30, 1874.

80. It has been suggested more than once that Prentice Mulford played a major role in writing *Life Amongst the Modocs*. In his eulogy of Mulford in the San Francisco *Call*, Miller attributes "the best part of" the book to Mulford, though he states in the same article that the book was written before he went to London (and also that he thought of the book as a novel rather than an autobiography). We should perhaps think of Miller's generosity in this regard as a reflection of his sympathy for Mulford whose life was a tragic affair in every respect. Scholars favorably inclined to Mulford do not ascribe the book to him, and anyone who studies the styles of the two authors will find that the impetuous surge of the prose and the sensuous diction are characteristic of Miller alone. It is quite improbable that Mulford could have written any page of the book fresh. Mulford learned how to polish and edit from Bret Harte, and it is surely in this regard that Mulford was of help to Miller. Though Mulford was Miller's secretary in London, the fine copy of *Life Amongst the Modocs*, according to the printer, was in Miller's handwriting. Resistance to Miller's work in America, initiated by William

Dean Howells, has lingered into the twentieth century. For instance, historian Richard Dillon has admitted to a prejudice against Miller whom he associates with Ernest Hemingway. In Dillon's view both writers over-emphasize their masculine feats. It is one thing to maintain a prejudice in private but another to make it into a public legacy (see the *California Historical Quarterly*, Vol. XIV, No. 2, p. 183; and Dillon's flip essay on Miller in *Humbugs and Heroes*). By repeating that Miller was a humbug and poseur, Dillon and the critic Franklin Walker have consistently underrated him as a writer and have over-simplified his character in the process. The manner in which they have ignored a large body of historical material that would confirm Miller's importance as an historical source has been confusing to students of history and writing. Neither Walker nor Dillon has any particular liking for the western transcendentalist school, and since this material has no appeal for them, they have misjudged it. Several generations of Californians have been encouraged by their scholarly neglect to bypass *My First Summer in the Sierra* and *John of the Mountains* by John Muir, and Miller's *Life Amongst the Modocs*. (In *San Francisco's Literary Frontier*, for example, Franklin Walker devotes less than one page to John Muir and his writings.)

81. See Hubbard, *So Here Then is a Little Journey to the Home of Joaquin Miller* (East Aurora, N.Y.: Roycrofters, 1903), p. 13.

82. Jung, *The Practice of Psychotherapy* (Princeton: Bollingen, 1954), p. 238. The remarks on Jung and the "shadow" personality are given in greater detail in Rosenus, "Joaquin Miller and His 'Shadow.'"

83. He has not become aware of the ambivalent side of his nature or of his "shadow," but he has understood the futility of violence and has gained respect for his limitations.

84. See his last novel, *The Building of the City Beautiful.*

85. *Joaquin Miller's Poems*, Bear Edition, Vol. 5, p. 221.

86. Hubbard, *So Here Then Is a Little Journey to the Home of Joaquin Miller*, p. 13.

87. *Joaquin Miller's Poems*, Bear Edition, Vol 5. p. 212.

Select Bibliography

Clemens, Samuel, *Mark Twain to Mrs. Fairbanks.* Ed. Dixon Wecter. San Marino, Calif.: Huntington Library, 1949.

Everson, William. *Archetype West.* Berkeley, Calif.: Oyez, 1976.

Frost, O.W. *Joaquin Miller.* New York: Twayne Publishers, 1967.

Giles, Rosena A. *Shasta County, California: A History.* Oakland, Calif.: Biobooks, 1949.

Guilford-Kardell, Margaret. "Joaquin Miller: Fact and Fiction." *The Californians* 9 (Nov./Dec., 1991): 7-13.

Longtin, Ray C. *Three Writers of the Far West: A Reference Guide.* Boston: G.K. Hall & Co., 1980.

Miller, Joaquin. *Selected Writings of Joaquin Miller.* Ed. Alan Rosenus. Eugene, Ore.: Urion Press, 1976.

Neasham, Ernest R. *Fall River Valley: A History.* Fall River Mills, Calif.: Privately printed, 1957.

Rhodehamel, Josephine DeWitt, and Raymund Francis Wood. *Ina Coolbrith.* Provo, Utah: Brigham Young University Press, 1973.

Rosenus, A.H. "Joaquin Miller and His 'Shadow.'" *Western American Literature* Vol. 11, No. 1 (May 1976),: pp. 51-59.

Southern, May Hazel. *Our Stories Landmarks.* Shasta County, Calif.: Privately printed, 1942.

Wagner, Harr. *Joaquin Miller and His Other Self.* San Francisco: Harr Wagner, 1929.

Wells, Harry L. *A History of Siskiyou County.* Oakland, Calif.: D.J. Stewart & Co., 1881.